Women and Bicycles
in America, 1868–1900

SELECTED OTHER WORKS BY KERRY SEGRAVE
AND FROM MCFARLAND

The Electric Car in America, 1890–1922: A Social History (2019)

"Masquerading in Male Attire": Women Passing as Men in America, 1844–1920 (2018)

The Women Who Got America Talking: Early Telephone Operators, 1878–1922 (2017)

The Hatpin Menace: American Women Armed and Fashionable, 1887–1920 (2016)

Police Violence in America, 1869–1920: 256 Incidents Involving Death or Injury (2016)

Chewing Gum in America, 1850–1920 (2015)

Wiretapping and Electronic Surveillance in America, 1862–1920 (2014)

Beware the Masher: Sexual Harassment in American Public Places, 1880–1930 (2014)

Policewomen: A History, 2d ed. (2014)

Extras of Early Hollywood: A History of the Crowd, 1913–1945 (2013)

Parking Cars in America, 1910–1945: A History (2012)

Begging in America, 1850–1940: The Needy, the Frauds, the Charities and the Law (2011)

Vision Aids in America: A Social History of Eyewear and Sight Correction Since 1900 (2011)

Lynchings of Women in the United States: The Recorded Cases, 1851–1946 (2010)

America Brushes Up: The Use and Marketing of Toothpaste and Toothbrushes in the Twentieth Century (2010)

Film Actors Organize: Union Formation Efforts in America, 1912–1937 (2009)

Parricide in the United States, 1840–1899 (2009)

Actors Organize: A History of Union Formation Efforts in America, 1880–1919 (2008)

Obesity in America, 1850–1939: A History of Social Attitudes and Treatment (2008)

Women and Capital Punishment in America, 1840–1899: Death Sentences and Executions in the United States and Canada (2008)

Women Swindlers in America, 1860–1920 (2007)

Ticket Scalping: An American History, 1850–2005 (2007)

America on Foot: Walking and Pedestrianism in the 20th Century (2006)

Suntanning in 20th Century America (2005)

Endorsements in Advertising: A Social History (2005)

Women and Smoking in America, 1880 to 1950 (2005)

Foreign Films in America: A History (2004)

Lie Detectors: A Social History (2004)

Product Placement in Hollywood Films: A History (2004)

Women and Bicycles in America, 1868–1900

KERRY SEGRAVE

McFarland & Company, Inc., Publishers
Jefferson, North Carolina

ISBN (print) 978-1-4766-7985-3
ISBN (ebook) 978-1-4766-3808-9

LIBRARY OF CONGRESS AND BRITISH LIBRARY
CATALOGUING DATA ARE AVAILABLE

© 2020 Kerry Segrave. All rights reserved

No part of this book may be reproduced or transmitted in any form or by any means, electronic or mechanical, including photocopying or recording, or by any information storage and retrieval system, without permission in writing from the publisher.

Front cover: print of "young woman standing beside bicycle near the water, 1896" (Library of Congress)

Printed in the United States of America

*McFarland & Company, Inc., Publishers
Box 611, Jefferson, North Carolina 28640
www.mcfarlandpub.com*

Table of Contents

Preface 1

Introduction 3

1. From the Dandy Horse to the Velocipede   5
2. The Tricycle   15
3. The Bicycle to 1889   36
4. 1890s—Popularity   62
5. 1890s—Health   105
6. 1890s—Morality and Propriety   123
7. 1890s—Fashion   151

Chapter Notes   205
Bibliography   213
Index   219

Preface

This book looks at women in the last third of the 19th century in America as they began in increasing numbers to take up the bicycle as an exercise, a sport, and an activity. Specifically the book covers the period 1868 to 1900. The first cycle craze to arrive in America took place in America from 1868 to about 1870 when the machine, known then as a "velocipede," reached the United States after its emergence in Europe. Men and women both took up the activity with women involved only to a minor degree. The velocipede was unacceptable for a variety of reasons and soon faded from the scene.

Improvements led to many advances in the machines with a focus on the tricycle and the bicycle. The former was developed mostly for women and children and it was to this cycle that women began taking up in greater numbers. At the same time the bicycle evolved into the high-wheeler machine with a huge front wheel and a tiny back wheel. Excluded from using that style of machine were men who were both not relatively young and athletic and all women. Thus the bicycle did not gain many adherents in the 1870s and through the middle of the 1880s. During that time women struggled with the heavy, hard-to-use tricycle. Developments in the period 1885 to 1887 led to the safety bike for men and then the safety bike for women, and at that point the craze for bicycles really took off. It heralded a golden period that lasted through the 1890s. By the turn of the 20th century, though, the fad was suddenly over as its usage dropped quickly and dramatically, killed by the automobile.

Taking up the bicycle was an important step for women as they struggled with the patriarchy to gain some measure of equality. For one thing it allowed women greater freedom and mobility and it was used by them in the movement away from the idea that they needed an escort or chaperon for almost any activity. The bicycle was also an important tool for women as they attempted to achieve dress reform and move away from the restrictive and controlling fashions that were everyday wear in this period. The major struggle for women in riding bicycles was the battle for the right to wear pants when they rode.

Research for this book was done using online databases with the Library of Congress' Chronicling America being the most useful. Also used was news paperarchive.com and various other online databases of newspapers covering that period of time.

Introduction

Chapter 1 looks briefly at the beginnings of the bicycle back around 1800 with the arrival of the hobby horse, or dandy horse. That was a machine without any pedals, with the rider using his feet to push off against the ground to make any headway. Mostly it seemed to have been a toy of the idle rich and little more. A pedal system was developed by sometime in the 1850s and in the middle 1860s the velocipede made its appearance first in Europe and then in America. From about 1868 to 1870 there was a craze for the velocipede (in its two-wheel, three-wheel, and four-wheel models) in America, which involved women to only a minor extent. The various deficiencies in the velocipede meant it quickly passed from sight. Despite the limited involvement of women with the velocipede, early marketers and advertising men tried to match the two in advertising material.

The focus of Chapter 2 is on the tricycle. After the velocipede fell from grace various developments in the industry took place with an emphasis on the tricycle and the bicycle. The tricycle enjoyed more popularity in Europe, especially England, than it did in America but it did get a greater number of women involved in the activity of cycling. Ultimately the tricycle failed due to its inherent limitations and followed the velocipede into oblivion, at least for adults.

Chapter 3 looks at the bicycle in the decade of the 1880s. The high-wheeler had been developed in the 1870s and dominated the two-wheel category. Its dominance continued into the 1880s. Women were only rarely mentioned in connection with the high-wheeler and then only usually as performers in circuses and other traveling shows that put on demonstrations on the high wire, and so on. In the last half of the 1880s the safety bicycle for men and women emerged, separately, and that brought about a large increase in usage by both men and women. Suddenly, men who were not young and athletic could ride a bicycle and so could all women. It was in 1888 that articles first began to appear in some number about women as cyclists.

The last four chapters of the book are given over to the decade of the 1890s. That was a boom time for the bicycle among both women and men. Popularity and usage of the machine are the topics of Chapter 4, while Chapter 5 is concerned with health issues that were raised in connection with women riding bicycles. In Chapter 6 the morality and propriety of females taking up cycling is considered. Many objections were raised against women taking up the activity as the patriarchy tried to retain its control over women. Those objections tended to fall into the inane and insane categories, such as a claim that biking made women poor dancers—it had no effect on male dancing ability—and to the idea that for women the bicycle was an agent of the devil.

Chapter 7 is devoted to fashion and the woman cyclist. Many of the articles on the subject were simply marketing ploys as corporations tried to sell women cyclists more articles of clothing, accessories, and so forth. In other words, it functioned much as today, with advertisers trying to get women to buy more stuff they really did not need. The other part of the fashion issue was more important and more political as women tried to achieve dress reform. A man of the 1890s could have easily worn his street clothing while he rode a bicycle (actually, though, he usually wore knickerbockers) while a woman who wore her street clothes of the 1890s faced great difficulties in biking. Some, in fact, did so. That was the reason for the introduction of the woman's safety bicycle, a vehicle that allowed a woman of the 1890s to wear street clothing, sort of. However, women fought against such constraints and adopted something else instead—slightly shorter skirts for one thing, and pants for another, although such were societal constraints that the word "pants" was virtually never used when discussing female attire. Divided skirts became a popular euphemism, as did bifurcated garments. They were pants, sort of, but when a woman stood up and was not moving in those garments they looked something like skirts, which, of course, was the point. By the end of this period women had not quite reached the stage where they could wear pants on bikes, but they got closer to that goal. They did, for the most part, forgo the corset to go cycling. Marketers tried to hawk a modified corset for cycling.

Bicycling was booming by around 1900, after a decade, and it is impossible to say how far it would have gone if it had been allowed to develop further. Cost was prohibitive and effectively blocked all the lower classes and probably a great deal of the middle classes from regular participation. But it did not matter because the automobile arrived. Suddenly the bicycle died and it would stay dead (except for kids) for a very long time.

1

From the Dandy Horse to the Velocipede

The first wheel was the "dandy horse," also called the "hobby horse," which was described in the *London Magazine* in 1769. The rider sat between two wheels, one of which ran behind the other, and touched the ground alternately with the toe of each foot pushing off against the ground, causing the machine to clumsily jerk forward. The rider propelled himself, then, the way a skateboarder does today, except the dandy horse rider used both feet, one after the other, while seated. These vehicles were seen in use later than 1820. The first velocipede (Latin for "fast foot" and a description for a human-powered land vehicle with one or more wheels) was an attempt to improve upon the dandy horse. What was practically the first bicycle, in the form of a type of the boneshaker pattern, was constructed and ridden by a cooper by the name of Gavin Dazell. It was improved upon but due to the great friction of the parts and the rough, jolting movements made evident to the rider, it did not command any great amount of public favor. During the 1860s the machines were made of handmade steel forgings with the wheels being of wood with flatiron tires. By 1872 in America the wooden velocipede was extinct, thanks to hollow steel frames, wire suspension wheels and solid rubber tires. With the machine improved by 1868, a craze developed for the velocipede that proved, however, to be short-lived. An 1884 account, referring to the end of the 1860s, noted, "The natural desire arose to extend the pleasures of the new mode of locomotion to the ladies and the result was the tricycle, three-wheel." Added the report, "Some day fashion will throw its powerful glance upon it, then the tricycle will become 'the rage' and gentlemen on bicycles escorting ladies on tricycles will be an every-day sight." Note the assumption involved in that statement: that no women would be riding the velocipedes and that no women would be cycling alone, without a male escort.[1]

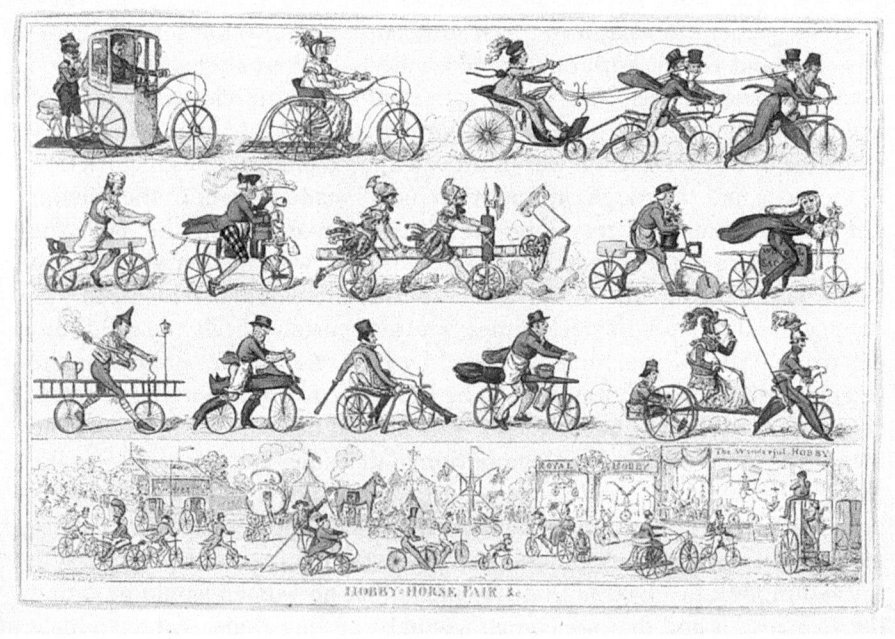

The top 1919 illustration shows two Quakers riding velocipedes while the bottom 1819 illustration depicts a hobby horse fair.

After the velocipede arrived on the scene in a major way, in the period 1868–1869 many predictions were made of better transportation for all, but as accidents increased, noted a journalist in 1890, "to such an extent that two new insurance companies sprang into existence, it began to be apparent that the velocipede was not all that it had been cracked up to be, and upon closer acquaintance it soon came to be eyed with suspicion, and was finally given the complete shake in certain circles to oblivion." Then came the bicycle, but it was the high-wheeler, or the "ordinary," and was definitely off-limits to women due to their mode of dress and to the image of women as somewhat frail and not physical, and so forth. The high-wheeler was limited to riders who were male and relatively young and athletic. Many men could not and would not ride the ordinary. Then came the safety bicycle, which opened the world of cycling to all males, and soon after that came the ladies' safety, or drop-frame design (now usually called a step-through frame) which opened the world of cycling to all females, at least potentially and theoretically. There were still moral and medical reasons advanced from many quarters as to why women should not be cyclists.[2]

However, before those improvements in the machine opened the way for greater numbers of female cyclists, if they could and would bear the opprobrium of society, they did interact somewhat with the velocipede during the machine's boom years of 1868 to about 1870. A brief item that appeared in a Southern newspaper in November 1867 stated, "The problem for modistes now is a garment that will permit females to bestride the velocipede." Throughout the period covered by this book the question of what the female cyclist could and should wear was the problem. In the fall of 1868 another brief account mentioned women in France by observing, "French ladies are taking to the velocipede. The empress [Eugenie] is an adept." A third brief item appeared in the newspapers in November 1868. It declared that "young women ride the bicycle astride in the streets of Detroit." (The term "bicycle" was sometimes used in the late 1860s but usually the devices were called "velocipedes.")[3]

Also in November 1868 the *New York Post* announced the complete success of a moonlight velocipede race, by ladies, which took place in that city earlier that month. The enterprise was planned by a young lady fresh from Paris "where she got inoculated by the velocipede mania." And, continued the article, "already the American manufacturers of these articles of locomotion have improved very much on the French models, and it is thought that velocipeding will become the fashion for ladies as well as gentlemen this season."[4]

Waxing eloquently about the new device, a journalist declared in January 1869 that the art of walking was becoming obsolete because of steamboats, railroads, horse cars, omnibuses "and last, and least in size though not least

An 1869 drawing of a velocipede that was supposedly made for women.

in importance, velocipedes." He went on to declare, "We have land velocipedes and water velocipedes; we still lack velocipedes for ice and air navigation. We have velocipedes with two wheels, and others with three, and even with four wheels; but the two-wheeled machines seem to be most in favor." Reportedly those machines were easy to learn to ride and in Paris, where the velocipede fad had started, "we learn that the number of these little vehicles has increased so much that they are required to carry lamps in the evening." Meanwhile, in New York City, "although we have heard of no police regulation requiring it, young gentlemen may be seen almost every night riding their velocipedes on some of our avenues with head lights attached." There were also said to be schools in New York City for velocipede exhibitions and instructions. One such recently opened institution was at 932 Broadway in New York City and was operated by the Pearsall Brothers. On any given weekday evening could be seen upwards of 150 men—doctors, bankers, merchants—engaged in the training school "prepatory [sic] to making their appearance upon the public streets and fashionable promenades." This journalist called the school a "velocinasium." And, he said, such schools "are coming rapidly into demand all over the country. There is a great call for improvement in these vehicles, by which their weight can be reduced, and their speed increased."[5]

This reporter had not mentioned that any women were at the instruction school he visited and the pupils were, presumably, all men. However, he went on to state, "we expect some ingenious inventor will soon bring out a velocipede upon which our ladies will be able to take their airings, and that, too, without the necessity of any considerable change in the present style of dress." He continued, "The pannier now so generally worn will serve to cushion the seat, and by the introduction of a shorter drew with flowing pants, which our ladies, who wish to enjoy robust exercise, may safely adopt, we may expect to see parties of both sexes making their morning visits to the Park mounted upon graceful velocipedes." It was said that a number of people were then using the velocipede to get back and forth from home to work. The Rev. Henry Ward Beecher owned two such American-made machines. Youngsters rode to school on them. The best speed attained by a velocipede to that date was a mile in a few seconds under four minutes. As a selling point in favor of the velocipede it was observed that a horse cost more to acquire and would "eat, kick, and die." The weight of a medium-sized velocipede was about 60 pounds, with the size of the driving wheel mostly in the range of 30 to 36 inches in diameter. Hills of more than one foot ascent in 20 (5 percent grade) could not be climbed without dismounting and leading the machine and, additionally, "the winter season is not favorable to velocipede riding."[6]

An editorial that appeared originally in a Boston newspaper and was reprinted in other papers offered the thought in February 1869 that the velocipede fad would grow as rapidly and as widely as the telegraph fad. "Teachers of riding this Trojan horse are opening their schools. Persons who make it the main point of their lives to cultivate ideas, clamber into the new style of scale and practise the contortions that are essential to propulsion," said the editor. "Even the ladies are curious, as usual, to know the secret of its attractiveness, and begin to talk of those equal rights which ought to produce velocipedes for their sex as well as the other." In conclusion the newspaperman enthused, "The velocipede is one of those modern inventions that is bound to go."[7]

Also in February 1869 a South Carolina newspaper noted, "It has been demonstrated out West, that women can ride the bicycle velocipedes by wearing bilegular garments." Not only could women not wear trousers or pants, but those words could not even be applied to describe a garment a woman might wear. In this case the non-existent word "bilegular" was concocted to describe what would later be called a divided skirt, or a bifurcated garment. Velocipede was a general term for a foot-powered land vehicle and referred to devices that could have one, two, three, four, or more wheels. Thus women could have ridden two-wheeled vehicles, at least in theory, but rarely did. That is, usual female dress of the period precluded them from riding a two-wheeled velocipede but not from cycling on a three- or four-wheeler.[8]

Still in February 1869 a different editor declared that civilization strove to "economize time by annihilating distance," and that led to such advances as the telegraph and the railway. Another step to overcome slow pedestrianism was for a person to make himself "a burden for beasts," and that led to the use of camels, horses, and so forth. Early in 1868 several factories in France began to supply the newly evolved and improved velocipedes, which soon found their way all over France. He thought France was particularly amenable to velocipedes because of their good asphalt roads that were smooth and hard. By 1869 such machines were being produced by American manufacturers. The most popular was the two-wheel machine, with the front wheel being about three feet high and the rear wheel being two and a half feet high. The rear wheel was generally smaller than the other, with the front wheel varying from two and a half to five feet in height. Two or three days was said to be long enough practice to master the machine, which was said to be capable of 19 miles per hour. The most popular machine, with two wheels, was called a "bicycle." Another variation, with two back wheels, "made for ladies and children is named 'tricycle.'"[9]

In March of 1869 the advertising industry was hardly in a mature status yet the marketing tie-ins between fads and products were already evident with respect to the velocipede. A newspaper editor observed, "We notice since the velocipede mania has taken hold of the people, that everything new is called 'velocipede.' For instance, in walking around town [Evansville, Indiana] we notice in a shoe store the 'velocipede boots' for young ladies; at a music store, 'Velocipede Galop.'" (Galop was a dance, like the tango or waltz).[10]

A somewhat vague report appeared in print in March 1869, wherein it was stated that the acme of at least one velocipede manufacturer's ambition was reached on March 24 in New York when, at a private exhibition at the Hanlon Brother's Hall in that city, a ladies velocipede was found to be a success. The report stated, "The machine was found to answer all the requisites of convenience and adaptability, and was built by a firm in this city." No details were provided as to just how the machine was built to be specifically for women.[11]

Exhibitions by velocipede "professional riders" were a common feature of 1869 and one account told of an exhibition that was given at the Opera House in Evansville, Indiana, at the beginning of April. The Velocipede Combination was composed of six people—three females and three males. "It will be quite a novelty to see ladies riding on a velocipede, but we are assured that they can handle them with infinite grace and skill," said an editor. He also thought the exhibition would draw a full house.[12]

Another exhibition took place in April 1869, this one in New Orleans. A day before the event it was reported that a young lady, the daughter of a well-known New Orleans citizen, would ride at the velocipede school located at 166 Canal Street in that city. "This is the first instance, we believe, of a New

Orleans young lady having mastered the bicycle. We understand that the lady, though but comparatively a recent worshipper of Velocis, is quite a proficient and manages her steed with all the skill and grace of an experienced rider," enthused the journalist. "Now that the movement is inaugurated, why should not the ladies generally participate in it?" On the day after the event it was reported to have been a very graceful exhibition. "As it was the first instance of the sort in this city there was quite a crowd present, gazing in open-eyed wonder and admiration at the strange sight of a lady on a bicycle," went the report. "As we have before suggested, there is no reason why this example should not be generally followed."[13]

The Empire City Rink in New York City was the site of a velocipede exhibition on April 14, 1869, given by a group from France known as the Parisian Velo Troupe. That group consisted of four riders, the two La Belle sisters and the two De Soto brothers. "Setting aside the dexterity exhibited in their many feats, credit is due to the female portion of the troupe for the strict conformity which was displayed in appearing in that rigid costume which theatrical managers have discovered to be the most efficacious means for filling their rapacious coffers. Young men were in ecstasies and cheered vociferously." Added the reporter, "But the propriety of ladies riding velocipedes in modern stage attire naturally suggested itself. That the morals of the rising generation would not be increased by the various evolutions displayed was very plain last night."[14]

Miss Edith Shuler, who was described as "one of the most accomplished female riders of the velocipede in the country," was engaged to give three public exhibitions at Dart's Hall in Rock Island, Illinois, in May 1869. The account that announced

Another ad from 1869, which was testament to the degree of popularity enjoyed by velocipedes in the brief period of 1868 to 1870. The ad herein was for a hair oil product.

the event assured its readers that "nothing will occur to offend the most refined sensibilities, and the ladies are especially invited to attend."[15]

An account that appeared in a New York City paper in April 1869 discussed the velocipede fad at some length. It declared that there was a condition running wild in the city, known as "velocipede fever." The Common Council resolution to prohibit the use of velocipedes in the public thoroughfares was to be debated in the near future, but this article urged that the resolution should be postponed indefinitely and the authorities should, instead of prohibiting the machines, adopt an ordinance regulating their use. Riding schools were being established all over New York. The Pearsall brothers were set to inaugurate their "gymnacyclidum" on the following night at the Apollo building. The arena had an area of 8,000 square feet and a gallery with seats that could hold 1,500 spectators. All of the various styles and types of velocipedes were to be on display there and experts would display their riding skills. A Miss Pearsall was to exhibit her skills on the Peerless, a new ladies velocipede. A man named Chase operated the Astor Velocipede Hall in Vestry Street while Perrego's Nassau Street School was reported to be a favorite place for lawyers, clerks, and downtown businessmen. Cammeyer's Amphycyclotheatron, on the Union grounds in Brooklyn, boasted of a one-quarter-mile open-air track. The "Velocipedrome on Hicks Street was intended for ladies as well as men and," noted the reporter, "all the leading halls are preparing for the introduction of the 'gentle sex.'" A velocipede rink had just opened in Omaha and was said to be drawing large crowds. As well, there were said to be 50 velocipede schools in Boston. "Straddle dresses" was the name given to the velocipede costume for women.[16]

A brief editorial at around the same time addressed the issue of women's clothing and bicycling—something that would remain an ongoing problem for women over the period covered by this book. Said the editor, "Dame Fashion says a 'real' lady will never ride the velocipede."[17]

Still, in April of 1869 a small item noted, "New Haven ladies ride the bicycle in the streets, attended by squires." That comment foretold one of the problems that cycling would go a long way to resolving for women. And that was the idea that they could go out and about on their own, or in all-female groups without the need of male escorts, or squires. That was not done in the short period of the velocipede craze but it would come to pass, at least to a large degree, during the most intense phase of the bicycle craze, in the 1890s.[18]

A report in May 1869 observed that the velocipede fad had come on with a rush and that it had been only some six months since the machines had been introduced into the United States. Then there were many varieties of two-wheeled velocipedes as well as one-wheeled machines and velocipedes for ladies. The most comfortable of all the machines was said to be a four-wheeler.[19]

One account that appeared in May 1869 directly addressed the subject of women on the velocipede. "The generally accepted reason for a woman's not riding a velocipede is shortly stated in the announcement that the gentle sex cannot straddle. That this movement is impossible? One doesn't see it very often, it is true.... It is something like that matter of voting. One needs to see it done before he will believe it can be well done," began the piece. "We have the testimony of the strong-minded that woman can vote with as much elegance and credit as a man and also that she can straddle the velocipede. Yesterday evening the latter was demonstrated in public at one of our fashionable velocipede rinks." Carrie Moore was the woman in question and she had worked the treadles of the new machine before an audience of Bostonians. "She did well; but, except for the fact that she was a woman who rode astride, there was nothing remarkable in her performance." Moore wore "loose pantaloons" that ended in ruffles where her boots began. The skirt of her tunic extended almost to the knee. However, this report also noted that it was to the bicycle schools that women had to look since the costume such as worn by Moore "would hardly be appropriate for these others." To solve that problem it was said that a dress had been invented for veloci-

Another illustration of a woman on a velocipede used to advertise a product, even though female riders were few and far between. This was from 1874 and was, again, for a tobacco product.

pede riding, a dress that was "both decorous and efficient." The outer skirt was made to button its entire length in front, and about halfway up behind. "When in place it has the appearance of an ordinary walking dress; but when arranged for ordinary velocipede exercise the buttons are loosened before and behind, the ends of each side are brought together between the legs."[20]

In the summer of 1869 a report from Paris described a velocipede race for ladies that had been held in Paris at the Hippodrome early in July. "The young ladies worked around the ring with that ugly and ridiculous movement of the legs which the velocipede exacts from its votaries, and 'never,' says a spectator, were the pretty round forms of pretty women made to look so laughably unattractive."[21]

An article that appeared in March 1870 remarked that a young lady had created a "sensation" at Velocipede Hall in Meriden, Connecticut, by her "graceful riding of the velocipede. She was dressed in bloomer costume, and was perfect mistress of the uncertain vehicle."[22]

But that was in 1870 and the velocipede craze took a rapid and dramatic crash that year and was not heard from again. Fourteen years later, in 1884, a journalist discussed the bicycle situation at the time and digressed to comment on the velocipede craze with the United States catching that fever in 1869. "Many of the riders of the present day caught the mania and did their best to utilize the machine, but it called for too much exertion on the road and was only suited for a plaything." The reporter added, "But people soon tired of it here [Washington] as they did in other cities, and in less than two years one could not be seen or found, except in a junk shop."[23]

The term "velocipede" rapidly fell out of usage in the language and was replaced entirely, in time, by the words which specifically noted the number of wheels on the device—unicycle, bicycle, tricycle and quadricycle. Since velocipede was a general term to describe one of the machines without regard to the number of wheels it contained, it was not possible to tell what sort of device those relatively few women rode or who rode a velocipede at all. Likely most of them rode a three- or four-wheeler. However, a couple of mentions of women astride indicated that at least some portion of the female velocipede riders did their riding on a two-wheeler. With the crash of velocipede popularity in 1870 it would be around 15 years before women would take to the bicycle. In between the tricycle craze would arrive and capture the interest of women before it, too, crashed out of favor. While the velocipede craze and the bicycle craze (starting in the mid–1880s) were widespread and affected men and women equally, the tricycle craze was limited to women.

2

The Tricycle

According to a correspondent writing to an American newspaper from London England in September 1880, in the west of London "it is no uncommon thing to meet a lady on a tricycle, which is getting to be for athletic young girls what the bicycle is to the young man. The vehicle is a queer looking thing." The journalist continued by stating, "The large driving wheel is at one side, with two small guiding wheels at the other, [and] a comfortable seat, like that of a sulky, being placed in the center. The propelling power is applied to two foot cranks in front. The speed attained by these three-wheeled conveyances is nearly fifteen miles an hour."[1]

Less than one year later, in July 1881 an account declared, "Tricycling has become the fashionable pursuit of the young men in England, and as the ladies never fail to follow in the wake of fashion when set by their admirers, the tricycle has been adopted by them with the greatest eagerness. At first it was considered 'rather fast,' and looked upon with shyness, but ever since the newspaper account of the ride taken by her majesty and the Princess Beatrice, each royal lady mounted on her iron horse," the endeavor has enjoyed great popularity. Readers were also advised, "It is urged that no danger can exist, as the queen, who is a heavy, fat old lady [Queen Victoria was then 62], was enabled to sit her steed with as much ease and confidence as when in former days she used to prance so proudly on her high nettled horse before the troops at review." In conclusion, it was reported, "And so professors of the bicycle and tricycle abound in London, and the racing and chasing along the suburban road at twilight and the laughing and chatting as the iron coursers shoot by, give quite a new aspect to the solitary walks round London."[2]

While the above account said that men had taken up tricycling they did not, apparently, do so to any great extent. The men who did turn to the tricycle were usually older men and/or men of any age who were not athletic or very fit. The high-wheeler bike then dominated the two-wheel vehicle market and that precluded women and all but reasonably young and fit males from riding a bicycle. What happened was that as men took up horseback riding and later bicycling they, to some extent, wanted their women to be able to accompany them. But the dreaded issue of women sitting astride had not been dealt with and could barely even be mentioned in the media. Out of all that came a way for women to accompany their men but in a way that patriarchal control and dominance was not threatened. In the case of horseback riding the sidesaddle was used. That meant the female rider could never best or outdo in any fashion her male companion who rode, naturally, astride his horse and had much better control over the animal. With respect to the bicycle it was a given that no self-respecting woman would ride astride one of those machines and so the tricycle was developed for use by women and children, as they were considered the two incompetent and inept classes of society. The tricycle did not last very long for many reasons. It was very heavy and very slow, for starters. Then the woman's bicycle (with the standard drop-frame still in use today) was developed. It was, compared to a man's bicycle, much heavier and of weaker construction. Thus, in both cases man was able to solve two problems. The sidesaddle, tricycle, and woman's bicycle all allowed a woman to accompany a man but ensured that the man would, in true patriarchal fashion, control every aspect of the activity.

According to one journalist the year 1882 promised to give an immense impetus to the sport of tricycling. Great improvements had been effected in the construction of these machines by the leading manufacturers, and the improved tricycles of 1882 were as far in advance of the 1879 machines as the present bicycle was ahead of the 1869 boneshaker. Machines strong enough to carry men weighing 200 pounds were then being built to weigh from 60 to 75 pounds (the average weight of a road bicycle today is roughly 20 pounds). Reportedly, many other improvements had also been made to the tricycle, including "the difficulty of propelling tricycles uphill, which formerly militated against their general adoption, is now fairly overcome." In 1881 the Prince of Wales (Albert, son of Queen Victoria and later King Edward VII) made tricycling very popular by purchasing one. There were supposedly, in 1882, about 60 distinct makes of tricycles on the market, with the number increasing daily. Also available were "sociable" tricycles that could carry two, three, or even four people at a time. Some of the early tandem bicycles were called "sociable" because the two people on a tricycle usually sat side by side instead of one behind the other, as was found with respect to the bicycle. Standard tandems such as found today, with one rider on front of the other, also could be found. It was estimated in 1882 that 25 percent of tricycle riders were ladies.[3]

Fashion issues and problems did not surface too often with respect to the tricycle since sitting astride never arose as a problem and the ordinary

THE TOURISTS.   LOVE'S YOUNG DREAM.

Two illustrations of "sociable" tandem trikes from the late 1880s. They were called sociable because the two riders sat side by side instead of one in front of the other, as was the case on the standard tandem of the era and of today.

walking clothing worn by women was suitable enough for a tricycle rider. However, one brief mention was made in 1883 to the fashion question: "Women who ride tricycles in England are beginning to wear trousers."[4]

The girl on the tricycle had made her appearance at the summer resorts of the United States, no later than the spring of 1883. As observed at Newport, Rhode Island, declared an article, "she sat between two wheels, which were connected by a short axletree, on a kind of a saddle—astride of it, but not so circumstanced as to make divided garments necessary, as in riding horseback fashion." And, it was noted, "her posture was not that of sitting, however, but her figure was suspended nearly perpendicular, and her legs were moved a great deal.... Her knees came up high, with an action more productive of good exercise than of grace. And yet she was a 'symmetrical and pleasing traveler.'" The prescribed costume was soft, thin flannel, with a blouse waist and a skirt reaching just to the gaiter tops. "It is obvious that the latter level could not be steadily maintained, in view of the high treading required to work the tricycle, without some special modifications of the garment," warned the piece. "This want has been supplied by taking an idea from the equestrian habit. Lengthwise of the skirt in front two gussets are set in at points where the knee will protrude into them in rising."[5]

A tricycle club was soon to be formed in Chicago, according to an August 1883 article, "of which many prominent ladies of that city will be members." This reporter thought that anything that would induce American women to take more outdoor exercise than they then did ought to be encouraged. "But aside from that, tricycle riding has many things to commend it, and there is no reason why it should not become as popular for women as bicycle riding has proved to be for men." He added that there was only one "dreadful obstacle" standing in the way of the speedy adoption of the tricycle by women and that had been expressed in print by an unnamed female. She said, "As tricycles are made the extremely ugly appearance cut by the rider, while working the machine, either front view or back, is enough to deter any lady from investing in one." It was the hope of the newspaperman that someone would soon reinvent the machine and thus combine the useful with the beautiful.[6]

Near the end of 1883 it was reported in a New York

An 1883 ad for a Columbia tricycle. A selling point was that it was equipped with 13 sets of ball bearings.

City newspaper that the use of the tricycle by women did not seem to have become so general in the United States, as the use of the bicycle by men. "This is a great pity, because American women should take more exercise than they do now; and tricycle riding seems to possess many advantages not so fully found elsewhere," said the journalist. "Were it once given the approval of fashion it is almost certain that it would become extremely popular with all classes of American women. It is the testimony of large numbers of English ladies that it is a delightful, pleasurable and healthful pastime." And with bicycling becoming so common among men it was only fair ladies should get a chance, he thought. "There are obvious reasons why they cannot get on the male bicycle; to follow on foot is out of the question, and even the naïve gallantry of the male cycler will not make it possible for him to stand still on his machine in a country road to talk with his lady friends." He went on to say, "The sidesaddle was designed to enable the ladies to accompany gentlemen on horseback. In the same way the tricycle seems to have been invented to enable them to accompany male humanity in the healthful exercise of bicycling." He also believed that it was quite possible that the tricycle might enlarge the sphere of woman's work in suburban town and country with the appointment of female tricyclers as letter carriers being a novel and picturesque feature of modern life, and doubtless in other ways the tricycle would be made the instrument "of women's emancipation from the thralldom of conventionality." In conclusion he asserted, "But seriously, while physicians, clergymen and business men are revelling in the newfound liberty of the bicycle, it is only fair that the ladies should have a chance to try the tricycle. Let some bold leader of her sex start the fashion in this country, and female tricyclers will soon be as numerous here as they are in England."[7]

On the morning of July 15, 1884 an enthusiastic wheelman told a reporter with a Washington, D.C., newspaper that seven young ladies in that city had recently adopted the tricycle as a mode of locomotion. That reporter saw one of those women on her tricycle and described her thusly: "Her costume was between a walking dress and a riding habit, and almost entirely conceded the movement that gave the motive power to the machine. There was not a shoetop, or a suspicion of hosiery to be seen, and the fair rider had an air about her that plainly indicated that custom and public opinion would soon confirm her choice of a vehicle if they had not already done do." Said the journalist, with reference to the first woman in Washington to ride a tricycle, "Mrs. Lockwood is no longer a curiosity or the object of impertinent observation and jest and it will not be six months before ladies on tricycles are far more numerous than ladies on horseback in the Washington streets." Also noted was that the double machine (tandem) and the family vehicle were great inventions and Washington, it was predicted, "will be treated to many novel sights in this direction. It will be quite an interesting sight to see a young lady and her pet dog, an artist and his easel and outfit, or a salesman and his stock sharing a tricycle." Concluding his piece, the reporter stated, "The possibilities of the tricycle are great, particularly in Washington, and it is soon going to be the proper thing for both ladies and gentlemen."[8]

Mrs. Belva A. Lockwood was reported to have been the first woman in Washington to have owned a tricycle, having purchased the machine in 1881. Several years later, in 1887, an account noted, "A few years ago Mrs. Belva Lockwood attracted much notice by appearing on the streets on a tricycle. She was the first woman to try it, and her independence, it is claimed, helped her considerably in her canvas against [James G.] Blaine and [Grover] Cleveland for the Presidency [in 1884], although she was not elected." He went on to add, "After Mrs. Lockwood appeared on the street some other venturesome women tried the machine and used to ride for pleasure, riding chiefly at night." Then a club was formed and a group of women could be seen on the streets, also usually at night. "Gradually, however, ladies began to appear singly on the street in broad day, and now a woman on tricycle attracts no more attention than a woman on a horse. Every week adds to the number of fair cyclers."[9]

In 1888 Belva Lockwood was running for the second time for the presidency of the United States on the ticket of the Equal Rights Party. She was a native of New York, having been born in Niagara County in 1830. At 14 years of age she undertook the care of a village school and at 18 she married Uriah H. McNall. He died, leaving her a widow at the age of 23. During the Civil War, Mrs. McNall did good service in the care of sick and wounded soldiers and in 1868 she married Dr. E. Lockwood. Mrs. Lockwood, having made up her mind to become a lawyer, and having been refused admittance to the Columbian Law School in Washington, entered the National University of that city and in September 1873 was admitted to practice law in the District of Columbia. Six years later she was admitted to practice at the bar of the United States Supreme Court. Since that time she had been engaged in practicing her profession and lecturing on women's rights. At that time, in 1888, observed a journalist, "Mrs. Lockwood is devoted to the tricycle. She rides that queer vehicle well and it is said that she introduced its use into Washington. Four years ago when she was running for President she was spoken of as 'sailing around Washington on her tricycle, showing her red stockings at every turn of the wheels, dressed in a brown cloth sacque [loose-fitting dress], which wrinkles in the back and puckers at the sleeves, making speeches now and then, and bowing to the crowds who have ironically greeted her with cheers and the waving of hats.'" In the 1884 United States presidential election Grover Cleveland beat James Blaine, with those two candidates combining for 97.13 percent of the total vote. The other five candidates, all running for a party, combined to share just 2.87 percent of the vote. In the 1888 presidential election Cleveland lost his bid for reelection, to Benjamin Harrison, although Cleveland won a plurality of votes. He lost in the electoral college. As in 1884 there were half a dozen or so minor parties running who split the 3.57 percent of the vote not taken by the two main candidates.[10]

An account that appeared in a Washington, D.C., newspaper in August 1884 enthused, "The tricycle, the near relative of the bicycle, is keeping pace with it in the growth in popular favor. It is particularly adopted to ladies and to persons who desire to make rapid progress without any risk of an ugly tumble, or to invalids who need some outdoor exercise." There were then said to be 350 different kinds of tricycles being manufactured. Then the reporter went on to state that the number of tricycles in use in the nation's capital was about 50. A tricycle club had recently been formed there and had a membership of about 20, consisting of a large portion of women. "Ladies of Washington were very slow in adopting the tricycle as a means of employment and exercise, being dissuaded from so doing by the unattractive appearance of the pioneer rider of their sex, who has for a number of years been a familiar figure upon the streets." Although not named in the piece, the woman is question was Lockwood. "In the shadow of the evening a few ladies tried the tricycles, which belonged to their husbands, and soon became so pleased with them that, putting aside all conventional ideas on the subject, they began riding as a regular exercise. Others soon followed their example, and now there are about a dozen lady tricyclers who ride regularly, and greatly enjoy it. Some ride singly, accompanied by their husbands on bicycles, and some use the popular 'sociable.'" According to this account it took 20 percent more power to drive the trike than the bike "and yet ladies when they have thoroughly mastered the machine, ride with ease in nearly every direction about Washington—7th street and 14th street hills offer no serious obstacles to a run to Brightwood." The first lady rider in Washington after Lockwood

Belva Lockwood was notorious as the first female tricycle rider in Washington, D.C. Some went so far as to blame her for impeding female progress with respect to the tricycle because she looked so unappealing on the machine. This photograph was from the 1880s.

was, he thought, Mrs. B.W. Hanna, wife of the captain of the Capitol Club; then followed Mrs. E.P. Hanna, Mrs. W.C. Scribner and Mrs. D.E. Fox. The sociable trikes, carrying two people side by side, were becoming very popular. A new machine called the Otto had arrived in America and was said to be in many respects like a tricycle, but similar to a bicycle in that it had only two wheels, but those wheels were side by side.[11]

As September arrived in 1884 a lengthy piece appeared that discussed the soon coming end of the summer season at resort hotels for the fashionable. Much material in the article was devoted to the kinds of dresses and costumes worn there, and so forth, which stated, "The 'divided skirt' has obtain[ed] such recognition as is to be found in its adoption by some lady tricyclists in England as part of the tricycle costume. It is not called by the name, but drawers corresponding with the dress, that is of the same material, are authoritatively recommended instead of underskirts for wear by lady tricyclers, and it is further recommended that the skirt of the dress be shortened a trifle above walking length and that the drawers be ruffled and allowed to project below." That was said to be all there was of Lady Frances Harberton's rational dress. With respect to America, wrote this reporter, "As yet changes in dress have not much interest for women from the tricycle point of view, no lady owning one yet in this country, it is said, and but few gentlemen." That was, of course, not true. There was said to be one tricycle that had been imported from Coventry, England, at a cost of $350, to be found at the resort of Long Branch. It attracted great attention when the male tricyclist owner went out with a friend "who is not infrequently a lady." That machine was a new version that could seat one or two occupants. But, concluded the piece, bicycles and tricycles require hard, smooth, macadam roads "such as are rarely found in this country."[12]

Another fashion-type article about the tricycle rider appeared in September 1884. It declared, "Ladies who use the tricycle in England wear a dress made of dark blue serge, the skirt kilted or tucked, with jersey waist and pantaloons for riding habits. This dress obviates the necessity of many undergarments and will not catch the dust. Compactness is the aim of these dresses."[13]

Still in September 1884 a profile of Washington's new tricycle club and its lady members was published. A reporter talked to a rider who declared that a good many bicyclists were giving up their bikes and getting trikes. A number of tricyclists formed a club known as the Potomac Tricycle Club on July 16 of that year. There were nine original members, three of whom were women. By late in September the club had 30 members, 10 of which were females. Several of the male members were described as "old bicyclists." The club had frequent runs for its members, starting at around 7 p.m. "The little platoon of ladies riding about the streets in the evening has attracted much notice recently. Such unfavorable comments as are heard generally come from ladies, who probably would not cast a very pretty figure on a bicycle," stated the newsman. The reporter was on hand at the start of a club run that month, with those runs being touted as being good exercise and good for health in general. One female tricyclist declared, "It is mock modesty that prevents many ladies from riding the tricycle. Some of them say that a woman sacrifices her dignity when she gets upon a tricycle.... Why, there is infinitely more dignity about a lady on a tricycle than a lady on horseback.... When a lady talks against tricycling either she is not able to get one or she cannot 'pull.'"[14]

That journalist went on to ask the female members assembled for their run about the question of dress. One woman said to him, "Well, I wear a skirt a little longer than an ordinary walking skirt. Some ladies, however, prefer short skirts. The ladies of the club have been discussing the idea of a uniform, but they are ladies, you know, and have not decided the matter yet. It is proposed to adopt the uniform of the cycling tourist clubs of England. That consists of a kilted skirt, a short cutaway coat and a half-beaver hat." The rider went on to explain, "The ladies do not wear any starched underclothing. Such clothing would impede the feet, of course. They wear dark trousers and the uniform is sensible and fitted for the purpose for which it was intended. There is no superfluous clothing. It is well to have a dress especially for riding, for it is apt to become greasy from the machine." And, she added, "one lady insisted on going out the first time she rode with her bustle on. Of course when the run was over the bustle was all out of shape and out of place, and she had to hurry into the house to fix it before she could appear on the street. Ladies now do their shopping on tricycles. I would advise every lady to try it."[15]

At the regular meeting of the Memphis Tennessee Bicycle Club that was held

An 1886 illustration of a woman on a trike. Some of these machines had the two large wheels in the back, but as do modern day tricycles, some had those big wheels located on the front end.

in October 1884 the tricycle came in for what was reported to be a considerable share of discussion. Though there were about 30 bicycles in the city of Memphis (counting only rubber-tired machines) there was just one tricycle. That machine had been recently purchased by Mr. W.L. Surprise. It had attracted much attention whenever it was seen in the city and the club hoped to add a tricycle section to its club "with the hope of inducing some of the ladies to join in this healthful and graceful exercise." According to the account, "Tricycles are used to a considerable extent by both ladies and gentlemen in the East and in Europe, and there are plenty of good streets in and about Memphis to make their use here pleasurable and profitable."[16]

Two weeks later another report from Memphis observed that another tricycle, at a cost of $160, had just been ordered by a Memphis man. A Memphis dealer who brought 12 girls' tricycles to Memphis a couple of weeks earlier had sold them out and then had an order for 40 more machines on his books. "The prejudice which has so long existed Memphis against bicycles has almost entirely disappeared," asserted the piece. Touting the role of his own newspaper the reporter said that in the spring of 1884, when his paper began the movement in favor of the wheel, there were just two bicycles in Memphis, and "there are now no less than thirty young men who are active wheelmen, besides about fifty boys and some fifteen girls from eight to fifteen years of age, who are riding tricycles."[17]

The subject of the girl who rode a tricycle in New York City was the topic of an article that appeared in print early in 1885. It began by announcing, "The newest performer in public is the girl who rides the tricycle. She has waited a long time before getting courage enough to make her rather unseasonable debut at Central Park, and only does so at length after much practice in more obscure places. She is an object of staring curiosity, and the horses are scared of her." The article added, "There is no Bloomerism in the costume which she has adopted. Knickerbocker trousers and a short skirt were originally prescribed for this service, but she is not such a fool as to think of seeking pleasure while looking like a fright." It was also reported, "Her bodice is covered nearly down to the elbows by fur, but the small girth of her waist is left in view. The skirt is woolen and dark, with plenty of wide bands of fur, so she looks warm, whether she is or not. Her shoes are solid and low." In the description of her costume the all-important question of modesty and propriety was not forgotten. "A concealed elastic cord contrasts the hem of her drapery and, therefore, the expectant observer might as well wait for the wind to blow up sunrise at midnight as to count on a relevant wafture of her petticoats. This safeguard to her modesty is requisite because there is no mass of underskirts which would impede her action in working the treadles [of the tricycle]." Those New York City female tricycle riders were usually to be seen in the forenoon "and there are as yet few duplicates of her; but she usually belongs to a family so eminent socially that she can do no wrong, and so her example will soon be numerously followed." In conclusion the article asserted, "I suppose we may expect, after a while, to see our approved heiress as frequently on the tricycle as we do now on horseback."[18]

In May 1885 a report out of Washington, D.C., mentioned the bicycle races at Athletic Park that were held that month. The report stated, "There is so much bicycling and tricycling here and it is so much indulged in by people of prominence and those holding rank in society that these races always attract attention." The journalist argued, "The use of the bicycle and tricycle is becoming extremely popular here. Large numbers of ladies now use the tricycle, and there is a tricycle club of some forty people." In this account Belva Lockwood was mentioned, but in a negative way. "The manufacturer believes that if it had not been for Belva Lockwood he would before this time have sold a thousand tricycles in Washington. He said the notoriety of Belva as a tricycle rider had prevented nearly everybody else from using them, especially women." That tricycle manufacturer added, with respect to the city's first female tricycler, "Now if it had only been Mrs. Logan who had bought a tricycle, then everybody there would have been using them before this time." Mrs. John A. Logan was socially prominent at that time and the wife of a well-known politician. John Logan was the vice presidential running mate in the losing campaign of 1884 on a ticket headed by James Blaine, who lost to Grover Cleveland. Lockwood, as previously mentioned, was a candidate for president in that campaign. The difference was clear and stark; had Mrs. Logan operated the first trike she would have been warmly received and emulated by many because she was an insider in Washington, a part of the system. However, Lockwood, even though she and Mrs. Logan were direct or indirect participants in the 1884 presidential campaign, was an outsider and not part of the system. Therefore when she operated the first trike she was stared at and mocked with nobody following her example.[19]

A writer who considered the topic of women and tricycles in July 1885, from Chicago, offered the opinion, "Although tricycles have been ridden by women for some time, yet the amusement (one of the most conducive to health ever introduced) has not increased in popular favor as much as it deserves to do." One reason for that situation perhaps lay in the cost of the activity because a good tricycle could not be had for less than $100, and that was a huge sum of money in 1885. "Another cause is the excessive disfavor with which a large section of society still regards the exercise. To hear the opinions of some people, it would appear to be almost criminal for a girl to appear on one of 'those velocipedes,' and the most unfounded charges are trumped up," he offered as another factor. "Another objection is that a tricycling woman must be 'fast.' The reason why is not very clear. Tennis-players are not considered so, neither are all who ride on horseback. The reason for this opinion must lie in the fact that some 'fast' girls have been very ready to adopt this mode of travelling, being rapid; and so their steady sisters who adopted the exercise for the good of health are given brevet rank as such." As a final thought he stated, "The tricycles most suitable for the use of women are the side geared ones. Those centrally geared can be used, but the first-mentioned are the most desirable, the central frame in the other kind dividing the skirt and causing an ugly appearance from the rear."[20]

One month after the above piece a writer out of Washington, D.C., observed, "The tricycle fever still rages among the people who lay claim to social prominence here. Washington is the paradise of the wheel, whether bicycle or tricycle, and the latter is daily becoming more popular." The Washington Tricycle Club had about 40 members with, among them, "some people of a good deal of prominence." The club made regular runs and its hall was open in the afternoons for the "exclusive use of ladies." A number of women who had male relatives in the Capital Bicycle Club had learned to ride the tricycle in order to accompany them in their runs. Most bicycle clubs of the time did not allow female members. The best most female riders could hope for was some sort of auxiliary organization, or annex, associated with the main club. Reportedly, a number of well-known physicians in Washington used the tricycle to make house calls. According to the story, "For some years tricycling as an exercise for women made very little progress here, but now the tide has turned and wheelmen, running through the quiet streets at twilight, meet ladies upon tricycles in groups and in pairs, accompanied by gentlemen at every turn." Meanwhile, the lady tricycle riders of Boston, while they had organized no clubs, had adopted some rules as to costume, which had to be of some neutral tint or

THE TRICYCLE.

Another 1886 drawing of a female on a trike, this time with the big wheels in the back.

shade, with hat, gloves and dress of the same. The jacket and sleeves were tight-fitting and the skirt was the ordinary walking dress length, made six inches longer behind, because sitting in the saddle would gather up the back breadth and made the skirt appear even all around. "With a skirt made like this not any more of the foot is shown in tricycling than in walking. Full skirts should be restricted by wearing thick, close-fitting underclothes, and the jockey hat is considered the most becoming to the tricycle lady riders," concluded the account.[21]

A September 1885 news item also told of the growing popularity of tricycling in New York City and Boston, with Central Park in New York and Commonwealth Avenue in Boston having become the main scene of tricycle riding for women. The report declared, "The fact is the tricycle has come to stay, and we may well mark with a special jubilate the era when the sewing machine goes out and the tricycle comes in." This journalist enthused over trikes because "of all forms of exercise the tricycle promises to be the most available—better than rowing, horse riding, and so forth. Boston women who looked on curiously a year ago to see women tricyclists at the Institute fair, and who no more dreamed of it for themselves than they dreamed of endeavoring to emulate Cavallazzi [a famous female ballet dancer of the time], are now adopting the tricycle and taking advantage of the deserted condition of the Back bay to practice up and down Commonwealth avenue." Concluding his story the reporter said, "By all means let the sewing machine and all that it stood for go out, and let the tricycle and all that it represents come in."[22]

"When the people get used to seeing girls and women riding upon tricycles, they will be no more surprised at it than they are now at the sight of a boy upon a bicycle," declared a newsman in June 1886, who went on to note that doctors pronounced tricycling to be "the most healthful of exercises." He also observed that "fashionable ladies in England used the tricycle very commonly over the long, pleasant country roads and in the small towns." It was, he thought, better than a horse, to which it was often compared for the tricycle did not get tired, it did not eat, it cost less to buy initially than a horse and cost next to nothing in upkeep. As well, the tricycle could hold shopping purchases as well as storing luggage.[23]

A report from Washington, D.C., in the following month remarked that the latest feature of life in the nation's capital was the adoption of the tricycle by ladies, in part due to the broad, smooth roads. "The fact that the appearance of a lady upon a tricycle would be likely to attract notice, and cause more or less comment, has until recently prevented their general adoption by the ladies. A number of tricycle clubs have, however, been formed among the ladies during the past few months," observed the journalist. But it was increasing in popularity daily and "it is safe to predict that the 'machine' will soon achieve an even greater popularity among the ladies than it has heretofore with the gentlemen."[24]

That same month an unidentified young woman praised tricycling as a better all-around sport and exercise than any alternative, who declared, "Just at first it's rather hard labor, but when you once get the knack of it you can do forty or fifty miles without feeling it, but you must have considerably practice first in making your weight do most of the work." She went on to say, "Some women object that it looks awkward from the short skirts, but there is really no need of them; they should not be shorter than the ankles, but they should be rather close and narrow, for a loose skirt is apt to tangle in the wheels. The first time I rode a tricycle my wide skirts were fluttered by the breeze of my swift motion against the rapidly revolving spokes, and in two minutes I was jerked off my seat and so tangled up in the wheel that I had to be combed out."[25]

Two illustrations from 1886 showing more typical tandems with the riders seated one in front of the other.

A reporter talked to a female cyclist in September 1886. The cyclist had learned to ride a trike in Liverpool, England, where she belonged to a club of 160 ladies but she was then the only representative of her sex in a local tricycle club on Long Island, New York. Said the reporter, "This gives pretty nearly the proportion, I suppose, of ladies riding tricycles in England and in America, the difference being due to the fact that we had the bicycle first from the mother country, and moreover to the great superiority of the English roads." That lack of decent roads in America had led to the use of a different version of the tricycle, in some cases. The three-wheel cycle with the front wheel being placed in a line midway between the two back wheels created a three-track vehicle that needed to find three clear tracks on the road. (The bicycle, with the two wheels in a line, only required the rider to search out one clear track as he cycled along.) On newer tricycle models that front wheel was placed to the side, aligned directly in front of one of the back wheels, thus creating a vehicle that needed only two clear tracks, instead of three. A tricycle at this time cost $120 to $150 for a "good outfit."[26]

In November 1886 it was reported that a well-known dealer in tricycles in Baltimore was seen to enter the White House grounds with one of his machines. Soon after he came out alone, without his machine. Apparently, the tricycle had been left behind. Some passersby at the White House that evening said they noticed a lady learning to ride a trike. Said a journalist, "This is a very fashionable sport in this city. A great number of ladies delight in riding up and down the smooth asphalt streets on the easygoing machines. They are seen at all hours of the day. Consequently a young lady on a tricycle is nothing unusual here, but it has caused comment from the people who have occasion to go past the White House grounds." Speculation was that the tricycle was for Mrs. Cleveland, and not for President Grover Cleveland "because the tricycle taken to the White House had a saddle arranged for a lady, and it is not likely the president would care to ride a machine 'lady-fashion.'"[27]

Women in this period were turning to various athletic pursuits and exercises. As one account detailed, "Of late years a great advance has been made by the women of this country in the direction of physical culture, and lawn tennis, rowing, horseback riding, tricycling, etc., have become more or less popular." And, continued the article, "among outdoor sports the tricycle is recognized as a useful and enjoyable means of exercise, and is numbered by Col. Higginson, William B. Howland and other enthusiasts as one of the greatest boons to American women the present century has brought." Howland had written in *Scientific American* that the practicability of the tricycle as a vehicle for the daily use of women was undoubted. Said Howland, "There is scarcely a large town in the land where there are not some ladies who use

THE LADY'S TRICYCLE.

An 1887 close-up of a lady's tricycle. Note that the front wheel is not directly in the middle of the two back wheels, as is the case today, but lined up with one of the back wheels. This was done to give the rider only two-wheel tracks to keep an eye on, as she traveled over very bad roads by today's standards, instead of three tracks on a regular tricycle, or just one track on a standard bicycle.

the tricycle as others do their horse and carriage. It is always ready at the door for an errand to the market, a call on a friend, a spin for pleasure or a journey to the next town."[28]

According to an article that appeared in July 1887 there had been a great increase in Washington, D.C., over the previous two to three years in the number of women who rode tricycles in that city. The first machine in the city was the one purchased by Lockwood just six years earlier, back in 1881, but it was described in 1887 as being old-fashioned. The article stated, "The tricycle of the day is made with crank and pedals, and a graceful woman who rides properly seems to acquire new grace upon it. Sitting erect, the movement is natural and easy, and she glides like a goddess." It was reported then that there were 500 women in Washington who rode tricycles. Many of them owned their own machines; others rented tricycles when they wanted to use them. There were single machines, and tandems, and sociables, "and tricycles of a great many different patterns."[29]

Illustrating the variety of tricycles was an ad for the machine that appeared in August 1887. It featured a machine designed for ladies and children, which looked somewhat like a wheelchair. Note that the machine had steel-wire wheels and steel tires.[30]

Another August 1887 article about the popularity of women on tricycles in Washington reported, "Probably five hundred of the 'very best' women residing in the city now take their exercise upon these vehicles many of them owning their own wheels."[31]

Yet three months later an article stated, "One hundred women ride tricycles in Washington." This piece went on to remark, "Most of the women have a special costume in the nature of a riding habit with the train cut off. Nevertheless it takes them a good while to get over their nervousness and their self-consciousness so as to really enjoy their ride. Very few of them ride in the daytime." Then the journalist waxed poetic and drifted into

An 1887 ad for "The Gem," a tricycle for women and children. It looked something like a wheelchair in the back area.

hyperbole: "These young ladies ride with perfect ease and grace. They show the possibilities of the tricycles to perfection as they sweep through the streets on noiseless wings. I have never seen better or more beautiful riding. They are the envy and the despair of their less successful rivals." Also noted was that many of those women owned their own machines but that a large number of them rented their tricycles by patronizing the "cycleries." As a final note he reinforced the fact that the patriarchy had not left the cycling arena by stating, "Of course, those who travel in the evening are always accompanied by gentlemen."³²

An 1886 sketch of a group of women setting off on a tricycle outing while a few spectators look on in wonder.

A month later a New York City reporter declared, "The number of lady members of the cycling clubs is growing, and those institutions are planting themselves everywhere along the parkside, where a woman may call, get her wheel, trundle it into the smooth parkways, enjoying an hour or two of exhilarating exercise and return it to cover again without a long journey over paved streets and jolting cobblestones."³³

Writing in a newspaper in February 1888 a journalist brought up a point that was not often mentioned. He wrote, "The women tricyclists who are becoming a numerous body and always belong to a wealthy, or at least well-to-do class, does not give a thought to the becomingness of their attire; it is what is most convenient, most comfortable and proves no obstacle to skimming along a road as fast as a man." Cycling in this period was the domain of rich and well-to-do women almost exclusively. Wheels in this period cost roughly $100 to $150 for a decent machine. Today, 130 or so years later, a woman can still get a machine in that price range, albeit the lower price range, at a store such as Walmart. Owning a machine was limited to the higher income class of women and even then it was often a husband or father, and so forth, who bought the machine for the female rider. Lower income women were limited in their cycling activity to renting a machine for an hour or two, if they could afford that. A poor woman of the time who eked out an existence as, for example, a laundress (which involved picking up and delivering clothing) would have benefited greatly from owning and using a tricycle in her business but had no hope of ever owning one. As well, all lower income women worked long and exhausting hours and likely had little energy left on a Sunday to rent a bike for an hour or two if, indeed, they had the funds.[34]

The Tricyclist Club of Philadelphia had 18 women members, as of February 1888, one of whom, Mrs. Lewis, was a candidate for the cup offered by the club for the best record in miles of travel made during the year. The record already exceeded 3,000 miles. Of England, it was said, "The Princesses of Wales are expert tricyclists, and the English club has more than a thousand women members."[35]

A May 1888 report from a New York City newspaper remarked that tricycling was becoming very popular with women in that city, with Central Park and various uptown drives the most popular spots. "Their great advantage is in opening up a new form of outdoor amusement and exercise for women. Physicians have not taken to advising tricycle riding as a cure for weak backs, broken nerves, dyspepsia, and many other ills that female flesh falls heir to," the reporter noted. In England the Queen and the Princess Beatrice had favored the wheel by riding through the Windsor lanes on tricycles, and the amusement has become very popular among the ladies of nobility. In the United States, Washington, D.C., was the most popular city for women on tricycles, with Boston next, followed by Brooklyn and New York. New York City "was slow in taking up tricycling, for the reason that until late last summer it was unlawful to ride in the parks in any vehicles not drawn by horses," explained the newsman. "As there were scarcely any smooth pavements outside of the parks, little riding was done in the city limits. A law went into effect last August, however, that admits all kinds of cycles to the parks. Since then the number of lady cycles has doubled, and is being increased every day." The bicycle clubs in New York did not have female members but allowed them "every privilege of the club-houses except that of membership." In Brooklyn the women formed a club of their own and were often seen on the avenues in groups of a dozen or more. "They frequently spin down the boulevard to Coney Island or out to Garden City and back." A woman riding a single tricycle could easily go 15 miles in an afternoon, and when riding a tandem with a man 20 to 30 miles was the usual distance traveled. This reporter went on to assert that a tricycle could go up a hill more easily than a bicycle. However, he did admit that a tricycle weighed about 25 percent more than a two-wheeler and "on a level road requires about 15 percent more exertion to propel it." The cost of a tricycle outfit, according to this account, was from $150 to $200.[36]

The city of Washington was said to have 300 women in the city who owned tricycles, in May 1888. Average price of these machines was said herein to be $100. Tricycle parties could be seen most every night. Those parties were made up of both men and women and one could rent a tricycle in Washington just as she would a horse at a livery stable. "A tandem rents for 75 cents for the first hour and 50 cents per hour thereafter. It is quite the thing now to take your lady friends out on wheels, and there are a number of little private clubs of ladies and gentlemen here who ride several times a week, and on Sunday evenings the streets have more bicycles and tricycles than [horse] carriages," explained the article.[37]

Several years passed with few mentions of the tricycle, as the fad had mostly passed. Writing in 1893 when the tricycle was rapidly on its way to being nothing but a memory and a junk item hidden away in a shed, a reporter noted that a woman on a tricycle could make "no sort of speed, the trike is fatiguing to operate and it is apt to rather soon make a creaking sound that sets sensitive nerves crazy." And despite what an earlier account had asserted, the tricycle was next to impos-

This 1886 sketch shows a woman on a trike followed by a man riding a high-wheeler bicycle, the latter by far the most popular style of bicycle then.

An 1882 view of Oldreive's new tricycle with a woman inside.

sible to power up a hill, even a slight grade. It was no wonder that the trike was abandoned for the bicycle. And that started to happen late in the 1880s, after a few developments, first of the safety bicycle and then of the ladies' bike (drop-frame) soon after that. According to this piece Ward McAllister permitted American young women to ride tricycles because the Princess of Wales and her daughters rode tricycles. But, said Ward, "it is highly improper

View of an 1887 cycling excursion. The men are all riding high-wheelers while the lone woman in the group is piloting a tricycle.

for young women to use bicycles." This reporter added, "If the Princess of Wales were to ride a bicycle, appearing just once upon it, Ward McAllister would see in bicycle riding henceforth the most modest and healthful of exercises for American girls and he knows it." Ward McAllister was the self-appointed arbiter of New York society from the 1860s to the early 1890s. He had married into money and sought, successfully, to be a tastemaker among New York's elite. He was the man who coined the term "The Four Hundred" denoting the approximate number of people who "really mattered" in that city.[38]

When the velocipede craze ended suddenly in 1870 little attention was paid to the bicycle for the rest of that decade. Work continued to be done to improve the machine; it was work that did not bear much fruit until around 1880 when the bicycle started to make a comeback in terms of usage, at least among men. It was never clear what percentage of women who used velocipedes in 1868–1870 used two, or three, or four wheelers. Most probably used the three or four wheelers. Thus the development of the machine was focused on two and three wheelers (bicycles and tricycles). Bicycles quickly evolved in the 1880s until the high-wheeler, or "ordinary" bicycle became the dominant type. It had a gigantic front wheel (often five feet or more in height) and a tiny back wheel (usually about 12 inches in height). Women gravitated toward the trike because it was easier to ride and the moral and fashion issues were less pronounced. Plus, of course, it was physically impossible for women to ride the ordinary, in any costume even remotely accepted in society. The ordinary also limited the spread of bicycling among men because only the young, fit and athletic male could ride them. Mounting an ordinary was very difficult and taking a fall off one was potentially very dangerous. While no woman would attempt an ordinary it was also true that no 45-year-old lawyer or 50-year-old physician would attempt it. Thus the bicycle limped along during the 1880s until later in that decade when the safety bicycle was in development, and soon after that came the ladies' bicycle, that is, the drop-frame, in much the same format as exists to this day. That caused the rapid decline of the high-wheeler or ordinary and the tricycle as men of all kinds flocked to the safety bicycle while women abandoned the trike to take up the ladies' bicycle, with the braver ones tackling the men's bicycle from time to time. The safety bicycle was so named because it was much closer to the ground and much safer to ride since a fall put the rider at much less risk of serious injury than existed in the case of a fall from an ordinary. The safety bicycle of the late 1880s was similar in size to a bicycle of today. Those high-wheelers are often called penny-farthing bicycles today but during their heyday they were never called by that term. It was only when the high-wheeler had faded away and was mostly a curiosity that the term "penny farthing" was applied to the machine.

3

The Bicycle to 1889

After the velocipede craze ended around 1870 development and improvement was concentrated on the three-wheeler machine (the tricycle for women and children principally) and the two-wheeler, the bicycle. What emerged as the most popular and favored bicycle was the high-wheeler, or "ordinary" as it was sometimes called. It was so-named because that was mostly the only machine available among the two-wheel devices. It was seen as the logical extension to the old boneshaker, with the front wheel enlarged to enable higher speeds while the rear wheel shrank and the frame was made lighter. Frenchman Eugene Meyer is regarded as the father of the high-wheel bicycle. That front wheel could, and often did, have a diameter up to 60 inches. It may have been fast but it was unsafe. That meant cycling became the preserve of adventurous and athletic young men. Older men and women preferred tricycles and sometimes quadricycles. The fact that older men took up the tricycle meant that the fad for tricycles was probably somewhat bigger and longer lasting than if women alone had turned to the tricycle. John Kemp Starley produced the first successful safety bike in 1885 and it revolutionized the cycling industry as it completely replaced the high-wheel machine by around 1890. Pneumatic bicycle tires in 1888 (replacing solid rubber tires) made for a much smoother ride while the diamond frame (the one used to this day, at least in men's machines) was found to be the strongest and most efficient design. The improvements in bicycle steering, safety, comfort and speed led to the craze for bicycling in the 1890s. Bear in mind that the bicycle craze was limited to the upper and middle classes of the population. Lower middle classes and the poor were effectively excluded from the activity due to the prohibitive cost involved. The ladies' safety bike was developed in the last few years of the 1880s. That was crucial to involving women in the activity since it allowed women to cycle who declined to adopt any of the "rational" costumes for riding a bike. Those women rode while wearing full skirts that

Safer than any Tricycle, faster and easier than any Bicycle ever made. Fitted with handles to turn for convenience in storing or shipping. Far and away the best hill-climber in the market.

MANUFACTURED BY

STARLEY & SUTTON,
METEOR WORKS, WEST ORCHARD, COVENTRY, ENGLAND.

In 1884 the first safety bike made its appearance from the Starley company in England.

came down to the top of the shoe or only a few inches from the ground. The safety bike for women (often called the drop-frame in this time period and referred to as a step-through frame today) allowed females to easily mount a bike while wearing standard clothing of the time. To ride a man's bike, while retaining a woman's dignity, modesty, and so forth, meant a woman had to adopt some form of a divided skirt, bloomers, short skirt, and so on; that is, move to a "rational" dress, something that was met with resistance from a lot of quarters.[1]

Almost nothing appeared in the media in the 1870s with respect to women and bicycles. One story published in New Orleans in March 1879 reported, "Bicycle riding by women promises to become fashionable in Detroit. The example was set by a wealthy and reputable young lady, who at first rode in secluded places, but afterwards took to the suburban roads." It was also said, "She uses the ordinary two-wheeled machine and sits astride, wearing very loose trousers, and is frequently accompanied by half a dozen female companions. A tumble resulting in a broken nose temporarily cooled her ardor, but the sport has more than regained the lost favor."[2]

In the early 1880s it was more usual to find women and bicycles mentioned, if mentioned at all, in connection with an exhibition in something like a circus, carnival, or some other traveling show. An ad for the Great Forepaugh Show that appeared in Jackson, Ohio, in October 1880 featured a high-wire artist billed as Zulia, the female Blondin who, among other things, rode a velocipede over a slender wire 100 feet in the air.[3]

An ad for W.W. Cole's traveling circus, appeared in September 1882 and featured among its attractions "A College of Bicycle Experts," male and female, who performed aerial bicycle riding. The word "velocipede" was just about gone. An advertisement from May 1884 for a different traveling show featured a female performer who rode a bicycle on a wire.[4]

A woman named Louise Armaindo appeared in San Antonio, Texas, in February 1885 to give a bicycle riding exhibition. An article subhead described her as "the champion bicycle rider of America." She was in the Texas city with the "male champions of America" to compete in a six-day race. Inter-

ZUILA, THE FEMALE BLONDIN,

Rides a Velocipede Over a Slender Wire, 100 Feet in MID AIR,

And wheels her babe over it and crosses the high wire 60 feet above the heads of the audience, blindfolded and with her feet encased in sacks. Only Exhibition using the new and wonderful

EDISON ELECTRIC LIGHT,

Requiring a 50-horse high pressure engine to produce the same. This is the largest and best show under the sun. Grand Free
BALLOON ASCENSIONS, each exhibition day. Mammoth Pavilion holding 10,000 spectators. The entire show transported on my own 3 Great Railway Trains.
Behold the Grand and Gorgeous Street PAGEANT!

An 1880 ad for a traveling show that featured Zulia, a female performing on a bicycle.

These ads, from 1882 and 1884, showed women performing on a high wire while riding a high-wheeler bicycle. That was about the only place one would have seen a woman riding one of these "ordinary" machines.

Zola Rides a Bicycle on 3-4 inch wire 100 Feet High.

viewed at her hotel by a reporter, Armaindo explained that she was born in Montreal, 24 years old, and began to ride a bicycle about five years earlier in Chicago. Armaindo had been an athlete before that as was her mother before her. Reportedly she had lifted 700 pounds dead weight.[5]

Despite the handicaps facing bicycling as it tried to gain popularity in the first half of the 1880s it did enjoy some increases in advocates. A report that appeared in June 1882 declared, "The bicycle has become a recognized institution. A bicycle convention has just been held, attended by three hundred persons, and they had a procession and an exhibition which were largely attended." In the opinion of this reporter, "There can be no doubt that these machines will become more popular and common every year, and it is equally certain that the tricycle, which has the great advantage of being safe from upsetting [the public and societal norms] and is therefore adapted to the great body of sober, middle-aged people who do not care to encounter the risk of broken arms or collarbones, will soon be adopted in this county as it has already been in Europe. There the tricycle is being employed quite extensively by business and professional men, and a new kind has recently been devised having a second seat, for a lady companion." Admitted by this account was the fact that the tricycle was not as fast as the bicycle but it was by no means slow. Ten miles an hour could be made on a tricycle with ease, and even as high as 15 miles per hour, it was said.[6]

"Five young ladies of Denver, Colorado, ride the bicycle 'man fashion,' clad in black velvet knee breeches, woolen high stockings, a polo cap, and a sack coat, with low cut bicycle shoes," reported a piece in May 1883. "The Denver masculines are all learning to ride so as to accompany the girls in their spins."[7]

A lengthy article that appeared originally in a New York City newspaper in December 1883 was about the prominent men who could be seen on bicycles in New York. The journalist also mentioned England, where letter carriers did their rounds on bicycles, policemen patrolled on bikes, physicians visited their patients using bicycles, as well as tax collectors, rent collectors and even sheriffs serving warrants using them. Plus many businessmen in England were said to be using them. Back in America nothing like that was happening, the reporter admitted, but he went on to say that many, many men used them for pleasure. The League of American Wheelman was said to have 4,000 members. Named in the piece were many doctors and other prominent men in the city. Men from other cities were also cited by name, as were racers and "trick" riders named. Despite such a large article only three women were named—all racers. They were Louise Armaindo, Elsa von Blumen, and Maggie Wallace.[8]

A journalist for a Washington, D.C., newspaper reported in August 1884 on the growth of bicycling in that city. He termed the rapid growth of the bicycle in Washington as being "astonishing" and went on to state, "It was only a few years ago that a bike was regarded as [a] great novelty and its rider as one too lazy to walk and to indigent to own a horse." The first Washington rider after the velocipede craze was said to be Charles G.W. Krauskopf, in 1878. He was the object of "a good deal of chatting and joking." In 1884 there was said to be two bicycle clubs in Washington, with one having 115 riding members while the other had 47. They were, the Capital Bicycle Club and the Washington Cycle Club, respectively. It was estimated then that the number of bicycles in constant use by men was 600. Of those about 400 were the upright machines and the remaining 200 were Stars, which had the little wheel in front (a high-wheeler in reverse).[9]

Another article that first appeared in a New York City publication, in August 1885, claimed that the latest craze among young ladies in the uptown districts of New York was bicycle riding. Harlem was one of those areas and one of those riders was 18-year-old Mamie Morrison. With her blonde hair and "perfect figure" she had "the admiration of all the high-collared young men who flock around to see her pass on her circle of steel." The costume worn by Morrison was manufactured by a Fifth Avenue modiste, according to designs furnished by Morrison. The loose-fitting dress was made somewhat upon the well-known bloomer costume. According to the story, "Miss Morrison predicts that in a short time every pretty girl will own her own bicycle and young men will not be needed to escort the fair ones to balls and theaters."[10]

A story in November 1885 from Washington observed that the city had a variety of machines in use, from unicycles and bicycles to tricycles and quadricycles. The smooth, hard roads of that city, estimated to be as many as 40 to 50 miles or even more, made the place a paradise for wheelmen. Tricycles sometimes carried whole families. It was said to have been a little over six years since the first bicycles made their appearance in the nation's capital, and "now there are hundreds and hundreds of them." The reporter felt the total number of bicycles and tricycles of all kinds then numbered up to about 1,500. Work was still said to be underway

This 1885 sketch depicted a woman riding a high wheeler machine in the city.

to develop the safety bike. "Within the past year tricycles have gained greatly in popularity. Two years ago you seldom saw one. A year ago they began to come into more general use, and now you see great numbers of them," the reporter noted. Tandem machines were also gaining in popularity with either two people sitting side by side or one in front of the other. Also mentioned was that tricycles would have been more popular earlier but for a single incident. That incident was the fact that the first woman to use a trike in

Washington was one whose name had been before the public a great deal within the previous 18 months. "Mrs. Lockwood is a talented woman, but she does not pride herself either upon her beauty or the size of her feet; and as the bicycle calls attention to both, her adopting of it did not tend to add to its popularity with the observing members of the gentler sex."[11]

THE FIRST SAFETY BICYCLE.

A sketch of what was supposedly the first safety bike. The date of the machine's arrival was not given, although it appeared in a 1900 newspaper account.

Six months later, in April 1886, Washington was again cited as the capital of the biking world, mostly due to its smooth roads. Boys and girls were going to school on bikes and trikes while men and women went shopping on bicycles (men) and tricycles (women). The journalist remarked that he saw "Belva [Lockwood] treading her beloved machine."[12]

A month after that a news story mentioned the popularity of cycling in Europe but lamented the activity was not as popular in America. "Ladies there patronize the tricycle far more than they do in this country," the report stated. Tandem machines were called "socials" because the objection had been made that bicycles and tricycles were "unsocial" since they were made for one person. That prompted the invention of the tandem and "all the world can now take its girl cycling along with it upon its steel steed."[13]

It was in this period, 1885–1886, that the safety bike for men appeared on the scene and was adopted enthusiastically by the high-wheel cyclists and embraced by all those men who wanted to cycle but had not attempted it when the high-wheel was the dominant machine. An article that appeared in a Washington, D.C., newspaper in March 1902 declared that the first bike ever made for a woman in Washington and possibly the first in the United States was built in 1883 by W.X. Stevens of Washington, for his wife. "It was ridden by Mrs. Stevens after dark," said the account, but the invention went no further at the time. "The idea of a woman riding a wheel was one not seriously entertained twenty years ago [1882]," said Stevens, in telling his story to a reporter. He continued by recounting that he had built a velocipede in 1868 that was almost exactly like the present wheel, but the frame was wooden instead of iron and of course it did not have rubber tires. It weighed, he thought, around 35 pounds. The old velocipede wheel was simply a wagon wheel. "An important defect of the velocipede was that it could not be made to travel up hill. The weight of the rider came entirely on the forward wheel. With present bicycles the rider's weight can be utilized as a motive force," explained Stevens. He was then asked by the reporter what the first woman's bike was like. He replied, "Almost exactly like the modern safety bicycle ridden by women. I ought to know, for I built it in 1883, for Mrs. Stevens. She demurred very much about riding it, for such a thing as a woman riding a bicycle was never thought of." It was like the modern machine but it was of wood. It had a drop frame even lower than at present—it came down within five inches of the ground. Stevens did not patent his device, which may explain why he does not seem to appear in any of the early material on bicycle history.[14]

An account that appeared in June 1895 remarked, of the period perhaps a decade earlier, "It affords the pioneer women cyclers no little amusement and satisfaction to recall the days when bicycle manufacturers, in reply to requests for women's wheels, would say with emphasis, 'We have never manufactured a woman's wheel and we never will.'" In the early days of wheeling, bicycles for American women were imported from England.[15]

An account from August 1894 remarked on the then-extensive use of the bicycle and that "it seems remarkable that half a generation ago the first

An ad from the early 1920s that compared the old high wheeler with the safety machine and pointed out the differences between them, and why women could never ride the former.

A ladies' safety bicycle, 1889. Note the large skirt guard on the back wheel. This added weight to the machine and the drop frame made it less sturdy, compared to the man's safety.

American-made cycle had not come into existence." The bicycle, as distinct from the old velocipede, made its advent in the United States in 1878. A single machine was made in 1877 for Colonel Albert A. Pope of Boston but it was in 1878 that the industry actually began, the Pope Manufacturing Company having made 50 bicycles in that year. The success of Pope and the rapid development of a general interest in cycling led others to engage in the business. Prior to 1878 "there was a small importation of English machines." The years 1887 and 1888 ushered in a new era in bicycling with the rear driving safety. (The high-wheeler machines were all front wheel driven. That meant that the steering wheel and the driving wheel were one and the same and that made them all the more dangerous and unstable. The safety bicycle of the late 1880s and through to today all are rear-driven with the driving wheel and the steering wheel being two separate and distinct wheels). In 1887 the Overman Wheel Company of Boston brought out a safety and other American makers brought out safeties in the following year and "it brought bicycling into favor with many people who had hitherto been deterred from it, an advantage very largely increased by the introduction of pneumatic tires a couple of seasons later." As well, noted the report, "a very important phase of the new era was the development of bicycling for women, who had been before this limited to the comparatively heavy tricycle, and thus placed at a disadvantage. Practically all the leading manufacturers now produce special patterns for ladies' use, and it is safe to say that the present number of riders of this sex is larger than the total number of wheelmen in the country ten years ago." A gradual reduction in the weight of the machines meant that by 1894 the safeties weighed from 28 to 35 pounds.[16]

Those first safeties built in America averaged about 60 pounds in weight. An article published in 1897 claimed, "One of the great steps in promoting the popularity of the bicycle was the invention by Owens of Washington of the lady's bicycle, in 1888. Heretofore the bicycle had been regarded by the female portion of the community as essentially a selfish sport for men and no invention in this or any other country has done so much for cycling as the invention of the drop-frame cycle for women."[17]

One bicycle dealer in the city of Washington estimated, in July 1887,

ONE OF THE NEW BICYCLE GIRLS.

An 1888 illustration of the new bicycle girl. Her costume is daring for the age and she stands ready to mount a man's bicycle, something very few women did at the time.

there were at least 1,500 to 2,000 wheels in his city. Bikes and trikes were used in Washington not for pleasure only but were also employed largely as a means of rapid transit for business purposes by professional men and businessmen such as physicians, insurance agents, newspaper reporters, collectors of various kinds, and ministers. Reportedly there had been a great increase within two or three years in the number of women who rode tricycles. "A novelty promised for this fall is a bicycle for lady riders. There are several fair riders in this city ready to take to this lady bicycle when it comes. It will be so arranged that a lady who will learn to ride it can do so with as much grace and propriety as she could ride a tricycle," declared the newsman. "It will be a modification of the Rover type of bicycle for gentlemen with the backbone or frame curved downward like the letter U between the wheels, so that when the lady sits upon the saddle there will be no obstruction in the way of her dress between her feet and the saddle." Said the dealer, "The only trouble will be in mounting. Ladies who ride will have to have gentlemen with them to assist them in mounting." The journalist added, "When the velocipede came out early in the century machines with the U shaped backbone were constructed for and used by the great grandmothers of the present race of tricyclers." With respect to bicycles, in 1887 the cost rose from $75 to $150 or $175.[18]

Writing in February 1897 a journalist remarked that bicycling had become so universal a method of outdoor exercise for women that it was difficult to realize only ten years had lapsed since the first of her sex had mounted a wheel. Back then, in 1887, he continued, Belva Lockwood had scandalized Washington by perambulating its streets on a tricycle a year earlier. In Brooklyn, New York, Mrs. Charlotte L. Bolton was a sufferer from ill health and was advised by her physician to learn horseback riding as a means of recovery. Instead, in 1887, she turned to the bicycle. Bolton took her initial ride on a machine down to Coney Island. She explained, "This was decidedly a new departure for a woman, an outrage, so considered, on all precedent, and a general defiance of public opinion." A newsman continued, about that ride, "It attracted wide attention and gave her very unpleasant notoriety. Small boys hooted and howled, threw sticks and stones, newspaper men wrote letters about it, the funny men found the woman cyclist material for unlimited jokes, and the cartoonist was never at a loss of a subject for his pencil." In was not long, however, before a few other women took heart and gradually braved public sentiment to become cyclists. In 1889 Mrs. Elliott Mason and Bolton were admitted to membership in the League of American Wheelmen, becoming the first women in that organization. By 1897 that group had 8,000 members with about 800 of them being females. When asked, in 1897, if she approved of the bloomer costume for women bikers Bolton said, "I certainly do not approve of those hideous garments. I believe in a woman preserving her individuality. When she appears in garments in which she cannot be distinguished from a man, she loses the dignity and grace of womanhood." Added Bolton, "I, as one of the first riders, at my home, have always worn a medium short skirt, equestrian trousers and high boots. I have never yet found any costume quite perfect." Concluded Bolton, "The advent of the bicycle has already done more to effect dress reform for women than all the lectures on the subject ever delivered. They now appreciate the freedom, cleanliness and comfort of a moderately short skirt. I have no sympathy whatever with the woman who apes the ways and manners of the opposite sex."[19]

A different account from 1897 also looked back to a time ten years earlier. It began by stating that in the beginning of cycling it was impossible for women to ride the high wheel

MRS. CHARLOTTE BOLTON.

An 1897 sketch of Charlotte Bolton.

"without sacrificing their dignity and reputation." And when Mrs. Smith of the city of Washington first rode the ladies' style of the low wheel (woman's safety), which her husband was the first to design and build, she rode at night, and it was many months, she told a reporter, before she dared to ride in daylight. In 1888 Mrs. Smith was the "pioneer missionary" and she persuaded many women to take up the wheel both for health and pleasure. (Smith may have been the same person as Stevens mentioned above.) This account also mentioned Charlotte L. Bolton of Brooklyn as being one of the first prominent women to adopt the wheel instead of the horse-drawn carriage.[20]

The years 1888 and 1889 marked the first time women received a considerable amount of media attention as cyclists. Articles dealing exclusively with female bikers began to appear in the press for the first time, in the lead-up to the full-blown bicycle craze of the 1890s. "Bicycles for ladies" was the title of an article that was published in March 1888. A reporter in the city of Washington asked a bicycle dealer about "those female bicyclists" to which the dealer replied, "What's the use of a lady riding a tricycle, the lightest of which weighs sixty pounds, when she can ride a bicycle that weighs only thirty-five pounds, and go a great deal faster with a smaller expenditure of force?" Then the reporter asked if bicycles were used by women anywhere else. Said the dealer, "Nowhere else in the world. I make these myself and put them on the market." Next, the reporter asked if women would use bikes anywhere else. Replied the dealer, "Of course they will. Washington will set the example. New York, Boston and Chicago will follow. Of course, no other city is quite so well adapted to their use as Washington is, because no other in the world has such smooth streets but others will use them. There are 14,000 cyclers in this city and these low [frame] bicycles will gradually supersede the tricycles. It must be so. The survival of the fittest requires it." When that journalist asked a professional lady of 45, who was described as a familiar figure around town on a tricycle, for her opinion, the woman replied, "I shall get a bi[cycle] if it will better answer my purpose. It involves no more exposure than my machine does. The talk of immodesty is all an affectation. Look at the way those bashful creatures 'dress' for a ball. Modesty is largely a question of fashion and temperature anyway." Concluded the journalist, "So woman is completing her conquest of the planet. She rows. She smokes. She preaches. She hazes. She shoots. She rides. And now she has lassoed the iron grasshopper that man has hitherto exclusively bestridden, and has fearlessly mounted it."[21]

Charlotte Bolton dressed and ready to go for a spin, 1897.

Two months later the Washington correspondent of a St. Louis newspaper wrote, "If my letter should show streaks of insanity in it, or sings of a mental paralysis on the part of the writer I beg you will make allowances. I saw a sight one evening last week calculated to sear the eyeballs of one whose optical orbs are usually in a condition of coolness bordering on congelation. I saw a woman go by on a bicycle! On a bicycle, I repeat; a vehicle with two wheels only, one of which was directly behind the other. Her feet—not to use a stronger term—were on both sides of the connecting bar, balancing precisely as a man would, and her lower extremities were flopping and kicking in a lively manner." The shocked newsman added, "I blushed and turned my face to the wall, resolved to gaze upon the dread[ful] sight no more; but I immediately turned back and resumed my investigations." When he withdrew his gaze but then turned it back he discovered there were then two female riders. "Both were dressed in all respects in the ordinary street costume of a lady.... But they were a pair of spectacles.... It was broad daylight, too." And, he continued, "it ought to be added, perhaps, that the bicycles were safety machines, that the connecting bar between the wheels was lower than usual ... the exposure of the rider is not so great as would at first be thought, especially in warm weather."[22]

Another piece in the spring of 1888 began by declaring, "The safety-bicycle has not only brought bicycling within a limit where it is looked upon with favor by conservative or timid men, but also seems to have solved the problem of the application of the bicycle to woman's use." A bicycle dealer who had just returned from a trip to Europe to assess cycling conditions spoke to a reporter with a Washington, D.C., newspaper. He expressed the opinion that bicycling would become very popular with the fair sex. There were then estimated to be about 500 women in the nation's capital who rode tricycles. Said the dealer, "As one by one these fair cyclers are induced to try bicycles—perhaps first in the seclusion of a bicycle schoolyard—and taste of the superior joys of the bicycle, they will become enthusiastic for two wheels instead of three." He added, "Already some of the more venturesome of the fair sex have appeared on the streets on ladies' bicycles, as they are called. The introduction of these bicycles will be made more easy by the appearance of the tandem bicycle. This is a machine for two riders, with two handlebars and two saddles or seats. The lady will sit in front and her escort in the rear. With a good rider as her escort a woman will soon acquire sufficient confidence and dexterity on a tandem to be able to pedal her own single bicycle." Explaining the new bicycle for females the dealer stated, "The woman's bicycle is the same as the man's bicycle, with a modification which removes all obstruction between the seat and the pedals, so that a woman's dress can fall to her feet, as on a tricycle. On the safety bicycles for men the frame is so constructed that there is a straight bar from the axle of the rear wheel to the post to which the handle bar is attached in front." And, he said, "of course such an arrangement offers an insuperable difficulty to a woman in her ordinary wearing apparel. The difficulty has been overcome by making this bar or backbone curve down and upward like the letter U," which allowed the dress to fall in a proper manner.[23]

Mounting that new woman's safety machine was made, said the dealer, "even more easily than on the masculine bicycle. Standing on the left side, with her hands upon the handle bars, the woman puts her right foot through the U and upon the right pedal. Then she raises herself on the pedal to the saddle, the movement giving a start to the machine." Also, the dealer argued that the safety bicycle was much safer than a tricycle and an accident to a female on a trike was apt to be more dangerous than an accident on a new-style bicycle. With respect to decorum, the dealer asserted, "There is really no more impropriety in riding a bicycle than a tricycle. In fact, on that score the preference should be given I think to the bicycle, for as I said, they are less liable to accidents of a kind that might subject a woman to mortification…. What ought to be understood, however, is that no woman should attempt to ride a bicycle unless she is suitably costumed." As far as the dealer was concerned, "the appearance on the street of a woman bicyclist with a bustle on would tend to bring the whole business into disrepute. What is a proper costume? Well, a lady rider should be dressed plainly in a costume of flannel, like an equestrienne habit without, however, having the extra length of skirt. It should be made of flannel, or some material of a heavy texture that would fall or drape gracefully to the feet." In conclusion the dealer offered the thought, "At first, I suppose, ladies will go out bicycle riding in clubs attended by gentlemen on tandems. In this way the ice will be broken."[24]

An article published in April 1888 declared that the bicycling rage was developing all over the country, and the report from the factories was that it was almost impossible to keep up with orders, even working night and day. "It had been supposed that the sport is the especial and exclusive prerogative of the genus homo of the masculine persuasion; but now comes the rumor from Washington that a ladies bicycle club has been organized there, which in a week numbered 30 members—chiefly artists and musicians," declared the reporter. The tricycle therefore, as a club member had reportedly said recently, was doomed, "for the prejudice against ladies riding the bicycle disappears the instant one sees a graceful female ride it. The tricycle is not graceful, while on the new bicycle only the toe and heel are exposed and the embarrassing awkwardness of the tricycle is entirely overcome." According to this piece, "The riding costume will be a tight fitting Norfolk jacket, full skirt, walking length, and riding hat and gloves. The ladies of the club will not appear in the streets except in riding costume and with permission of their teacher, and will not ride in parade."[25]

A reporter writing in May 1888 declared that Washington, perhaps, had more wheelmen than any other city of its size in the United States. There were estimated to be about 4,000 riders of machines of one kind or another in that city and that 3,000 men owned bicycles. The average price of those bicycles was put at $100 each. Credit for the popularity of the machines was given over the wide, smooth streets that existed in the nation's capital, with a cyclist being able to ride 279 miles through Washington's streets and not go outside of the city or go over the same ground twice. There were reported to be 60,000 wheelmen in America and the League of American Wheelmen had 11,000 members. The various safety machines then on the market were fast driving the other machines out of the market. Those safeties had the two wheels about even in size (a dramatic change from the high-wheeler machines), were much closer to the ground than other machines and thus there was less danger from serious accidents in riding them. Nearly all the stores in Washington that made considerable numbers of deliveries of small packages used tricycles for that purpose. Drug stores, notion stores, laundries, and boot and shoe stores sent out their goods by way of a messenger on a tricycle.[26]

Yet another article from the spring of 1888 noted that one of the newest things under the sun was the Woman's Bicycle Club of Washington and that the nation's capital "is the great woman bicycle center. Tricyclists and the man on his bicycle are seen everywhere in the civilized world. But the woman bicyclist belongs to the national capital, and is exclusively a Washington novelty." In the two months since the club was organized its membership number had reached upward of 70. There were half a dozen young girls of 15, twice that number of young women under 25 and the rest are older women (about 52), and mostly married women. The members were elected by ballot, and one black ball rejected the candidate. The club uniform or habit was of dark blue cloth. The skirt was walking length, hung full from the waistline, and "of course, the full skirt has no draperies, and it is quite full enough at the back to allow a small bustle, if desired." Mrs. Harriette Mills, the club president, was described as a woman of culture and common sense and of being an enthusiast of the bicycle as a promoter of health and a source of pleasant recreation for women. "There is a delightful little air of mystery about the woman's club. It is exclusive, reserved, and averse to any notoriety. It has conquered the bicycle, and will make it fashionable," declared the journalist. The ladies' safety was described as having a 30-inch driving wheel in the rear and a 24-inch steering wheel in the front but, said the newsman, the wheels looked to be almost the same size when they were in motion. This account also declared the tricycle to be on the way out as it had no grace or style while "the tandem bicycle or double machine meets the wants of the timid woman, or the woman who prefers an escort on the street."[27]

In this account Belva Lockwood was also mentioned as having appeared on the streets of Washington some six years earlier on a tricycle. Also noted was that she would never make the tricycle popular with her sex. Said an enthusiastic lady bicyclist, "Mrs. Lockwood holds on to that clumsy, heavy old machine with an obstinacy worthy of a better cause. It is just such tricycling that has put the bicycle back three years. It is, in fact, the stumbling block. Women say, 'Oh, we can't bring ourselves to look so awkward. We can't expose our feet, and go blowing along the streets in that fashion.'" That woman went on to add, "But when we get a woman once to try the bicycle, she offers no such objection. But Mrs. Lockwood is in a tight place now. She knows her old machine has already cost a great deal to keep it in repair, and that it isn't worth keeping up any longer. Why, the bicyclists here would rather make a present of a bicycle to Mrs. Lockwood than ever see her on that old tricycle again.... Mrs. Lockwood is a progressive, and we cannot understand why she sticks to that old tricycle as she does." Reportedly a visitor to Lockwood said to her, "It is the ungraceful appearance and the exposure of the feet, Mrs. Lockwood, that women object to." Replied Lockwood, "Ah, yes, well, women have feet. I don't know why they should be ashamed of their feet. They don't mind showing their feet when walking. But I grant that the new bicycle is the more graceful, light and beautiful machine. On many occasion I should like it. But it would not serve my purposes as well as the tricycle. I could not stop at a moment and remain stationary for five or ten minutes without dismounting." Lockwood continued, "I do not want to dismount and then mount again every time I stop in the street. Now, that is the single and only objection I have to the woman's bicycle.... Women who ride for pleasure or healthful exercise will of course use the bicycle." According to this story there were about 100 bicycles in use by women and "nearly all are in Washington."[28]

A MEMBER OF THE CLUB.

This 1888 sketch showed a woman setting off on a ride wearing normal clothing of the time. Her very long skirt was, of course, difficult and dangerous with respect to riding a machine, even a ladies' bike.

"You may wonder how a lady can mount a bicycle gracefully, but it's quite easy," began a piece that appeared in September 1888. "You know a man puts his left foot on the pedal or step and throws his right leg over the rear of the saddle. A moment's reflection will convince you that this would never do for a lady wearing skirts." Bicycle inventors were said to have racked their brains for a long time to invent a woman's bicycle and the appearance of the low machine with chain gearing and wheels of equal size solved the problem. "All that remained to be done was to get the 'backbone' between the handles and the seat out of the way so the lady could step on the pedal and thrown her right leg around in front of the saddle instead of behind. This was easily done, and the fate of the ladies' tricycle was sealed." This newsman concluded by observing, "I see almost every day a lady of at least forty-five years, who only a few months ago took her first lesson, and she now cuts graceful capers on her machine and skims about like a swallow."[29]

An article out of Chicago about Pauline Hall was published in November 1888. Declared the item's subhead, "She has a lady's safety machine and whirls away at an astonishing rate of speed—the dudes admire her and the experts tire out in trying to keep up—Pauline has never taken a 'header.'" Hall was one of the most popular turn-of-the-century prima donnas in America. It was also said that ladies on bicycles had been seen before in Chicago. Bertha von Berg once rode professionally in the skating rinks, and there was another female professional also, who was wont to turn the faces of all gazers backward in surprise when she sped up an avenue on a regulation wheel, clad in velvet knickerbockers and black stockings. The cyclist was not named. The ladies' safety had possibly half a dozen female riders in Chicago in the summer of 1888. "Miss Hall, however, is the first actress or singer who has been seen 'wheeling it' and though she and her devoted attendants—for Pauline must always be attended, of course—have sought secluded avenues at hours when observation was least probably, they have been seen, and the fair rider has been recognized." Hall rode one of those ladies' safeties and "vulgar trousers or strong-minded but none the less ugly bifurcated skirts are not necessary to the enjoyment of the healthy and exhilarating sport as she enjoys it. Just a neat riding habit, rather short, abbreviated enough to show an entrancing glimpse of twinkling ankles, rounded and graceful—that is all the costume necessary. Of course the habit is bustleless." This account described the woman's bike by observing that "the connecting rods between the wheels are dropped sufficiently to avoid the necessity of 'bifurcating' the rider's nether garments.... All in all, the bicycle is a very lady-like affair, and its requirements are remarkably modest." Other famous figures, however, had not followed Hall's lead. "Marie Jensen doesn't ride a bicycle; she prefers a cab. So does Lillian Russell, and most of the rest of the stars of opéra comique. Pauline Hall is unique in several things, and going out with the boys on a

ON THE ROAD.

PAULINE HALL.

The two sketches from 1888 show famed prima donna Pauline Hall posing and riding.

cycling jaunt is one of them." Concluded the article, "Her example will doubtless find many disciples in and out of the profession ere long, but for the present the pretty, graceful prima donna has the distinction all to herself, and has never been known to so disgrace herself as to take a 'header,' a feat which older wheelmen of the sterner sex accomplish with varying frequency."[30]

A report out of Philadelphia in December 1888 said that bicycling was becoming quite popular among the women of that city. Two of the leading clubs, the Philadelphia and the Pennsylvania, had already opened their doors to "the gentler sex" and each had the names of several young women on its membership rolls. Each club had also set apart one room in the house for the use of the lady members and their friends. "It is only recently that Philadelphia's fair daughters took to the bicycle and there are now at least half a hundred riders in the city. Perhaps one-third of the whole number were taught to manage the wheel at the Park Bicycle Rink at Belmont and Elm Avenues," said the reporter. George S. Hart was the manager of that rink and the instructor. The reporter asked Hart about his female students, to which he responded, "On the whole I think they learn much more rapidly than do men. To be sure, they are somewhat timid at the start, but with a little encouragement they soon get confidence in themselves and handle the wheel with perfect ease," Hart explained. "You see with the safety bicycle they cannot get much of a fall, even if they should get out of the saddle. They only have to take their foot from the pedal and step to the floor, a distance of about five or six inches, thereby saving themselves a fall." When the journalist asked Hall how the women mounted the machine the instructor replied, "I find this is the most difficult thing to teach them. In the first place, let me remove a popular impression that the ladies must sit astride a wheel just as the men do. That is not the case at all. The ladies' bicycle, instead of having a straight bar running down from the handle-post has a U-shaped bar. This, you see, permits a lady to step right into the saddle, and there is nothing to interfere with her skirts." And, Hall added, "in getting on the ladies' wheel you make a standing pedal mount. Every pupil has some trouble in mastering this, but by constant practice she learns to mount the wheel very skillfully and gracefully." In conclusion Hall told the reporter, "By the way, I want to tell you that the men will have to look about or the young women will leave them behind. They are much more graceful riders than men, and it will not be a great while before they will get the speed."[31]

A six-day bicycle race between a dozen women took place at Madison Square Garden in New York City in February 1889. Several such contests had reportedly already taken place in various parts of the country and there had been more of them even this early (in 1889) than in previous years. The publicity generated from such events had likely advanced the cause of bicycling for women, even though the bicycle racers used the high-wheeler style of machine, the overwhelmingly favorite type of machine through the 1880s. It would rapidly fall from popularity by the early 1890s, due to the dominance of the safety bike—for both men's and women's machines. "The girls, perched on wheels larger than the driving wheel of a passenger locomotive, but light and flimsy as the air, are all eagerness [sic] in their efforts to outdo each other and to gain the plaudits of the spectators, and when it is considered that they are riding at a speed of twelve to sixteen miles an hour, and that they must, perforce, be close upon one another on the forty-yard track, the danger of mishap is apparent." The named women racers in the illustration were all regular racers through this period of time; that is, from early to mid–1880s onward, to at least 1889.[32]

"No other American city, not even New York, has so many bicycles as Washington. Four thousand wheels are owned in this city. Two years ago there were but three thousand. Washington street scenes resemble those old cartoons of the first velocipede craze which swept over the country," began an account from May 1889. The usual reasons for such a state were given; that is, the roads were very good and there were many miles of them. Men were described as "bold" riders and "even the women here ride boldly—for

This 1889 illustration depicts 10 female bicycle racers by name who were all well-known at the time. All of them raced on high wheeler machines. None of the costumes shown would have ever been worn by a woman riding her bicycle on city streets, as all of those costumes would have compromised her dignity, respectability, and so forth.

Washington women have taken to the wheel in greater numbers than their sisters of any other city. There are said to be five hundred women riders in the capital.... Very pretty and graceful figures they make, with stray locks flying, a ribbon or two showing color and skirts so modestly and delicately managed." It was also reported that a great majority of the women riders scorned the feminine tricycle as too slow and ungainly: "Hundreds ride the 'safety' machine, which has two small wheels of nearly equal size like the old velocipede, and which they mount and bestride like men ... the skirts are managed as gracefully as the habit an equestrienne, and with as much modesty." Occasionally, after dark and in the outskirts of the city, one could see an adventurous young woman riding a large wheel, and "the first woman in America to ride a bicycle was Mrs. Smith, still one of Washington's daring and rapid riders." Many of the women clerks in the government departments and agencies rode wheels to and from their work and "all classes of residents ride wheels and it is not uncommon to see a young woman from the aristocratic West End ride down Pennsylvania avenue on a shopping tour; but it is a singular fact that none of the members of congress or important officials of government indulges in the popular pastime. Perhaps they think it is not dignified." A large business was said to be operating in Washington every Sunday that rented bicycles. One establishment kept 150 machines for that purpose, and on pleasant Sundays all of them were rented. The charge was 50 cents an hour or $1.50 for an afternoon. Wheels were used for business in Washington also. Mail carriers, small laundries, florists, stationers, shoe dealers, and other tradesmen kept cycles fitted with baskets or boxes for use in delivery. Newsboys and newspaper carriers also used them in their work. What was thought to be the only bicycle passenger car in America was used in Washington. A man had rigged up a five-wheeled vehicle with seats for six passengers, besides himself, and used it as a transit vehicle, charging 10 cents per passenger.[33]

This 1889 illustration depicts some of the commercial uses that were made of the bicycle in the United States.

Writing about the fad in general in May 1889 a newsman noted the demand for children's safeties had become quite large. With respect to the Salt Lake Cycle Club in Utah, he reported, "The most radical departure is the admission of ladies to membership, and its advisability has been strongly questioned by a number of the members. That the fair sex are a most decided acquisition, the experience of the staid old Philadelphia Bicycle Club has proved beyond a doubt, and the Pennsylvanians are taking in ladies at the last few meetings."[34]

Writing out of Boston in May 1889 a reporter remarked, "Washington is the banner city for lady bicycle riders. At the present time there are nearly two hundred. There is also a ladies' club composed of sixty riders, with a clubhouse of its own." In Philadelphia there were said to be about fifty lady bicyclists and Chicago reportedly had about the same number. Buffalo started this season with several riders on the new machines. New York City had a riding-school for ladies on the safety bicycle and "Boston has comparatively few lady riders, but their number is fast increasing and Lynn and Salem each boast one who can ride any wheel. Rhode Island wheelmen have an honorary membership composed of lady riders, and they are taking an active interest in the ladies' bicycles."[35]

A lady on a tricycle in Los Angeles was described as a rarity in June 1889, and "for any member of the feminine gender, except stage performers to appear on a bicycle was, until yesterday afternoon unheard of. Miss Daisy, one of the employees in Mr. Robinson's store, made her appearance, however, on Franklin Street, soon after 5 o'clock, on one of the two-wheeled machines." And, continued the article, "for the benefit of those who might think such a performance would involve anything indelicate it must be stated that the cycle was a newly contrived machine whereby the rider can sit in the saddle without having to go a-straddle, the seat being placed about one and a half feet back of the handle with an open space between."[36]

Bessie Bramble wrote an article in September 1889 about the "present rage" among women for athletic sports: ladies who hunted, rowed and sailed. She declared, "If the present rage of women for athletic sports is kept up for a few years, it is very plain that the fragility and feebleness—or rather to say delicacy of organization—with which American women have so long been credited, will speedily disappear." All of that would mean that dress reform would be inevitable. "Manifestly long skirts, tight waists and the regulation fashionable rig of trains and trimmings must seem doubly irksome and trying after the freedom of the short skirts and trousers of the yachting costumes," wrote Bramble. "Another form of athletic exercise which is growing in favor with women is bicycling. Little of this is seen in Pittsburgh, but it may be attributed to the ill-paved streets and rough roads all round about. In Washington with its smooth asphalt streets women may be seen flying around on 'Safeties' all over town, and in such numbers that they have ceased to provoke

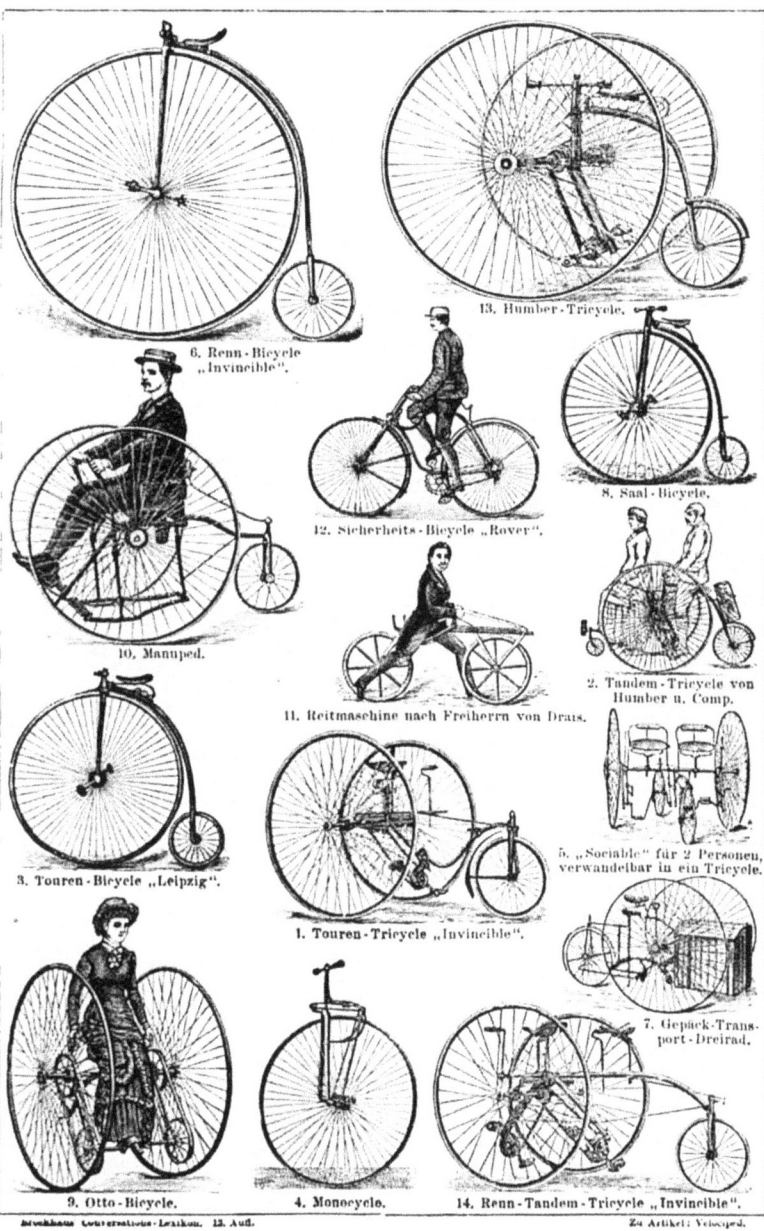

This illustration came from a German encyclopedia in the 1880s and showed many of the types of cycles that were in vogue at one time or another in that decade, and earlier.

a stare or excite remarks save from the green-horn visitors, who never in all their 'born days' saw such a sight before."[37]

According to journalist Robert Graves, writing in September 1889, "Washington girls set the fashion in bicycles for the entire country. They were the first to abandon the somewhat awkward tricycle and take to the more comfortable and graceful 'safety.' That this was a machine which its rider had to bestride man fashion did not in the least disconcert them." Graves added, "Having mastered the art of riding with skirts hanging modestly and becomingly on both sides of the frame of her steed, having learned how to wear loose blouses and the prettiest of flannel skirts ... having mastered all these acts the Washington bicycle girl has sighed for more worlds to conquer, for other means of reaching the masculine heart."[38]

An 1889 newspaper ad that depicted the three machines that dominated the field in the 1880s: the rapidly outgoing high wheeler and the incoming safety machines (male and female) that then dominated the field and fueled the bicycle craze of the 1890s.

A PET ON THE WHEEL.

A novel aspect of the bicycling fad was shown in this 1889 sketch with a female out for a bike ride who was taking her pet bird along with her.

An advertisement that appeared in a Seattle newspaper in October 1889 captured the changing face of bicycling in America, just before the boom decade of the 1890s began. The ad featured the ladies' safety bike, the men's safety, and the "ordinary," or high-wheeler. The first two had just started to sweep the market while the third was on the way out and would be dead within a few years.[39]

4

1890s—Popularity

The decade of the 1890s was indeed the golden decade for the bicycle, for men and for women. The arrival of the safety bicycle and the women's safety bicycle during the final few years of the 1880s opened up bicycling, physically, to both sexes. Older, and not-so-athletic males could comfortably handle the safety while they could not handle the high-wheeler with much comfort. The ladies' safety allowed women to step through the bike to mount it rather than having her throw a leg over the upper bar. That allowed her to maintain her dignity and maintain propriety and so forth. As the number of female bikers increased dramatically during the 1890s the number of critics, and the amount of criticism directed at women, decreased. But, of course, by no means did that criticism disappear.

Bicycle schools flourished in this period and many women learned to ride a wheel at one of those institutions. One such academy was the Ladies Bicycle Riding School in Minneapolis at Snow's Bicycle House, 611 First Avenue South. According to a May 1890 advertisement, "A class of 30 ladies will graduate this week, and they are planning a street parade in uniform this coming week." A trial lesson was given for 50 cents while a full evening of instruction was offered for one dollar. A full course of instruction consisted of 10 evenings for a total of five dollars, which included the use of a bicycle. Any tuition paid could be applied toward the purchase of a wheel at Snow's bicycle shop.[1]

A May 1890 article that originated in St. Louis announced, "The number of feminine bicyclists in St. Louis is gaining surely and rapidly. The exercise, as vouched for by Miss Mabel Jenness [physical culture guru of the day] is both scientific and healthful, as well as a graceful and delightful mode of locomotion. The wheelmen of the past had the delights of the bicycle solely to themselves." And, it was noted, "then came the advent of the tricycle for women, its gradual overthrow, the lull of the ladies' cycling, and then vive le

Ladies' Bicycle Riding School.

A class of 30 ladies will graduate this week, and they are planning for a street parade in uniform the coming week. Trial lessons, 50 cents; full evening, $1; full course, 10 evenings, $5, including use of bicycle. Tuition will be applied on purchase of wheel. Call or address Snow's Bicycle House, 611 First avenue south, Minneapolis. Illustrated Catalogue and Price sent free on application.

LADIES' BICYCLE SCHOOL!

Jackson St. Rink (Afternoons).

Strictly Private to the Learner and Her Friends.

EXPERIENCED INSTRUCTORS IN CHARGE.

For tickets, choice of hours and all information, call on or address

S. F. HEATH, Ag't Columbia Bicycles,
95 E. Fourth Street, St. Paul.

These two ads are from 1890 and tout the advantages of two different bicycle schools in Minnesota where women could enroll to learn to ride a bike. These schools were just for women and such institutions became increasingly popular and pervasive in the 1890s.

SHE LEARNS EASILY.   THE WAY SHE MOUNTS.

These two sketches from 1890 illustrate women learning to ride bicycles.

bicycle for ladies, just as well as for men.... Now the three-wheeled affairs, known as the tricycles, are things of the past, and the ladies' bicycles are high in the favor of the wheelwomen of St. Louis, as well as elsewhere. The fair riders mount the wheel with the agility of the wheelman himself, set the machine going and spin away with the fleetness of a bird." Then the journalist declared, "At present there are at least fifteen women bicycle riders in town, whilst candidates for the honor in the shape of amateurs in process of study are constantly on the increase." Profiled in the piece was the individual Delia Hardcastle, granddaughter of the late Colonel Calvin Case who was described as a prominent member of society. Concluded the story, "She rides for pleasure every day a distance of fifteen to twenty miles without experiencing the least fatigue.... She dresses in taste and dainty fashion though while on the wheel she always wears the Jenness-Miller [famous fashion house] style of dress."[2]

According to a September 1890 news account the first thing a visitor noticed in Rochester, New York, was the large number of bicyclists in the street. The second surprise came when the observer noted the varied sorts of people who used cycles. And, added the story, "finally he is astonished to see women of diversified ages and conditions upon wheels—not half a dozen or a score of women, but literally hundreds of them. Occasionally one will meet in a block more men and women on bicycles than on foot." It was said to be a fact that hundreds of the most prominent businessmen of Rochester, such as mill owners, brokers, bankers, lawyers and wholesale dealers in many lines of trade, went to business in the morning regularly upon bicycles and used their wheels constantly during the day. A respectable bicycle dealer in Rochester had recently told the journalist that there were at least 4,000 bicycles in daily use in Rochester and that a large proportion of them belonged to businessmen. The dealer also said there were 400 female riders in Rochester.[3]

Miss Carlotta Cole, it was reported in November 1890, had the distinction of being the first female in Brooklyn to have ridden the ladies' tandem bicycle. She said, "It shows 'go' in a girl to ride a bicycle instead of a heavy, slow tricycle, and it requires pluck, too. I remember well the attention I attracted when I first rode the ladies' tandem bicycle with my brother, but the sport is now becoming very general." Cole added, "It is a difficult thing to learn how to ride a bicycle with people looking at you, and so my most profitable lessons were taken at night.... Nerve is all a girl needs to make wheeling enjoyable, and I am glad to see so many plucky young women using the tandem bicycle." Concluded Cole, "To look graceful a girl must sit erect, and sail along as if she were a part of the machine and were enjoying the ride, instead of leaning first right, then left, with questionable bodily jerks, groping the handles with death like grasp, and putting a scared, wearied expression on her face."[4]

There were more female riders in Washington, D.C., than in any other American city, or so it was reported in December 1890. Even so, many women apparently held back, as one report stated, "Many a woman hesitates long before she attempts the difficult task of managing the untamed steed of steel and it is, perhaps, true that a great many graceful riders are lost to the world simply because the wheel looks so dangerous." According to this account, "Washington has the honor of having harbored the mind that conceived the idea of making a bicycle suitable for a lady's use, as well as of owning, as one of its fair citizens, the first lady who had the courage to brave the world and push pedals from a saddle hung between two wheels instead of three. Women on wheels had then long been an ordinary sight on the streets, but there were always more than two wheels to each woman." It was also stated that by 1890 there was less wonder than there was before at the spectacle of a lady gliding over the smooth streets of Washington on her own wheel, without what "the sex is sometimes pleased to call the humiliating presence of a man to help along. Many a lady has braved public opinion, as well as her own fears, and now the appearance of such a rider elicits much less comment than did the first 'bicycles with the little wheels in front' two months after their introduction." A well-known bicycle dealer there said there were at least 1,000 lady riders in Washington yet, still, "it is with great difficulty that a lady can be induced to even think of the idea of mounting a wheel and riding along the street in the face of the world. It makes her blush for shame. She would rather die than think of doing it and she almost grows hysterical at the mere suggestion." The biggest worry for this journalist was the question of dress. As noted, "The day for sewing bunches of [buck]shot into the skirts of dresses intended for riding wheels has gone by. Ladies' tailors may still put them into riding habits, but the masters of wheeling schools will never advise the use of weights in the skirt. All that is needed to preserve the natural order of things, and it is very essential that they should be preserved, is that a lady who rides must keep her dignity at the same time that she does her balance." Sewing buckshot into dresses was done, of course, to give them greater weight and, hopefully, keep them from riding or flying up when a woman in a skirt was cycling. Of the estimated 1,000 female riders, it was believed that 800 learned in the past year. The reporter noted, "It is very seldom that it is at all necessary to give more than five lessons—each lesson being of half an hour—in order to teach a lady to ride." The usual number of lessons needed was said to be three.[5]

Writing in April 1891 a reporter by the name of John Heaton remarked, "A few years ago there came a time when cycling seemed to reach its limit. One would have said that it was likely to remain stationary, or even to decline in public favor." Since then, though, he argued, there had been some changes: "The perfection of the safety wheel has made it possible to ride without the constant fear of a broken nose.... The invention of the ladies' bicycle has relieved the weaker sex of the burden of a third wheel and set women all over the country to cycling. The pneumatic tire has placed the bicycle racer abreast of the trotting horse for short distances and away ahead of it for long ones." The price of machines was reported to have dropped as their quality had improved. As well, the improvement of the common roads "has been due largely to the persistent clamour of cyclists and reacts to increase their number." By this newsman's estimate there were between 250,000 and 300,000 wheels in the United States, not counting the myriads of children's machines. As some of the cycles were rented out and some owned in partnership and some were tandems that carried double, "there may be not so many short of half a million regular or occasional wheelman in the country." The safety bicycle was then the overwhelmingly favorite machine with men and women alike. The reporter then discussed motivation by noting, "Perhaps the most interesting feature of the present cycling outlook is the number of women who wheel. Here the difference of motive in the sexes comes out strong. Men wheel because they want to, women because others do."[6]

Heaton spoke to Mr. Richards, the manager of the large Columbia bicycle manufacturing firm. With respect to women riders Richards observed that it made an immense difference whether bicycling started right or wrong in a town. He said, "If women of character and prominence happen to take to the wheel first in a place, the dealers are happy in plenty of orders. If the sport 'starts wrong' it may languish for years unless the leaders happen to take hold of it." In other words it was a class distinction that was involved in making cycling popular with women. Richards added, "The cycle makers in England and America could afford to present the Princess of Wales a wheel in solid gold for her part in popularizing the sport." He continued, "When men began to ride bicycles they at once, as a rule, adopted practically the costume they now wear—something resembling a baseball player's suit with the addition of a sack coat. Minutiae, such as rubber-soled shoes and club caps, came later. With women the question of dress comes first of all, and it has been practically decided that while she can wear almost any variety of dress it is better to have one designed especially for the wheel." The English publication *Bicycling News* reported that a ladies' college debated the question whether wheeling was a proper sport for women. Afterward the women voted on it with 32 favoring the activity, 14 denouncing it, and seven hedging. Concluded this account, "It is diffi-

This 1891 ad for a New York City bicycle dealer featured ladies' safety bikes for a price of from $75 to $140. The fine print told the reader the dealer also rented cycles.

"CYCLING INFORMATION."

SAFETY BICYCLES.

$75 TO $140.

All leading makes, COLUMBIAS, Victors, Tourist, Warwick, Kenwood, Psychos, and many others. In fact, we supply any Bicycle in the market worthy of our guarantee, at manufacturers' prices.

$75 TO $140.

LADIES' BICYCLES, ALL MAKES.

$20 to $45.

Youths' Bicycles, the best that can be produced and fully guaranteed.

CYCLE INSTRUCTION.

Our facilities for safe and correct instruction are unequalled. We have a large hall especially equipped. We have COMPETENT INSTRUCTORS. Our lessons are private (no spectators) and by appointment. LADIES especially appreciate this system of Cycle Instruction.

IN OUR RENTING DEPARTMENT may be found NEW BICYCLES of ALL LEADING MAKES. 1891 patterns COLUMBIAS, Warwicks, Kenwoods, Tourists, Psychos, &c., &c.

AS WE ARE NOT CONFINED TO ONE MANUFACTURE, and show a general line, our customers are enabled to make comparisons and satisfactory selection, without prejudice.

Our pamphlet, "Cycling Information," will be mailed on application, giving further particulars, with rates.

A visit to our new Cycling and Athletic Building and inspection of Salesroom and Instruction Hall is solicited.

GEORGE R. BIDWELL CYCLE CO.,

306, 308, and 310 West 59th St.

Open Evenings.

NEAR 8TH AV. ENTRANCE TO CENTRAL PARK.

cult to see why anyone should wish to negative such a question, provided the woman has time, money and strength. Or rather, time and money alone. The strength comes by using it."[7]

Minneapolis was described as being a "great wheel town," in April 1891. During the course of 1890 there were 250 riders added to any already large list. The 1891 season was expected to double that number. There were said to be about 800 riders then in Minneapolis "exclusive of the small boy" with the advent of the safety machine being credited with chief responsibility for those numbers. In the United States over the previous 18 months, 62 firms had been established to manufacture the safety machine. High-grade safety bicycles cost from $125 to $150. There were dozens of cheaper wheels that sold for from $25 to $110 but they were described as being of poor quality. In 1890 there were an estimated 40 or more female bikers and the account predicted, "This year will see 200 females astride the safety." The Ladies Cycling League in Minneapolis was exclusively for women and founded in February 1891. Among its members it numbered about half of all female riders in the city—that is, about 20. This piece concluded, enthusiastically, "The lady rider has come to stay, and I am glad to see the prudish notions of a lot of old maids have not been sufficiently strong to prevent our pretty girls from enjoying the best of all sports." The tricycle had all but vanished from Minneapolis by this time with that machine having "just 3 admirers in the city—all men."[8]

A reporter by the name of G.W. Weippiert noted in October 1891, "A few years ago wheeling was considered a fad practiced by would-be athletic young men. To-day staid heads of families and dignified women can be seen in every city and village mounted on wheels, accompanied by their sons and daughters, similarly equipped.... In the course of five years the bicycle, which has already risen from a fad to a convenience, will have become a necessity." He also observed that everywhere roads were beginning to be improved, giving more impetus for people to take up cycling. "The Chicago wheelwoman is daring, pretty and graceful, and so are her sisters in hundreds of western cities and villages where cycling has become a popular pastime," he stated, with reference to his home city. "A few old-fashioned fellows who have failed to progress with the times may cast slurs upon girls addicted to bicycle riding, but the common-sense people—and they constitute the majority in this enlightened country—are glad to see that American women everywhere are beginning to cultivate an exercise which has proved of tremendous benefit to their sex in England, France and Germany, where the sport has been popular for many years."[9]

A journalist with a different view as to the popularity of biking wrote in January 1892, "Cycling as an amusement for ladies and girls, has, it is true, scarcely made the progress into public favor which its votaries predicted." He thought that was because of one or all of four reasons: (1) that tricycling was at best somewhat heavy work for everybody who was not strong, (2) that for most people cycling was a somewhat expensive pastime, (3) that, for lack of a suitable dress and machine, few females looked well when they were riding, and finally, (4) "till comparatively recently, cycle manufacturers have paid but slight attention to the requirements of women in the matter of machines specially constructed to meet their needs in weight and suitability." Then he declared that the first and fourth reasons "which have perhaps prevented this healthy and delightful pastime from becoming as popular as it deserves with women and girls, are fast being rendered invalid as ladies' bicycles of a suitable and convenient pattern can now be obtained from most of the leading makers, all of which devote attention to the needs of ladies." He concluded by writing, "Manufacturers are at last recognizing that, should bicycling be made possible for ladies and become popular, there is another vast field opened for their enterprise."[10]

An article in January 1892 showed how far bicycling for women had come. It was a profile of women who had made 100 miles on bicycles in 16 hours or less. Writing from Chicago the journalist noted, "Bicycling is a favorite diversion of the Chicago girls. No other city in the country has developed so many expert lady riders. There are no less than half a dozen of them here who have covered 100 miles within 16 hours." Alice Waugh, a Chicago schoolteacher, had the distinction of being the first female in Illinois to make a century run within that time limit. Waugh was 21 and she achieved her feat after she had been riding for about five months. All of the women profiled in the piece were accompanied by a male rider on their century rides.[11]

This 1892 sketch showed Chicago's Alice Waugh, supposedly the first woman in Illinois to complete a century (100 miles) ride. Women who accomplished such feats were profiled more often as the popularity of the activity among women increased.

"Outdoor exercise is constantly recommended by physicians for women who are afflicted with nervous complaints and other illness. It is upon these recommendations that the bicycle has become so widely used by females," stated a journalist, writing in January 1892. "Up to within the past two years the exercise was confined to the tricycle, but shortly afterward the safety wheel was introduced and at once became an established favorite. To-day women bicyclists outnumber women equestrians almost two to one." A woman cyclist who had gained widespread prominence through some "remarkable performances" on the wheel was Margaret Kirkwood of Boston. She was described as an expert of long distances. Every week she took long rides in Boston along with her brother. By then she had completed many centuries. Chicago then had six female century riders and, reportedly, another dozen or so were to be found in various other cities. "The riding schools in this city [New York City] and Brooklyn are largely patronized by women. The teachers in the various schools say that the number of pupils who take to wheeling increases each year," he said. "Many women who are taught to become expert riders in the riding academies very seldom venture to ride in public." (Many of those schools had large private areas where cyclists who knew how to ride could cycle. These areas were sometimes indoors and sometimes outdoors. It meant a female cyclist who, for whatever reason, did not wish to cycle in public could do all her cycling in one of these private spaces.[12])

"The female bicyclist gradually grows more numerous. She is on our streets. She airily glides along, darts over the crossings, sweeps around a corner as on the wings of the dove, playing her pedal extremities firmly, gracefully, and with a coolness and skill commensurate with that mastery of anything she does well because she is naturally fitted therefor," so wrote a reporter in March 1892, with no little hyperbole. "Slender women and bicyclists are not naturally drawn together. They are the most exciting and graceful combination that has appeared in public in the nineteenth century." He went on to argue, "Excitement has a far greater fascination for women than for men.... Women gamblers and horse-racers and female dissipaters are more fiercely addicted to their passions than men. Having once bestrode the bicycle, she will never relinquish it." In conclusion he stated, "The fatal excitement of balancing like a bird in the air and gracefully skimming along like a swallow before a storm, links her in the future to the wheel. We may expect soon to see our sidewalks ornamented with an equal number of male and female cyclists."[13]

Several bicycle dealers in Washington, D.C., interviewed by a newspaper reporter of that city told the newsman in May 1892 that the output of ladies' wheels that season had been considerably larger than heretofore, and "they attributed the increased sales to the fact that ladies can ride along the streets nowadays without attracting any more attention than a male rider, and also because the wheel is recommended by many physicians to be one of the most healthful exercises known." However, the journalist also observed that there

The Start.
Copyright 1897 by R. Y. Young.

An 1897 woman ready to ride her bike, dressed in a style that was likely to cause comment from many quarters.

were few female members of bicycle clubs in Washington and that "Ladies' races have been looked upon with disfavor by the average wheelmen for a long time, notwithstanding that such a race is heard of now and then."[14]

Writing from Hackensack, New Jersey, in August 1892 an observer noted, "Three years ago the only women who dared [to] brave public opinion and ride a wheel in Hackensack was Mrs. Kittie Schmults, who was seen frequently propelling herself on a tricycle in the streets of the sleepy old town. That method of locomotion caused the village matrons and maids to look askance at their plump neighbor, and subjected her to not a little criticism from the sterner sex under a belief that there was just a shade of immodesty in the sight of a woman on a tricycle." When the safety bike appeared Schmults discarded her three-wheeler for a two-wheeler "and if the natives of Hackensack were surprised to see her on the first machine they were astounded at what they declared to be an act of brazen boldness. Some very mature maidens would not even gaze at the bold bicyclist—although they were assured by less prudish sisters that there was not the least hint of indelicacy in the picture formed by Mrs. Schmults on her wheel." He continued, "The men who appreciate attractiveness in the female form admired her jaunty make-up. Her riding skirt is cut just the proper length to permit the free play and necessary exposure of dainty feet that work the pedals with racing skill." A year earlier in Hackensack, it was reported, several young men and less than half a dozen girls were seen occasionally in the city streets imitating the example of Schmults, to "the horror of sewing circles and Dorcas societies." (A Dorcas society is a group of local people, usually church-based, with a mission of providing clothing to the poor). In the spring of 1892 a bicycle agency was established in Hackensack and wheeling "became epidemic. Old and young, male and female, were attacked by the malady; and many of those who were most ungenerous in their criticism of Mrs. Schmults were the first to succumb to the infection." The local press took shots at those beginners and one of them stated, "Ladies with large feet should never ride a bicycle." And, said the author of this piece, "that had the effect of bringing the divided skirt into use by many of the female bicyclists because it can be adjusted more readily to cover the feet." During the summer of 1892 the bicycle craze took hold in Hackensack to the extent that authorities in the city passed an ordinance requiring bikers to carry a bell, to have lights and have them on from sunset to sunrise, and to keep off the city sidewalks while bicycle riding.[15]

According to a report in January 1893 there were then over 1,000 female bikers in the city of San Francisco and another 500 located across the bay in Oakland and Alameda, while nearly every other city in California "has its quota. The public has been completely won over, and none but the overprudish and incurably dyspeptic are left to rail against it." And that meant a dramatic change in the lives of those women. "Now all is changed. Now with her bicycle she can go where she will, when she will and the way she will... . Everything has changed since she has learned to ride." In San Francisco there were bicycle "livery stables" where one could rent bicycles, and "these are called cycleries on wheeleries. A cyclery is generally a riding-school and a wheel-renting establishment in one." Thomas J. Cullen, an instructor at one such establishment, said, "In the past year we have taught about 300 ladies how to ride a bicycle. The pupil is given her first lesson on a safety tandem [with the instructor in the other seat]." Both the San Francisco Bicycle Club and the Alameda Bicycle and Athletic Club had a ladies' annex (which meant, of course, that females were not allowed to be full members of either club). According to the article, ladies' bicycle clubs do not seem to thrive very well. Miss L.D. Hill had been a cyclist for about 30 months and she remarked, "I think I was one of the first four ladies who rode a bicycle in San Francisco. I can remember the first day I went out there how all the men stared at me as if I was a curiosity. Now they take it as a matter of course, I suppose." By the estimate of this writer there were then over 30,000 women cyclists in the United States. The first woman to take to the wheel on this side of the Atlantic was, reportedly, Mrs. W.E. Smith of New York. "The fad, or whatever it pleases you to call it, is on the increase as nothing of its kind ever was before," said the newsman. "The list includes many well-known women such as Pauline Hall the actress, Mrs. Kendal, Miss Drexel, Kate Field, as well as leading society women in every city in the country." It was a singular fact though, he noted, "that very few ladies' clubs have had a lengthened existence. They have either died in their incipiency or were disbanded shortly after organization. Noteworthy examples of this are Washington, Providence, Philadelphia, Chicago and Minneapolis. It is only that New York City has developed a successful organization." The only other successful women's bicycle clubs then in existence were said to be in Omaha; Hartford; Houston; West Somerville, Massachusetts; Worcester, Massachusetts; Toronto; Ansonia, Connecticut; Wyoming, Pennsylvania; Rosedale, Massachusetts; Buffalo; and Brooklyn.[16]

Kittie Schmults, depicted here in 1892, was reported to have been the first woman in Hackensack, New Jersey, to appear on the city streets on a cycle. She started with a tricycle but soon moved on to a bicycle.

More hyperbole was engaged in by an eminent (but unnamed) physician in August 1893. "I have frequently had opportunities to notice the difference between the riding of men and women bicyclists, and I have been much surprised at the contrast between the two. The women, as a rule, are graceful, dignified and easy. The men in the majority of instances have looked more like agitated grasshoppers than anything else that I could imagine." He went on to add, "I think it safe to say that not one man in twenty-five rides really well, The women almost—if not altogether—reverse this rule, for a very ungraceful rider among them I rarely see."[17]

When reporter Isabella Proctor discussed the subject in August 1893 she noted that lessons cost 50 cents for 30 minutes and five lessons "are often sufficient" to produce a female biker, although "a woman less strong and courageous than the average will of course require more. Mounting and dismounting unassisted are the most difficult things to learn and are not taught until the pupil has gained control of the machine when in the saddle." Proctor claimed there were then almost 100 bicycle manufacturers in the United States. She concluded, "fortunately the woman's machine can be ridden by either sex, so if but one wheel is to be owned in the family let it have a drop frame that the weary housekeeper may enjoy her share of the change and exercise occasionally."[18]

Brooklyn, New York, was said to have been hit by the bicycle craze, where, in May 1894, "the officials, the clergy, the school teachers, even the middle-aged women have surrendered to the epidemic. There are 2 large schools in the Bedford district. The school makes money by guaranteeing to turn out a finished rider for $5–50 cents per half-hour lesson." Those female students preferred to ride at night, "but the darkness does something more than attract beginners who prefer not to be seen too distinctly when they are tumbling 'round. It also coaxes out the women who wear bloomers and are a little timid about showing them to too many persons at once. The manufacturers of one popular wheel declare that in five years there will not be a woman rider wearing skirts in this country. They say that every day the number of women in bloomers increases. This interesting and pretty development is apparent in Brooklyn. At times as many as half a dozen women in bloomers are seen on one asphalt block."[19]

A journalist writing in a New York City newspaper in June 1894 said

Top, left and right: Two 1894 sketches of bloomer-wearing cyclists. The question of whether or not to wear that garment while biking was a never-ending one during the period covered by this book. *Bottom, left and right and following page:* Out in Stanford University in Palo Alto, California, in 1894 the question of what to wear was supposedly settled with the convertible outfit. The female cyclist went out for a ride wearing knickerbockers but carried a skirt along with her. If she needed to stop to visit or to shop she put that skirt on and, in a flash, she was decent again and fit for human society.

4. 1890s—Popularity

MANY WOMEN WEAR BLOOMERS.

LONG AND SHORT BLOOMERS.

The Stanford Girl in Wheeling Trim

The Wheel-Girl in Her "Quick Change" Skirt.

WOMEN CYCLISTS.

They Are Organizing at Palo Alto

FOR SOME ENERGETIC WORK

The Wheel-Girl's Inventions in Rational Dress

AND A "PRESTO CHANGE" SKIRT

How the Bicycle Craze Has Struck the University—The Athletic Association.

that two of the leading firms of bicycle manufacturers in America had recently expressed the opinion that within five years there would be no difference between the cycles used by men and women, and that "in other words, they believe the day is not far off when all women devoted to wheeling will discard skirts on the road, and wear what is now usually referred to as the 'rational' or 'reformed' dress." And, he added, "they say there is no reason why women who wear costumes designed to enhance the comfort, enjoyment, and safety of bicycling should not have wheels equal in every respect to those the men ride. In other words, the sex of the rider will cut no figure in the manufacture of bicycles, and women will no longer have to put up with wheels whose mode, specially designed for skirt wearers, is necessarily inferior to those made for men in strength, lightness, and ease of propulsion." He felt that era had just about arrived. It was heralded by a cycle that was just beginning to appear in the streets of New York City and Brooklyn that was intended for women, "though it has the diamond frame heretofore seen only in the safeties made for men. In no respect does it differ from the finest high-grade, and high-priced roadsters used by the sterner sex except that the diameter of both wheels is from two to four inches smaller than that of the men's machines, and the frame is accordingly so much nearer the ground. The wheel is mounted by the step or pedal mount in vogue among men riders and is, of course, intended only for those women who wear the 'rational' dress." It was possible that few women patrons of the wheel would look askance at that innovation, he thought, "but if they will take the trouble to compare it with their own wheels they are certain to agree that it has its advantages." Women were not as physically strong as men yet the wheels they rode weighed from five to eight pounds more than men's roadsters. "This is a discrimination against the fair sex reaching the proportions of a grievance. If women are not to be allowed to enjoy the exhilarating and health-giving bicycle on equal terms with the men, they have wrongs that Miss [Susan B.] Anthony has not included in her category," he argued.[20]

He went on to declare, "The new wheel, however, weighs only twenty-eight pounds, which is two to five pounds less than most of the high-grade men's roadsters of exactly the same strength of frame. This is the crowning advantage and it is secured chiefly by doing away with the skirt guards which are the unsightly and not wholly protective feature of women's bicycles, and by saving the extra weight required for the unscientific and clumsy frames devised for riders wearing skirts." Undoubtedly, he believed, there were many women who, as much as they enjoyed bicycling, would rather give up their wheels than appear in costumes more comfortable and safer than those they were then wearing. "Every one of them will say, however, that bicycling in its present phase places limitations upon their enjoyment of it that are not imposed upon their husbands and brothers. It is an interesting and an important question how to surmount the difficulties and make all men and women free and equal bicyclers." And the solution to that problem was to be found "in a sensible bicycle for women" and he did not think American women "will be slower than their sisters in Europe to recognize the advantages of a bicycle dress reform and to dress accordingly." Concluding his piece the newsman stated, "The young women who are perfectly certain that they would rather die than wear one of the modest and tasteful bicycle suits which are now seen by scores on our streets are likely, before they are married, to see them so commonly in use that they will not call for special remarks…. We predict that the new bicycle, or something like it, will soon be a recognized feature in the wheeling world."[21]

One week later that same newspaper ran an editorial on the above topic, the special female diamond-frame machine. "Most people of taste and refinement will object to the use by women of bicycles constructed on the same pattern as those ridden by the sterner sex. This is the latest fad in bicycling, a woman's wheel with the regulation diamond frame having just been put on the market [for] her." he thundered. "Of course, in riding such a bicycle a woman is compelled to wear Turkish trousers, or something of that sort, and to mount from the axle step, just as a man does." It was claimed that these bikes were lighter than those usually made for women, the editor explained, "but this is true to only a limited extent, and practically the additional four or five or six pounds made necessary by the difference in construction are of no consequence in ordinary riding. In racing and in long-distance riding lightness is an essential factor; but women ride for health and pleasure—not to make records. Hence it cannot be successfully maintained that they are discriminated against by the bicycle-makers." However, then the editor began to reveal what was perhaps the real reason for his hostility. "The new fad is to be regretted because its inevitable tendency will be to increase the prejudice against women's riding which already exists in certain minds. Most women will not ride unless they can do so modestly and without making themselves conspicuous," he asserted. "This, of course, is very easy, and it is unfortunate that anything should arise to create the contrary view. Experienced lady riders assert that it is entirely safe to ride with a slight modification of the ordinary skirt, and that to enjoy the wheel thoroughly and get the best good out of it is not necessary for women to make their apparel approximate that of men in any degree."[22]

The importance of class issues in popularizing biking among women was evident in this October 1894 report out of Richmond, Virginia, which stated, "The perfectly unreasonable prejudice which exists here in some moss grown corners relative to bicycling for women is about to be ridden straight over by one of the city's belles…. All that has been wanted to make the bicycle popular among Richmond women has been its introduction by a social leader, for beautiful women, as has been well said, are their 'own law and gospel.'" That social leader was not identified. Continued the account, "The exercise is beneficial, and how the charge of immodesty could ever be brought against it is inconceivable only to the superfluously sensitive morale of those persons who find tables unpleasant because they have legs and offer no apology for them in the way of drapery. These people, unless I am mistaken, are of that class of whom Swift says—'Nice people—yes—people who are always thinking nasty things.'" In conclusion the reporter enthused, "The girl on the bicycle is a vigorous, bright, and womanly one, and long may she roll!"[23]

One week later a report out of Minnesota also alluded to class issues. In that account it was reported that the bicycle craze had at last reached St. Paul, Minnesota, "though one has long known that it was only a question of time. To mention the names of women bicyclists would be to give a list of St. Paul's four hundred." And, added the report, "clubs are being formed, and it is not an uncommon sight on Summit Avenue these moonlight nights to see a parade of men and women perched on wheels. The asphalt pavements are a joy to the souls of the bicyclists."[24]

An account that appeared in a California newspaper in November 1894 remarked, "The bicycle craze has struck Palo Alto and struck it hard.... It is not only the boys who fly about on wheels. The girls do it, too. This term the wheel-girls are becoming so numerous that they have thought it high time to organize for mutual pleasure and encouragement." Mostly the article was about women bikers at Stanford University in Palo Alto. An attempt at organizing a bicycle club had been undertaken a year earlier "but the time was not ripe for it and the bicycle club formed then lingered on awhile and then died a natural death." The new female club was formed in 1894 to be a branch of the Woman's Athletic Association and it was said 30 to 40 girls were members of that new club. With respect to the bicycle costume, "the club does not intend to impose any uniform. Many students wear the ordinary gymnasium dress consisting of full knickerbockers of the Turkish variety, with a loose blouse. Others put less material into the folds of their Turkish garments, while a few wear the divided skirt and others ordinary skirts." Celia Mosher, one of the faculty members of the university, had invented a "quick change" costume for wheelwomen. In the gymnasium and on their wheels they were clad very much like the ordinary wheelmen, wearing "black woolen stockings and tan shoes, knickerbockers and a smart Norfolk jacket worn over a starched shirt.... Matching that costume, however, is a trim tailor-made skirt of ordinary walking length. It buttoned down the side and could be slipped on in a few moments, giving the wearer the appearance of the every-day tailor-made girl." When the women who wore that combination went out on their bikes they took the skirt along with them. "When the cyclists approach any town where they feel that, in deference to public opinion, they must wear the clinging feminine skirt, or if they want to get off their wheels to shop or pay visits, they button on the skirt and, presto, the cyclist is transformed into a girl in ordinary walking dress." It was also pointed out that usually rows of buttons on skirts were merely there for decorative purpose, "but the Palo Alto buttons serve a purpose—they save the wearer stepping into the garment to which they belong or having to throw it over her head. 'That, you see,' explained one of the student, 'would be too suggestive of dressing in the streets.'"[25]

Pauline Pry wrote in a Washington, D.C., newspaper in November 1894, giving details about how she spent a recent morning learning how to ride a bicycle. At the school where she received instruction there were 200 women in attendance with women learning to ride with lessons being given from 7 a.m. until 10 p.m. She also mentioned the society and diplomatic men who had taken to the bicycle. The talk of the females at the riding school, said Pry, "revealed that while Washington girls are wearing bloomers on their bicycles after dark, they haven't yet dared to repeat their summer successes in them by daylight."[26]

Appearing late in December 1894 was another account that brought up the factor of class that stated, "The bicycle 'fad,' if 'fad' it can be called, has taken a firm hold on fashionable society must certainly be accepted without question at the present time. The evidence is so complete that it would be absurd to attempt to stem the rush of cycling's popularity or to deny that society has the craze." He went on to assert, "Of course, it may be held that, like others of society's passing pleasures, cycling will have its day, die and be buried with no mourners at the funeral. But then the history of cycling's entrance and progress into society's ranks does not show any indications that such shall be the case." As far as this journalist was concerned the progress of the activity had been too slow to be classified as a fad. It had not boomed its way into fashionable society's arms "with the glare and noise of trumpets and fireworks, but its advance has been slow and steady, so slow, in fact, that until lately it might have been classed with the pace of the snail." There were many reasons for this, argued the newsman, "among them being a natural aversion to the publicity of the thing in the days when even a man riding a bicycle was stared at in the streets, while people stopped and gazed with open-eyed wonderment at the strange sight of a woman speeding along on a wheel; and she did not have to wear bloomers, either, to create a sensation, nor need she be anything but a model of propriety and modesty." According to this account, "The mere fact that a woman was riding a bicycle was enough to collect a crowd of curious people in the front windows of the houses along her ladyship's route. Then, again, bicycle-riding was thought by many to be dangerous and even unhealthful, and essays and stories were written by alleged authorities to prove this." But time passed "and now the approach of a bicycle in the street excites not the slightest interest unless ridden by a woman, and even then only the passing notice due to her sex at all times."[27]

As far as this newsman was concerned, "The conservatism of society did not permit it to adopt the bicycle craze at the start, neither was it first taken up by the poorer people of society. It was too costly a pleasure for the latter to think of indulging in." And, he continued, the middle classes were the first to accept the bicycle with open arms, "and so the bicycle craze grew until there is at least one bicycle in almost every house occupied by the middle class, while it many of the houses every member of an entire family has one." Among those who had recently purchased and learned to ride bicycles were Mrs. William H. Vanderbilt, Mrs. William Jay, and Dr. Carroll Dunham. Many other names, both men and women, were listed in the article. "This list, it will be seen, includes prominent people in society, physicians and lawyers, actors and actresses, authors and men well known in business circles." Then a list of a dozen or two names of prominent people "in high circles" abroad, in England, who had taken up the activity were given, proving how "as in this country, the bicycle novice among the upper classes of society abroad patronizes the schools, of which a considerable number have recently sprung into existence." In New York City most of the first class bicycle instruction schools were on the Upper West Side, in the neighborhood of Central Park. About a dozen such first class schools could then be found in New York. A novice in such a school had a belt buckled around the waist with a loop attached. The attendant grasped that loop and walked around on the inner side of the track, steadying the novice. The newsman said that a conservative estimate of the number of bicycle riders in New York and Brooklyn was 40,000. For the entire United States, one estimate put the total number of bike riders at one million. There were then some 150 or more factories in America that manufactured around 500,000 cycles per year. The output of a single factory ranged from 40 machines a year to 40,000.[28]

A brief item that appeared in February 1895 also touched on class topics. It declared, "One peculiar feature of the wheeling craze is the emancipation of the waiting-maid. Well-to-do women have their maids instructed so they can ride in the street and rink with them."[29]

Writing in the early spring of 1894 a reporter in Minnesota declared, "All the girls are bicycle girls this spring. A girl who is a bicycle girl is self-conceited, eccentric, and anxious for undue prominence. Such a girl will refuse to wear violets. Beware of her." He went on to add, "The swellest trotting saddle horse that can be imported, or the smoothest 'single-foot' pacer that ever nibbled blue grass, will not induce St. Paul young women to ride a block this year. The most dashing village cart, dog cart, or cart of any other sort, will not induce them to drive. Jenness-Miller will be unable to persuade them to walk. They will ride a wheel or 'never go out as long as they live. So there!'"[30]

An article extolling the popularity of bicycling in New York City appeared in April 1895, calling the activity "a sport for everybody" and adding, "Men and women, young and old, alike are enthusiastic about riding." Within a year the act of riding on two wheels "has ceased to rank as a sport, and has taken its place among the recognized forms of travel." The mania for this swift, graceful, noiseless mode of progress had provided epidemic to a remarkable degree, and neither age nor sex was spared, he enthused. "The railroads have made special provision for bicycles, the ferries provide special transportation for them, elevated trains in Brooklyn now run bicycle cars, and even the saloons and restaurants along the thoroughfares most favored by the riders have catered to bicyclists by signs announcing themselves as 'The Bicycler's Rest,' 'The Wheelers' Retreat.'" According to this account there were then 280 distinct brands of bikes on the market, many of which were inexpensive machines; this article put the average price of bicycles at $85. The first bicycle school in New York City was said to have been established at the corner of Fulton Street and Broadway in 1880. By 1895 there were dozens of schools in the city and they were busy from 8:30 a.m. until 10:30 p.m. Purchasers of bikes received a free course of instruction in all the schools, that is, those that were affiliated with dealers. "Society women looked with disfavor upon cycling at first, but its recognition at Newport last summer gave it a big impetus in the city last fall and this spring. The majority of pupils at the various academies are women. They attend early in the forenoon and frequently return in the afternoon and evening for two or three lessons a day." A single lesson cost 50 cents and lessons on the road that lasted one hour cost two dollars. Usually five lessons were needed to learn to cycle. In this reporter's opinion the most popular costume was a snug-fitting waist, with bloomers, leather leggings reaching to the knees and a skirt reaching to the shoe tops over the bloomers. "The long, heavy skirt seems to have passed out of date, and while the advocates of the out and out bloomer costume are very numerous, most women will prefer to wear a skirt reaching to the shoe tops over the bloomers. Such a skirt does not interfere with the pedals or wheels," concluded the article.[31]

A New York City paper presented a panoramic view of female cyclists that were seen on Riverside Drive on May 5, 1895. The more fashionable cyclists wore "Scotch suits" with knickerbockers that bagged like bloomers. Reportedly, about one in ten of those women seen wore bloomers.[32]

An ad for a bicycle school that appeared in a Lincoln, Nebraska, paper in May 1895 was pitched directly to women. The school was located on the

This panoramic sketch from 1895 showed the different types of female riders that were seen on Riverside Drive in New York City on one particular day.

second floor over the company's main business, its music store. The ad declared that the school wished to train 1,000 females to ride a bicycle that season.[33]

One month later the same paper in Lincoln presented an enthusiastic article that stated, "The bicycle epidemic is sweeping over the whole country. It is estimated that during the coming summer the votaries of the wheel in New York City alone will number 200,000." According to this article, "In many cities the bicycle has inaugurated a serious rivalry with the street car, and in Denver the effect has been so unmistakable that the local street railway company has cut the wages of its employees in order to meet the great reduction in its income. The daily receipts of the car lines have never been so low, and that the drop is caused entirely by the introduction of bicycles is beyond a doubt." One estimate was that 4,000 wheels were sold in Denver in 1894 and, he thought, the estimate of 10,000 in use in Denver "is probably extremely low. The use of the bicycle has apparently but just begun to fairly take hold on the popular fancy, and it is prophesized that before long the majority of people will just as soon think of doing business without their bicycles as their watches."[34]

A report in June 1895 observed that bicycle "stables" had sprung up. They charged one dollar a month, and cleaning the machine and keeping it in running order were included in the fee. Businessmen, for example, who rode his machine to work usually had no place to leave it. Those stables also rented machines. This article brought up the topic of women instructors at riding schools. Said the mother of one young female pupil, "You are right about the woman instructor; she is a necessity. I have been allowing my daughters to ride there,

An ad for a bicycle school from 1895.

More Ladies

Are learning every day that not only pleasure but health and strength are to be found on the wheel and as a consequence

ARE LEARNING TO RIDE

at CURTICE CO'S. bicycle school over their music store on South Eleventh st.

Bicycles

are a healthful, rational mode of hardening the muscles, improving the complexion, and a ride

Every Day

goes very far toward keeping the mental faculties in the best working order.

OUR SCHOOL

is now open and scores of ladies are learning to ride. It is not difficult if the pupil

IS UNDER A COMPETENT TEACHER

and we have one. Many do not ride gracefully because not properly taught.

WE WANT TO TEACH A THOUSAND LADIES

this season. It's the ladies we want specially. Make an appointment and look

AT OUR SCHOOL

and cycles.

THE

N. P. CURTICE CO.

207 South Eleventh St.

although I had scruples about their doing so with only strange men for instructors. One day I happened in just as a young woman fainted and fell off her wheel. Every instructor in the place rushed up to her, and, while I recognized the fact that all had only the kindest intentions, it flashed over me as they lifted her out that there ought to be a woman in an official position around. The thing made such an impression on me that I wouldn't allow my girls to come here anymore until I hear that the managers had engaged a woman instructor." (This, of course, brought up the idea of a chaperon.) Overhearing that remark at the academy, a young woman at the school learning to ride responded, "Let the old women talk all they want, but I don't need any chaperon." In this account roadster bicycles were said to weigh 22 to 24 pounds.[35]

Victor Bicycles Lead

THE BEST PEOPLE RIDE THE BEST WHEELS.
RIDING A '95 VICTORIA IS THE SUREST GUARANTEE
THAT YOU BELONG TO THE "FOUR HUNDRED"

'95 VICTORIA
The Only Perfect Drop-frame Bicycle

Strong

As It Is

Graceful

No Wonder They Run Light
See That Crank=Hanger

Scientific construction, the finest material only, and a rigid testing of every part, are key-notes of Victor Success.
ABSOLUTELY PERFECT.

OVERMAN WHEEL CO., Makers of Victor Bicycles,
Cor. Fourth and Main.   WESTMINSTER HOTEL BLK.

In 1895 this Los Angeles bicycle dealer advertised the Victor ladies' wheel.

One of the celebrities who endorsed bicycling for women was famed actress Lillian Russell who wrote an article in July 1895 in praise of bicycling. She said, "I could not help recalling the days not so very long ago—surely within a year—when women looked longingly at their brothers spinning a wheel, but scarcely dared to attempt the same themselves, unless strictly within the walls of a selected academy. Now women cyclists are the rule, and those who are not learning to ride the great exception." Russell concluded, "The cycle supplies the place of tonics and society, professional and working women alike find it gives them the peculiar 'just something' which their system lacked."[36]

Testament to the popularity of women and cycling was the fact that a stage play on the topic surfaced in 1896. Louis Harrison's musical farce *The Bicycle Girl* received its first performance in St. Paul, Minnesota, on January 19, 1896. Said a reporter, "It serves as a vehicle of exploitation of the new woman, the coming man and the bicycle craze. The cast was led by Nellie McHenry, who played the bicycle girl. The first act, which showed the interior of the Briarwood Bicycle Club, 'warrants the appearance of the ladies strictly up-to-date wheeling costume.'" The play featured a conventional love story in which two men courted bicycle girl Grace Fordyce, carrying the audience through three acts, who were left wondering which of the suitors the bicycle girl preferred. Ending the play was a bicycle race that was won by the bicycle girl. The play toured the country for some time. For example, it played in Hutchinson, Kansas, on April 15, 1896. Reviews were reported to be mixed.[37]

In May 1896 an advertisement appeared in the papers that tied the phenomenon of the bicycle girl to a product called Lightning Hot Drops, a patent medicine of the time. That product was billed as an external remedy for pains, sprains, cuts, scratches, and so on. It was an early example of a corporation attempting to sell more products by linking it to a societal fad, even when the two had no relationship at all.[38]

So popular was the bicycle that it spawned a stage play, *The Bicycle Girl*, that toured the nation in 1896. This sketch is of the play's star, Nellie McHenry.

MEDICINAL.

The Bicycle Girl

Or Man—
will find—
that the—

LIGHTNING HOT DROPS

Is their friend as an external remedy for Pains, Sprains, Cuts, Scratches and Bruises and all like accidental ailments.

CARRY A BOTTLE ALONG.

You'll find it of particular use when Gripes, Pains in the Stomach come on—nothing better for Cramps or Cholera Morbus.

50c size holds twice as much as the 25c size.

**HERB MEDICINE COMPANY,
SPRINGFIELD, OHIO.**

Marketing tie-ins were used even back as far as 1896 as this one for a patent medicine.

It was said in May 1896 that in the previous year there were 850 different names [brands] of bicycles on the market in the United States (though some manufacturers made more than one brand). In February 1896 there were 1,143 different kinds of wheels made and registered in America. Within three months, these 300 new makes of bicycles were placed on the market. The article then wondered why it was that jewelers sold bicycles. As a general rule, the explanation went, those jewelers were not the sole agents for the wheel but were simply subagents for the bicycle dealer who represented the manufacturer. In explaining the situation a prominent jeweler in St. Paul, Minnesota, said, "We are doing it in self-defence. The average young man, in former years, when going on a trip would purchase a watch; on his sweetheart's birthday he would purchase a lady's watch.... The young man does not buy watches or bracelets or brooches anymore; he buys bicycles instead." The jeweler continued, "Count the number of young ladies riding on the boulevard or through the parks on some fine days and then think that not one in a hundred of those ladies bought their own wheels. They were given to them by brothers, fathers or their sweethearts instead of jewelry. We have decided to keep in front of the procession as before, and now, if we cannot suit a young man or young lady with some article of jewelry, we have a bicycle which 'runs like a watch' that we can offer instead." One novelty item for female cyclists then on the market was a bicycle screen for "modest maidens" that hid bloomer girls' legs.[39]

Summarizing the "new woman" in May 1896 a reporter declared, "Not so long ago the ideal woman was the helpless, strengthless creature who must be protected from the faintest breath of air and from the slightest exertion. She was beautifully and confidingly dependent upon the manly 'oak' to which she clung." And, he added, "she passed from an utter dependence upon her father and brothers to any equally utter dependence upon a husband. She had little self-reliance; and still less ability to take care of herself. And now, of late years, there has been a change—and we hear of a 'New Woman.'" In the opinion of this account the bicycle girl epitomized that new woman.[40]

According to a May 1896 story there were four million bike riders in the United States. The number of cyclists who passed a given point in 16 hours was computed by an actual count at the corner of Seventy-Second Street and the Boulevard (unnamed) in New York City on a Thursday in May between the hours of 7 a.m. and 11 p.m. An average of 879 riders passed that corner each hour. A total of 14,052 riders was composed of 10,536 men, 2,501 women and 1,015 children. Those riders sailed by mounted mostly on safety bikes. Seven rode tricycles of the "youths' pattern," 193 were on tandems, six were on the duplex machines (a three-wheel vehicle with two riders seated side by side), and four doubles' machines. All other machines being ridden past the point were safety bicycles. With respect to costumes, the majority of

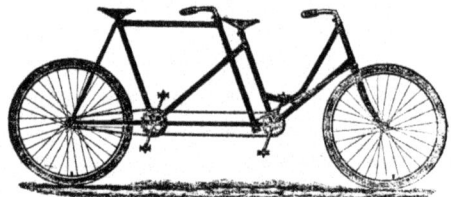

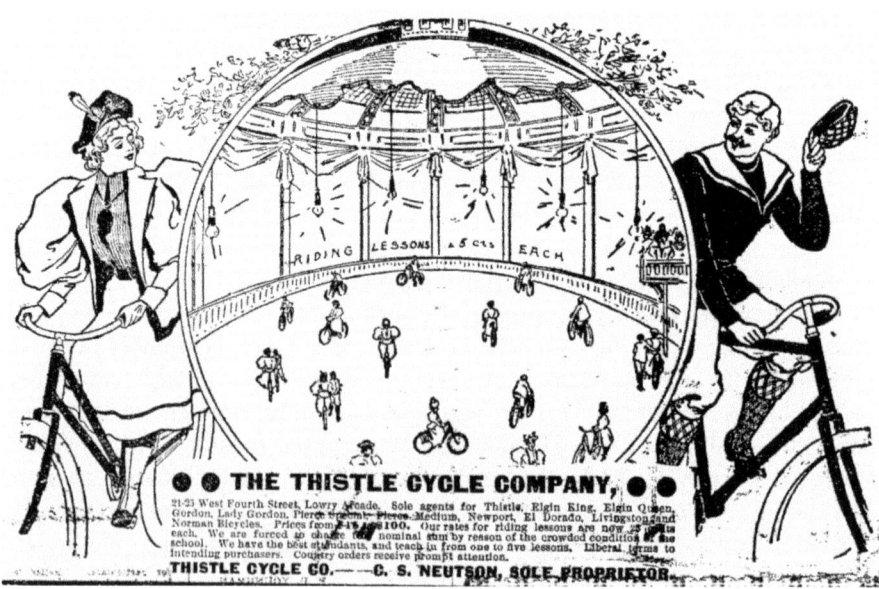

wheelmen "wore the ordinary street costume" with perhaps an exception in the matter of head covering, with caps being almost the exceptional rule for both sexes. There were 2,997 men in bicycle costumes more or less marked—knickerbockers, golf hose, sack coats and Scotch caps being the usual outfit. Among the women 660 were in costume, with the divided skirt being the favorite; additionally, "the bloomer was present, but conspicuous by its rarity. There were only sixty-three of them." In the city of New York there were estimated to be nearly 200,000 bicycle riders of whom 80,000 were members of various clubs. In America there were said, in this account, to be at least 250 cycle manufacturers with their output expected to hit one million machines in 1896. The price of bicycles varied from $50 to $100 and upward and often involved additional cost for extras, for example, five dollars for a bicycle lantern (lamp) and $20 for a suit of bicycle clothing. The average cost of maintaining a bicycle was put at one dollar a week, excluding the initial purchase price.[41]

When opera star Emma Calvé arrived in Chicago in June 1896 she had little or no experience in bicycling. She spoke to opera star Nellie Melba, who was performing in the same company as she, and found

SCREEN FOR MODEST MAIDENS.

Opposite, top and bottom and right, top and bottom: Three of these 1896 illustrations showed ads for bicycle makers that targeted female consumers. The fourth illustration showed a special modesty guard that could be bought and mounted on a woman's machine so she could completely hide her legs and thus retain her modesty, dignity, and so forth.

This illustration supposedly captured the difference between the "new woman" (who was active, on the move, a bicycle rider), and the "old woman" (who was inactive, frail, listless, and so on).

her to be in a similar condition. However, they were both interested in bicycling and decided to take up the activity together. When Calvé was asked why she took up the activity she replied, "Oh, partly for pleasure, and then again, all professional people must have some sort of exercise, don't you know." Then she was asked why she did not do it before, to which she responded, "Well, when I was in New York the weather was too cold, and besides I didn't see as many women riding bicycles in that city as I have seen in Chicago." Next she was asked if she would continue with the activity when she returned home to Europe, to which she responded, "Yes indeed. Every artist in Paris owns a bicycle, even Sarah Bernhardt, and any number of well-known professional people can be seen on the boulevards there riding along on their wheels." Finally, she was asked if she was going to follow the idea of Chicago's new woman and wear the bloomer costume. Calvé asserted, "Nay, nay, you don't catch me out on the streets in anything like that. I will wear a short skirt that will reach to my shoe tops and then, besides, I have bought a low frame woman's wheel, and that will overcome the necessity of my wearing the divided skirt." When those two opera stars took up cycling Melba was 35 and Calvé was 37.[42]

One of the more bizarre stories related to women and bicycling surfaced in June 1896 in an account that provided a description of a new sport—bicycle tennis for women. Reportedly this fad had started in England and by the spring of 1896 it had arrived in the United States where it was adopted in some summer resorts. Needless to say, it never caught on and died a quick death, almost before it was born.[43]

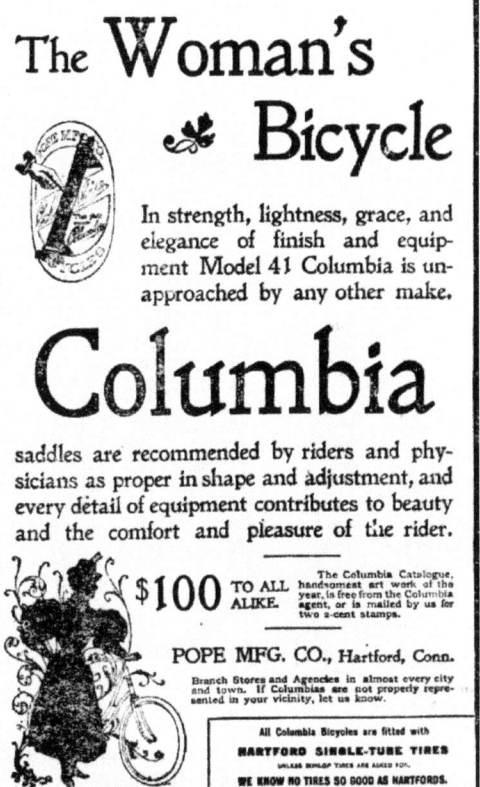

This 1896 ad touted the Columbia woman's machine and emphasized that the saddle on the woman's bike was different than the saddle on a man's cycle.

By late 1896 it was reported that the bicycle girl had discovered what to do with last season's bicycle wheel: "This winter will see a change in the home of the bicycle girl. From cellar to roof her home will look 'bicycle-y,' to coin a word. Golden mural wheels will greet the eyes in the drawing-room, silvered chains that once groaned with dust and grease will be draped on the mantel piece, and every part of a bike's anatomy, beribboned and ornamented, will serve a decorative and useful purpose." At this time a low-end bicycle could be bought new for $20. Also, needless to say, the fad of using old bicycle parts as items of home decoration never caught on.[44]

TENNIS ON WHEELS.

An 1896 drawing of women engaging in the newest sport, bicycle tennis. It died a very quick and unlamented death.

That same month, November 1896, another article appeared that was concerned with trivial so-called aspects of females and cycling. This one was about pins, bracelets and garter buckles that were said to be the latest fad of wheelwomen, which stated, "The bicycle girl, her needs and her fads, is a positive influence in the various departments of commercial enterprise." A variety of scarf pins, bicycle jewelry, stick pins and garter buckles were detailed in the account. "And this does not end the list of the bicycle girl's fads, for the craze is spreading. A bicycle clock is seen on the wheelwoman's dressing table and a bicycle paper weight is found on her desk. Her beautiful ivory toilet set has a silver wheel on the back of each pin in place of the customary monogram, and her stationary is stamped with a tiny machine in her club colors." All articles such as these indicated that women and bicycles were a mature industry now and that meant that more and more unrelated business concerns tried to tie themselves to the bikers in order to sell them more and more product that was unrelated to bicycling itself.[45]

In January 1897 an article began by saying that two or three years earlier a man connected with a large bicycle establishment remarked in conversation

The Bicycle Girl and Her Last Season's Wheel

She Takes It Apart, Paints and Polishes It and Then Makes It Serve for Decorative Purposes

WHEELS FOR MURAL DECORATION.

Another example of an attempt to produce false fads was this 1896 illustration that urged readers of the attached article to take apart old bicycles and to use the pieces to stick up on the walls as an element of home decoration. This fad lasted about as long as did the one for bicycle tennis.

that he believed the time would soon come—and the limit he set was three or four years—when no bicycles would be built specially for women, but all women riders would be using diamond-frame wheels. But in 1897, declared a reporter, there was no indication that that prediction was coming true, and "on the contrary, there are many signs that what is termed 'rational' costume for women has had its day and is on the decline in this country." Observations during the previous year had showed, reportedly, fewer bloomers worn by women than in earlier times, although the number of women riders had greatly increased. The writer of the piece then wondered if there was any demand for diamond-frames for women. To find out he asked that question at the headquarters of the various bicycle companies. A spokesman at one company told him, "No, there is scarcely any demand at all. So far as I can judge, I should say there is a smaller demand this year than there was last, and less then than in the year before. Our women haven't taken to trousers or divided skirts. With frames made as they now are, there is no reason why they should. The loop frame is very stiff and practically as rigid as the diamond; in fact, the loop has a tendency to take up the vibrations." He added, "Besides a woman riding such a wheel is able to get off much quicker in case of an emergency. Women are not in the habit of swinging their feet round as men are, and consequently when mounted on a diamond frame they cannot get off so quickly and easily as a man can. I should say that not one woman in fifty of those who come in here looking for bicycles even suggests a diamond frame as a possibility."[46]

Writing in a Washington, D.C., newspaper in February 1897 an observer remarked, "The bicycle has emancipated woman" and said women should give thanks "upon the head of him who first made a wheel which a woman could ride." He pointed out that those thanks should go to either the late Mr. W.E. Smith or Bert Owen, "both of them being given the credit of making the first woman's wheel." Among other benefits women received from the bicycle was that "it means that she has a certain freedom never before dreamed of." With respect to costume, he asserted, "The use of the rational costume is in its infancy as yet, but the day will come when the female rider will dress to suit her own ideas; when Dame Fashion will make a sudden swerve and style of dress suitable for cycling decreed to be the rage." With the "loose corset" endorsed and accepted by all physicians and riders the reporter predicted, "It is natural to conclude, too, that a woman, after enjoying freedom from the constraints of tight lacing while on the wheel, will not torture herself with small corsets while on the street or in the house, but will give to her vital organs on all occasion that freedom from repression which is imperatively demanded while she is having a spin of a few miles over some favorite driveway."[47]

Journalist Amos Cummings observed in July 1897 that many members

The Cycling Maiden of Today.

Cycling Maiden of the Future.

These 1897 sketches show the bicycle girl of the present and of the future.

of Congress had taken to riding the bicycle, which he took as testament to its popularity in the nation's capital, a city that had earned the nickname "the heaven of bicycles." Workers all over the city used them and most government departments and agencies set aside places to park and store the machines for the working day, while "theaters advertise them checked and stored without charge." It was then estimated that 12,000 to 15,000 people employed in Washington used their wheels in going to and returning from work. Nearly 20,000 people were employed in government departments and estimates had it that over 25 percent of those use the wheel. When an "old fogey" scoffed at a young friend and expressed astonishment that the younger man had a wheel that younger man declared, "In a quarter of a century you will see one hundred wheelmen where you now see one." Replied the older man, "You are crazy, it is simply a fad. Within ten years it will die out, and you will not see one wheel where you now see a hundred."[48]

Charlotte Bolton was one of the first women to take to cycling back in the late 1880s. In September 1897 a reporter asked her to give an account of her experiences and beliefs. She said, "I was one of the first to ride a lady's safety bicycle, my first wheel being a New Rapid, with hard tires, which I purchased in Manchester, England, in 1889. It weighed some forty pounds, which was light at that time." Bolton continued, "That the use of the wheel is making women more courageous, more self-reliant, stronger and healthier

THE CYCLE OF TIME.

Miss Antique—I have been in two centuries.
Miss Guy—If you live until nineteen hundred, you will have been in three.

This 1897 illustration also shows the old and the new bicycle girl.

is illustrated every day. I do not approve of hard, long-distance riding, but preach moderation. Whatever prejudice may have existed against bicycling for women is rapidly disappearing as the subject becomes better understood." In conclusion Bolton stated, "I have found that a lady can dress and care for herself as gracefully on a wheel as in a drawing room. To all women who have not already taken to the bicycle I say, delay not another moment, for you cannot imagine how much of life's joys you are missing."[49]

Bicycle tennis for women was a strange idea, but something equally weird was reported on in September 1897. The "gymkhana" was a sort of bicycle tournament that English women, and men too, began to indulge in a year or two earlier. The feats of the gymkhana could be performed out in the open or in a large hall. Events included a musical ride, a potato race, fancy riding, winding of a May pole, an obstacle race, and various other things, all while the participant was riding her bike. This, too, was an idea that did not catch on and died at birth.[50]

Over in Paris, France, at the end of 1897 it was reported that an old house had been leased by the Misses Jardine and its floors were devoted to bicycle instruction. Mignon and Felice Jardine were the sisters running the place. They felt that since deciding to take up the activity the women "hesitate about riding because they must learn from a man, and natural pride keeps a woman from wanting to appear ridiculous in masculine eyes." Added the journalist, "They also reasoned that a woman could teach the wheel better than a man, because of her highly sensitive organization, which makes her shudder at the thought of a fall, even though the fall may not be hers." The matter of costume was considered important and the Jardines reasoned that women could learn the trick of balance more quickly in bloomers and therefore when a pupil started to learn at their school "she is told to take off her skirts and put on baggy trousers for the first few lessons."[51]

TILT IN THE BICYCLE GYMKHANA.

Like bicycle tennis this bizarre sport, called bicycle gymkhana, comprised of performing various athletic endeavors while on a bicycle, was doomed to immediate failure.

The growing tendency to admit women to membership in bicycle clubs was reported to be a sign of the times, as reported in February 1898, "The fair sex are on an equal footing with the sterner sex in many such organiza-

This 1898 illustration accompanied an article about a bicycle school for women that was run by women, a rarity at the time.

tions, particularly in the larger cities." Other bicycle clubs, which do not go so far as to admit women to active membership, "in many cases make special arrangements for their entertainment on certain days of the week or month. It is safe to say that women riders are welcomed to participate in the regular runs of at least one-third of the clubs in and around the principal cities."[52]

A high point for the bicycle craze of the 1890s occurred when the *New York Tribune* newspaper issued a special section of the newspaper on February 22, 1898, to celebrate the bicycle. It was a 19-page supplement that featured an illustration of a woman bicyclist on the cover. Inside, however, there was only one page devoted to women, with the other pages all given over to men bikers, wheelmen clubs, advertisements and so forth. Subheads on the

This page and following two pages: The popularity of bicycling women was such that the subject warranted a cover spread in the media, for *Scribner's Magazine* in 1896, and a full supplemental section in the *New York Tribune* in 1898. However, with respect to the latter section, just one page of 19 was devoted to women and cycles, and much of that was given over to inane fashion comment, as in the last sketch.

woman's page included "prominent women give their views of the exercise," and "Doctors, lecturers, society women and scientists heartily approve." That supplement was, of course, a measure of the popularity and persuasiveness of bicycling in society. However, there were also half a dozen illustrations of the latest fashionable costumes for the female biker, as the supplement was little more than a marketing opportunity.[53]

Superstar actor and singer Lillian Russell gave a series of five lessons in a New York City newspaper in July 1901, in which she discussed three sources of beauty, including the use of a medicine ball, the gymnasium and bicycling.[54]

An account from August 1901 remarked that the 19th century had brought about the bicycle girl, and that "the bicycle girl brought about the common sense girl, the every-day up-to-date girl, the general utility girl. The girl who can ride the bicycle with grace and endurance can and will do most anything that comes to hand, even to, in many instances, making a living for her worthless husband."[55]

But then, suddenly, the craze was over. The culprit—the killer—was, of course, the automobile. An early omen was reported in February 1897 when a reporter remarked, "The bicycle will have a potent rival on the Continent this coming season, for the tourist now promises to take to the auto-car and leave the cycle to rust and decay." And, he continued, "so it is not at all improbable that before many months the bicycle girl will have evolved into the auto-car girl." One possible drawback noted in attaining that goal was the cost of the auto-car.[56]

"Cycling costume of blue serge, trimmed with bands of white cloth."

This photograph showed a main street in Philadelphia in 1897. In the lower foreground two women can be seen making their way on bicycles, with a few horse-drawn carriages also on the street. The automobile was nowhere to be seen, a circumstance that would soon end.

A few years later, in October 1906 a journalist wondered, "Who has seen a lady on a bike?" She was said to then be as scarce in Spokane, Washington, "as hen's teeth in a barnyard or any other place…. The time was not very long ago when the lady bicyclist used to pass up and down the streets at a good pace, but nowadays one may watch for hours without seeing a lady awheel, or even a little girl." He wondered where they had all gone, stating, "There used to be hundreds of them in this city. Today it is doubted if there are 25. Evidently the ladies have shook the bicycle for good." With respect to male cyclists he observed, "Oh sure, they ride yet, but not nearly so many of them." No reason for the bicycle's demise was speculated upon by this reporter.[57]

In June 1907 a lengthy article appeared about the auto craze. It estimated that there were maybe 10,000 women motorists in America, or even more. Carrie Nation ("the great temperance crank") was said to be learning to drive and Mrs. Marjorie Gould (a member of New York's Four Hundred, which was a list of New York's society during the Gilded Age) was described as an enthusiastic autoist. Mrs. William K. Vanderbilt had recently purchased a new car "and hundreds of leading society women of America are devotees of

Here Is the Auto-Car Which Promises to Be a Dangerous Rival of the Bike

Top: **This humorous drawing from 1897 warned of the coming automobile and how it would erode the popularity of the bicycle, something that did happen rapidly and dramatically.** *Bottom:* **Women on bicycles in late 19th century America.**

the sport." During the period covered by this book, the upper and middle classes were the women who rode bicycles. The lower classes were mostly absent. They just did not have the money. When the automobile arrived in a serious way those relatively wealthy women could and did switch rapidly from being ardent and devoted bicyclists to being ardent and devoted autoists.

The "new woman" and her bicycle, and the several varieties of her, as depicted by the English publication *Puck*.

Between roughly 1901 and 1905 or 1906 the bicycle passed from a craze enjoyed by many thousands to a dusty relic found only in a garage or shed, if found at all. It was completely dead and would remain so—at least with respect to adults—for many, many decades to come. That was just one more blessing bestowed upon us by the automobile.[58]

5

1890s—Health

The issue of cycling and the health of women was often discussed in the media. From the beginning most of the accounts were favorable to the idea and advocated that females take up cycling as an excellent form of exercise and as an endeavor that would improve their health. However, that idea was often challenged in print, sometimes in bizarre fashion. In March 1889 a woman cyclist wrote of having read an article as to why women should ride a lady's bicycle. She agreed with that article, remarking, "From my own experience I have found it improves my health and complexion very much. I have only been riding since June, but I am stronger now, and enjoy living much better than ever I did before that time. The pains and the doctors have both gone, where I don't know and care less, so long as they have gone and so long as I still have my bicycle and can take my ride every day." She went on to observe, "I sometimes get a trifle angry when I hear some old feminine fuss and feathers say, 'Oh, isn't that disgraceful to see a woman riding a man's bicycle.'" This female cyclist declared that her husband was very much pleased that she rode "and here I will mention that the advantage in having a lady's safety is that either can ride…. I am growing old gracefully as I ought to."[1]

One of the stranger health items that appeared in print occurred late in December 1889 when a reporter wrote of a woman by the name of Harriet H. Mills, who had once been prominent in a ladies' bicycle club. Mills was described as a singer who devoted much of her time to music. Reportedly, Mills declared, "the judicious use of a bicycle will not only help a woman's voice by the proper exercise of her muscles, but also materially improve a woman's health and disposition."[2]

Writing in the summer of 1892 a journalist remarked, "Five years ago the prophet who should have predicted the spectacle of thousands of 1892 ladies riding bicycles would have been mobbed by innumerable Mrs. Grundies. [Mrs. Grundy was a fictional English character who personified

PROPER POSITION.

This 1893 sketch illustrated the proper position a woman should assume on a bicycle for optimum health.

the censorship found in everyday life from conventional opinion; also, an extreme prig.] Even now the voice of bigotry is occasionally heard crying in the wilderness—lone voices, however, that count as nothing against the overwhelming testimony of the girl riders themselves, their fond mothers and watchful family physicians." Also noted was that just a short time earlier at a meeting of homeopathic physicians in Chicago, it was unanimously decided that bicycle riding was "one of the most wholesome and exhilarating forms of exercise that women can indulge in…. In some cases ailments and weaknesses peculiar to the sex had been permanently cured by reasonable and judicious bicycling." According to the journalist it was the easiest thing in the world for a woman to learn to ride the "ladies safety and all riding teachers agree that women learn quicker than men." Then the journalist lapsed into hyperbole when he wrote, "It is claimed that the bicycling girl is, all things considered, the most irresistible of any. Who can resist the witchery of a creature in form a fairy, in motion a cherub on the wing, whoever seems on the point of soaring away skyward, to be lost forever to mere human life."[3]

Critics of bicycle riding for women regularly made their voices heard, pointing out the harm the activity produced, with respect to health concerns. There was never any truth to the nonsense they spouted, but the threat posed by cycling for women, in their fight for emancipation (in the form of freedom and independence of movement) and in their fight for dress reform, caused much distress in the halls of the patriarchy. Attacks on cycling for women, which accused the activity of a destroying their health and morals, were all related to controlling women and keeping them in their place. In the summer of 1892 a young woman wrote to a St. Paul, Minnesota, newspaper to ask whether the paper thought bicycle riding by young women was safe. To that query the paper declared that "it depends. If one is athletic and quick in movement there is no particular occasion for alarm, but for one advanced in years or absent-minded when on the street, bicycle riding by young women is always dangerous and often fatal."[4]

Doctor T. Gaillard Thomas declared, in May 1893, "I have made a study for some time of this very question, and I say without hesitation that the effect upon women of judicious bicycle riding is beneficial rather than injurious. Women in the past have taken far too little exercise. The bicycle fills their requirements in this respect. I have never had a patient who was injured by riding, except by accidents, and I frequently recommend it to my patients." Dr. Emmett, described as a well-known specialist in women's diseases, said he had never seen a case of injury to a woman from bicycle riding and considered the activity to be very beneficial to women. The reporter doing the piece said he then tried to find doctors to give testimony to the other side of the issue but declared, of that quest, "It was not successful. Some physicians seen admitted that they had heard of specialists who did not approve of women and girls riding the bicycle, but none of them could give any names, and not a single one of these somewhat mythical personages could be found."[5]

On every fair night in August 1893, declared a reporter, there could be seen in Lincoln, Nebraska, numbers of men and women on bicycles whirling through the city's streets. "It is worth spending some time to watch the frog-like bend of the male riders, who look as if preparing to leap into a pond, and the oscillating feet and rebellious skirts of the women. There will come necessarily visions of spinal diseases and muscular contraction for males and of the ailments which overtake females and which often baffle the skill of the doctors." As well, the journalist noted that doctors had long given the advice that women "abstain from the too frequent and consequently unhealthy use of the feet at sewing machines, which frequently produce ill-health and often untimely death. Very [much] like the treadmill action necessary to operating a sewing machine is the movement of the feet by females on bicycles. Of course it is conceded that the bicycle is here to stay." He went on to fret that doctors would have enough to do in the future unless "women cease to use the single wheel with its stingy little pad altogether. The female form was not made to ride straddle." And, the newsman concluded, "men like to accompany females, but how many of the former would marry the heroine of a bicycular adventure? One look at the ungraceful attitude of the rider would cause most men to seek wives among women who still cling to the side saddle, the modest contrivance of their mothers and grandmothers. If Eros does not laugh he certainly must weep when he sees beauty on a single wheel."[6]

Reporter Isabella Proctor wrote, in August 1893, "There has been much discussion on the healthfulness and unhealthfulness of bicycling for women. Carried to excess it doubtless proves injurious, as does immoderate indulgence in any sort of bodily exercise." On the other hand, said Proctor, "many doctors recommend the moderate use of the bicycle to persons having delicate lungs, nervous dyspepsia, melancholia (which is often another name for it) or a rheumatic tendency. Fortunately women have not adopted the stooping style of riding, which is one of the main counts against bicycling in opposing physicians' eyes. As long as the woman rider sits upright, with her chest well out and her shoulders thrown back, so long will she be a strong argument in favor of the wheel." An hour's ride at sunset "will do wonders toward counteracting the mental and physical irritability consequent on a long day's sewing or writing and makes the probability of a quiet night's rest twice as good." Proctor added, "The habit of wearing tight clothing while riding cannot too strongly be reprehended.... Easy fitting garments and not too many of them should be the rule." She argued that the skirt should be narrow enough so that it would run no danger of blowing back sufficiently far to become entangled in the gearing, and it should be heavy enough not to spread and weave at every gust of wind. "As to color and style," she wrote, "a woman's own good taste and modesty will teach her that the less conspicuous she is the better she will appear while riding. Black, dark blue and dust colors all look well, and the blazer suit and shirt waist are suitable for summer wear." Bicycling was an easy accomplishment to acquire but, concluded Proctor, "considering the impedimental nature of a woman's dress, it is a bad plan for her to attempt to learn without a professional teacher."[7]

Physical culture for women in the 1890s was increasing with a variety of athletics being promoted. A large dry-goods merchant in Boston, in 1893, had arranged to give, at his own expense, one hour a day of physical culture for his employees, most of whom were women. At the Berkeley Ladies Athletic Club in New York City there were then more than 375 members. The medical director at that institution, Dr. Mary Bissell, favored wheeling for women and a large number of those who were members of the club were taking bike riding lessons. "There are hundreds and hundreds of female bicyclists to be seen on the smooth paved streets of New York."[8]

From the *British Medical Journal* in 1894 came the story of the death of a lady cyclist from syncope (fainting, sometimes due to a rapid fall in blood pressure) after a bicycle ride and it was, said the account, "of course the text for many fraternal warnings and advice to lady bicyclists to give up the enjoyment of an exercise in which it is feared they may indulge to excess. They are, of course, told by some that bicycling is unladylike, if not unwomanly, and that women do not know how to practice the careful restraint in such matters to which men are accustomed." But, the article went on to say, "so far from being unsuited for women, bicycling is an exercise in which they may indulge with perfect security and generally with much advantage. We are persuaded that they are as little prone to excess in athletics as are the generality of men, and within reasonable bounds we should like to see cycling as generally practiced by women as by men, and it would be greatly to the advantage of many cycling clubs and cycling resorts that the ladylike element should be more largely introduced."[9]

Dr. Douglas Hogg, of Paris, requested in the fall of 1894, in the columns of a medical journal, the opinions of medical men as to whether bicycling was unhealthy or injurious to women. It was reported that Hogg "has received forty-eight answers to his question from distinguished English, French, and other physicians. Of these, thirty-six approve of the exercise, if practiced in moderation, three recommended it under certain conditions, while nine are totally opposed to bicycling for women."[10]

Mrs. Mary Sargent Hopkins, at a meeting of the Professional Woman's League on December 21, 1894, gave a lecture to women who "sacrificed" their health and beauty through "unnecessary devotion to home or society." Hopkins was from Boston and was described as "an ardent advocate of bicycling for women." She said, "It is the greatest cure for insomnia ever known. As a soother of nerves unstrung it has no equal, and as a banisher of wrinkles and rejuvenator of age it is wonderfully efficacious."[11]

Dr. Mary T. Bissell wrote an article on the subject of the bicycle for women which appeared in newspapers in January 1895. She declared, "The mention of the bicycle for women opens a field of mild controversy which is only important because some of the objections to its use are taken from the hygienic standpoint as well as from the social. Many objectors contend that the wheel is as undesirable for women as the sewing machine, while the majority of patients seriously object to what they feel to be the unpleasant publicity of the exercise." Bissell said she had made inquiries among women who used the wheel regarding the effects of the exercise upon them and had failed to discover a single case of injury or poor health resulting from its use. On the contrary, she declared, the testimony to its exhilarating and healthful effect is universal and that several American physicians "have warmly commended its use."[12]

Said an unnamed girl to a reporter in May 1895, "I am having such a time over the bicycle question. Mother says it isn't proper and father insists that it is not a healthful sport for women; so what am I to do?" The reporter then sought out medical opinion on the subject. Dr. Osborn, a female physician, said, "Certainly I am in favor of the bicycle for women, especially those nervously inclined who are apt to dwell upon their petty trials to the detriment of their health and the discomfort of those around them. There are undoubtedly women riding, who, from certain conditions of the system, have no right upon a wheel, but to the average woman it brings health and strength." Osborn continued, "I favor the bloomer costume worn without a corset.... Women are apt to become too enthusiastic and go to excess in this, as well as horseback-riding; then either exercise is made injurious. Our women must have something to draw them into the open air and the bicycle supplies this need." Another female physician, Dr. Meade, declared, "The bicycle will never be a success until a new seat is brought into use, the present one being unphysiological. A saddle made to bring the pressure upon the muscles intended to bear the weight is what is needed. I have taken no interest in the question, so have no opinion as regards the costume, except that all of the muscles should have perfect freedom." Dr. Carrie Gross asserted, "I think the most modest costume to be worn upon the wheel is a short skirt and bloomers. I favor the exercise and consider it decidedly beneficial.... I do not favor a woman becoming masculine in taking up these sports. She can enjoy them and still retain the feminine modesty, which is her chief charm." Added Gross, "So many who object to the exercise contend that there is no difference between running a sewing machine and riding a wheel. In the former only the muscles below the abdomen are brought into use, while in the latter every muscle in the body is exercised. Surely there can be no comparison." All those opinions caused the female journalist to think it all over and one of her conclusions was that "the wheel is as proper for women as for men. A woman on a bicycle in street costume looks almost as well as one would on horseback in evening dress." She continued, "We have simply reached that point of our existence where we are going to be sensible enough to dress for the occasion. We surely would not appear at an afternoon tea in bloomers or attend the Governor's reception in a dainty morning gown. Then why ride a wheel in [a] walking gown? Until we enlarge our ideas beyond the limit of 'They say' we shall simply be miserable failures as anything but pretty, useless dolls who die when the sawdust [society] escapes us." One evening that journalist was out walking in her hometown of San Jose, California, when some of the members of the ladies' cycling club appeared on the scene, and she noted, "I counted ten of them, with two [male] bodyguards."[13]

Writing in May 1895 a journalist asserted, "For some time before cycling became a distinctive fad among women, public opinion was almost evenly divided as to the physical benefits and dangers accruing from it. To-day it is hard to find a man, woman or child who will admit that there is a possibility of the slightest danger to the health of a rider, male or female."[14]

One month later a female physician in New York City was asked if she thought the bicycle craze would last. She replied, "Indeed, I think the women will stick to their wheels even if the men should tire of them, because the bicycle has introduced a means of rational outdoor exercise for women which they felt the need of and the men did not. Men, from the nature of the active life they lead, do not find the novel delight in an outing that a woman does."[15]

A lengthy piece that appeared in newspapers in August 1895 featured "scientific people" giving some practical reasons in favor of the moderate use of the wheel. The article began by declaring, "For while it is true that it is injurious for all women sometimes and for some women all the time to ride the wheel, just as it is bad for all men all the time unless used in moderation, still there are excellent reasons why all women who can without injury use the wheel as a means of exercise should do so, and these reasons give hope new life for a great reform." An unnamed Boston physician pointed out why mature women who can use it, should use it, namely, that all women need more of outdoor exercise. "Nearly all women suffer from lack of open air movement, and from the restraints of clothing, notably the corset which, however much men may inveigh against it, seems to have foreclosed a mortgage of possession upon our women." The wheel got the women into the open air a great deal and "it induces her to relax the martyrdom of tight and confining clothing." The doctor also argued that biking increased the woman's physical exercise without increasing her fatigue. "Almost any woman in fair health can ride six miles on a wheel with less fatigue than she can walk one mile, and if she walks in modern costume with corsets and tight clothing and impeding skirts the burden of opinion seems to justify the judgment that the bicycle will do her less harm than the walk, even if she is not physically sound."[16]

Those words from the Boston physician could be accepted, claimed the reporter, "without rejecting the warning that no woman should take to the bicycle who has any doubts of, or reason to doubt its beneficial character in her use of it. Nor should young girls use it, those who are as yet unformed and not fully developed, except with such extreme moderation as to deprive it of any pleasure or benefit. As a rule, it may be stated that the burden of wise opinion and of professional advice is against the use of the bicycle by girls at all." Going on, the reporter declared, "The wheel, then, is doing two important things for the physical well-being of woman; and these lead to two other things equally as important, namely, they awaken women to the truth that there is no absolute need to be the slave of the corset and tight clothing, and that there is such a thing as being free and independent and still lovely and graceful. This then may lead, and let us hope that it will, to the emancipation of American women from a slavery that their husbands and brothers have inveighed against steadily but hopelessly. Even if some women 'did not and should not' take to the wheel for exercise, its influence is going to be felt among all women and actually bring about a reform, an emancipation, that will mean good health for American women where poor health is the rule." In conclusion, the newsman wrote, "It may be that the wheel is to some the greatest boon to our womankind that we could possibly devise for them, since it may free them from slavery and teach them the possibilities of health, long life and happiness, that reside in physical well-being."[17]

Dr. Langdon Carter Gray, a neurologist in New York City, was interviewed in the fall of 1895 on the subject of cycling and health, to which he said, "Bicycling is at present a mental epidemic and everybody, old, young, and middle-aged, is riding, without regard to physical effects.... Notwithstanding the fact that women have taken up this sport indiscriminately, it has been of wonderful benefit to them, for it has carried millions out into the fresh air and kept them out of our abominable public conveyances that the great distances in New York necessitate." Gray continued by saying, "Women are naturally better riders than men. This is because they are lighter and sit much more erectly and they do not attempt to race or scorch as a rule." He did mention overexertion as a possible bad effect that could strike women but concluded, "I am inclined to think that the benefit is greater than the bad effects, and consider it a most healthful exercise for women if they will assume a proper position and ride along easily, covering not more than six miles an hour and not bending themselves over the handle bars like a jackknife and go scorching along like would-be sports and young boys anxious to make or break records." Dr. A.M. Phelps, an orthopedist, believed in wheeling and was an ardent cyclist himself. But he did not believe in the indiscriminate use of the wheel by women. "Some women and girls should be most emphatically prohibited from riding the bicycle immoderately, if at all," Phelps explained. "For men and healthy women I consider it one of the most healthful exercises in the world, because it brings into action every muscle of the body. I doubt whether young girls at the age of puberty, particularly those of extremely rapid growth, should use the wheel at all, and if so they should exercise in great moderation. It is at this age that we see various curvatures of the spine, and the position assumed while riding would be likely to produce such troubles, and also steeped shoulders and contracted chests, which interfere with respiration if the exercise is carried to extremes."

The reporter producing the article spoke to a couple more doctors, unnamed, and said that they had nothing but praise for women and cycling. Concluded the journalist, "The doctors quoted coincided on four points. They are all violently opposed to women making long runs, to their covering more than six or seven miles an hour, and to their assuming other than an erect position on the wheel." And, added the newsman, "experience has taught the enthusiasts that the medical fraternity is right on these points, for the majority of them now declare that after riding twenty miles wheeling becomes work."[18]

Writing in the first month of 1896 a reporter stated, "Probably no other single question regarding the welfare of American women has been so thoroughly discussed in public for the past two years as the question [of] whether the bicycle was a proper vehicle for feminine use," and "physicians, clergymen, social 'reformers,' and all sorts and conditions of women themselves, from the advanced female suffragist to the frivolous favorites of the variety stage, have given their views pro and con on the subject, until the debate has threatened to become a perennial feature in newspapers and magazines." One of the latest to give his opinion was Dr. Henry J. Garrigues, a consulting surgeon in the New York Maternity Hospital. He stated, "The arguments of the pessimists who declare that wheeling itself is dangerous to womanly health are entirely fallacious. Moderate and judicious indulgence in this form of exercise he declares to be not only harmless but highly beneficial to women in general." According to Garrigues, when pursued intelligently and prudently, cycling "has a distinct curative effort upon the nervous affections which are responsible for so much headache, insomnia and neuralgia among the feminine sex."[19]

In July 1896 a reporter wondered if the medical doctors all agreed on the subject of women and cycling. The answer he gave himself was "Well, hardly! They scatter in their views regarding the wheel's effects on the health of the people almost as much as the ministers do regarding its influence on the morals of the public." Then he cited an example from New York City, of Dr. Forbes Winslow, that "famous" London, England specialist—then attending a medical conference in New York City—"has expressed himself as uncompromisingly opposed to bicycling by women." Winslow said, "No woman should ever be allowed to exercise in that manner. It is dangerous to health and is injurious to morals." He added, "I am fearful for the next generation if this bicycle craze keeps on, for it is then that the full effects of the evil will be absolutely demonstrated to the public. Abnormal conditions must be expected to exist when the causes for their development are so universally used. The exercise is too violent for the physical construction of women." Dr. Championiere, a distinguished French physician, did not agree with Winslow. After a four-year study Championiere concluded, "The bicycle is of direct benefit to women in increasing muscular strength, lung capacity, healthy action of the heart, and that its effect on the mind is most excellent. Women riders are less nervous and more confident, walk with [a] more certain step and are altogether improved." Said the reporter, "Dr. Winslow's attack suggests an animus that comes not from a scientific study of the bicycle, but from a conservatism as to what is called women's real place. This, he says sharply, is in the nursery." The journalist added, "Women who ride the bicycle are, other things being equal, far better fitted for the duties of the nursery than those who have kept themselves there to satisfy the contentions of the men who believe a woman's sphere should be as narrow as the man's sphere is broad."[20]

Dr. Forbes Winslow in 1898. With regard to women riding bikes he said, "It is dangerous to health and is injurious to morals."

At the beginning of 1897 a journalist started his piece of the subject of cycling and health by asserting, "The bicycle girl has been forced to confess that the wheel is an injury to her. This has been brought about by the winter dancing season, and the way it happened is that the young woman who, during the summer and fall, has indulged in a daily spin, finds that the dance to her is no longer what it was and that instead of having grace in every motion, she finds it very difficult to develop even the proper motion." According to this account it had long been a matter of discussion whether or not the muscles and all that made up the legs of a bicycle girl were permanently affected by the exercise on the wheel, and "the young woman who has plighted her affections to the bike in the season when it was particularly in evidence, suddenly discovers that while in her mind she is thoroughly familiar with just what she ought to do [on the dance floor], she is absolutely incapable of performing proper action. The muscles of her limbs seem to have lost their cunning ... and her partner wonders what on earth is the matter with the young woman who the year before danced as if she were a sylph." This supposed problem was said to have been particularly apparent in the waltz and "the bicycle girl finds it absolutely impossible to execute the steady glide.... The polka, the schottische, and the quadrille are almost as difficult." And, it was also reported, "careful inquiry among the

WOE FOR THE BICYCLE GIRL

Her Long Rides Unfit Her For the Ballroom—Her Limbs Seem Like Wood—Can No Longer Take the Dainty Steps.

An 1897 headline giving a dire warning about how the bicycle rider would, to her horror, find she could no longer dance. Curiously, the dancing ability of bike riding men was not impaired.

young women who ride the bicycle shows it to be an actual fact that exercise on the wheel seems to deaden and stiffen the set of muscles that come into play in dancing."[21]

With respect to the "dancing problem," doctors, the reader was led to believe, could not explain the issue. "So general has been the practice of riding wheels by young women the past season that this curious affectation of the dancing muscles is a matter of almost national interest," claimed the journalist. "Go into any ballroom, where the young women of ordinary society are to be found, and watch the movements of the dancers. There will at once be apparent that lack of grace and lithesomeness that is usually characteristic of the American girl. There is a dragging movement about the feet as if a tendon was out of order, or something of that nature." Apparently the best way to observe and appreciate the differences of the wheel upon the dancer was to observe the dancing of the girl who bikes and the girl who does not. That was said to tell the story: "The one moves through the waltz as if she rather floated than made her way about on a plebeian floor. The other traverses the waxed floor as if it was considerable of an effort, and that she would be very glad when it was all over." The bicycle contingent was wondering if this problem was a new form of bicycle leg. "The bicycle leg has had so many different diagnoses that it is difficult to say just what the term really means," the journalist stated. "So it is safe to say that the newly discovered affection that has laid hold upon the young women votaries of the wheel can be more properly termed the non-dancing leg." This lengthy article did not once mention the obvious question, that is, what about men and dancing? Then the account answered that question in just two sentences: "The queerest part of it all is that the dancing powers of men are not injured. It is one of those ills to which women alone are heir."[22]

The dancing problem was continued in the press a couple of months

Sorrows of the Bicycle Girl in the Ballroom.

An 1897 sketch connecting the dots of the dreaded loss of dancing ability. Bike riding led to muscular legs which led to awkward and clumsy movement on the dance floor.

later when a reporter noted, "More than one girl who last summer devoted great attention to wheeling has made the disagreeable discovery that her indulgence in bicycle exercise must be curbed if she would retain the graceful ease of motion necessary to a good dancer. Society girls not a few have been puzzled to find that the graceful movements of former seasons were almost if not quite impossible during the winder just closed." One unnamed doctor was said to have told a suffering woman, "You will remember that I warned you against overindulgence in wheeling. I am afraid you did not heed the warning. You see, big muscular development does not accompany grace." He added, "It is also probably that many women, who have become infatuated with the wheel, indulge in the sport to excess, neglecting dancing altogether."

According to this account, "The young women who dance at the theaters ruefully admit that their affection for the wheel has caused them no end of trouble." In this article no mention was made about men.[23]

A positive article about the effect of cycling on health appeared in May 1897. At the last quarterly meeting of the American Statistical Association, Dr. S.W. Abbott, secretary of the Massachusetts Board of Health, presented some figures regarding the proportion of pulmonary tuberculosis in females to that of males in Massachusetts. The rate in 1851 was 1,451 females to 1,000 males; in 1890, 1,055 females to 1,000 males; and in 1896 only 874 females to 1,000 males. That year (1896) was the first year in which the number of deaths from tuberculosis in females was smaller than that in males. According to the article, "The fact that a uniform reduction in the rate of female deaths began some five years ago, about the time when women were beginning to ride the bicycle extensively. Dr. Abbott considers it significant, and he is inclined to attribute the decrease in the death rate to the great increase in open air exercise among women which has been inaugurated by the use of the bicycle."[24]

If the idea of the dancing problem was odd (and it was), something weirder was on the way. A report came from Paris in June 1897 that stated, "The doctors of France are puzzled by a new mania which is afflicting women who ride bicycles. The feminine bicyclists are becoming extremely cruel. Medical men who have made a study of the matter are inclined to ascribe it to a form of insanity, the cause of which is to them an absolute mystery. There are in Paris a number of physicians who call themselves bicycle specialists, meaning that they have made an especial study of nervous and other troubles resulting from the use of the wheel. These men are completely mystified." The first such case that came to general notice was that of Mme Eugenie Chantilly, wife of Desire Chantilly, a well-known silk manufacturer of Lyons. Once when she was on her bicycle "the strange affliction came upon her." She was in Paris and riding with her friend Mme Henry Fournier. During that ride Fournier sped up and began to pull away from Chantilly. Fournier looked back over her shoulder and laughingly said, "Adieu, mon amie." Then she looked back to see her friend Chantilly speed up and deliberately run into her. Chantilly collided with Fournier and knocked her down. Then Chantilly rode back speedily and "actually rode over the prostate form of Fournier. She attempted to arise but was repeatedly knocked down again by her friend and it was not until others came to her rescue that the assaults ended. She was removed by her husband to Lyons where she has remained in seclusion." Reportedly, Fournier received a broken right arm (between the wrist and the elbow) and several internal injuries. The two doctors involved in the incident, one for each woman, considered the case and "determined that they had discovered a brand new disease which was due solely to the bicycle. This determination was arrived at from the fact that the symptoms and the mania were entirely different, even in the smallest detail, from all that pertains to cases of insanity among women resulting from conditions known to medical men."[25]

This drawing from 1897 illustrated another illness inflicted on bike riding females. It made them cruel and ready to run over other women cyclists. Curiously, here also, the sanity of bike riding men was not impaired in the slightest.

Those doctors, it was said, looked around to see if there were any similar cases and "they found seventeen women who had been seized with the same irrepressible desire to injure all cyclists of their own sex whenever possible, at such times as they were awheel. The desire apparently took the same form in every instance, the first action being a violent collision, and then repeated attempts to ride over the form of the fallen cyclist." The doctors also found that not only did the desire to ride down other wheelwomen appear "but there was plenty of additional evidence that the mania inspired a keen delight in all things savoring of cruelty. In some of the instances, women indicated this fact by torturing their pet dogs or cats in the most frightful fashion, although previous to the time the mania afflicted them, they had been kindness itself to the animals." That it was cycling that brought the mania on "there seems to be no question. Only wheelwomen have been afflicted with it, and oddly enough, in every instance, they have been over 30 years of age." The other theory advanced as to the cause which has been seriously considered was that it was "the result of the effect upon the nervous system of the intense exhilaration rapid riding brings about. French wheelwomen ride at a high pace. They are all embryo scorchers [fast riders], much more so than their sisters in other countries. This being the case, it is suggested that the practice of scorching by women is likely to bring about a new form of insanity corresponding to that which afflicts the unfortunate French women." In conclusion, said the article, "It is, therefore, thought probable that if women are not forced to ride at a slower pace on their wheels, this remarkable mania will make its appearance in the wheeling countries other than France. The worst feature of it all is that there has thus far been found no method which would result in curing a patient or even rendering the mania less violent." In this lengthy piece no mention was made of male cyclists. Their sanity was apparently unimpaired by cycling, as was their dancing ability.[26]

In July 1897 Dr. Lewis A. Sayre of New York City declared, "Women do well to ride the wheel. It means a stronger healthier race of men and women for the coming generation. Women were going into decline. Their nervous force was wearing out. That means a great deal, for the decay of a nation begins always with the breaking up of the nervous system of its women." With respect to bicycle riding Sayre added, "It is giving women healthy diversion, teaching them self-control and self-reliance, and making them fit physically to be the mothers of a race of giants." And, he added, "I know that some of the woman reformers have objected to wheels, and with justice, too; but now that saddles adapted for women are a specialty with saddle makers, the chief grounds for objection are removed.... Saddles for men and saddles for women should be different. The ordinary saddle, modeled for men, is not at all suitable for women. It is more likely to do them serious physical harm, but with a properly formed saddle there is no danger whatever." Sayre continued by saying, "They leave off their corsets when they ride, though they will not do so at any other time. Perhaps the bicycle will kill corsets. That would be a grand victory for the wheel.... No amount of preaching about dress reform has the influence of the bicycle. Theory is good and logic is good, but putting a woman on a wheel and letting her go out on our smooth roads, where she has a freedom she has not thought of before, is an argument that is effective. It wins her to freedom." Dr. Sayre argued that the cycle taught self-reliance, something that a great many women needed. "A woman guiding herself along the streets learns that she is able to take care of herself, even if there is not a man at her elbow. She is surprised, probably, to find this out, but if she keeps at wheeling she will learn that she is every bit as strong as a man physically as well as mentally. She can develop physical power quite equal to man's, and she can use it to a continuous advantage. The bicycle will prove this to her satisfaction and to the benefit of her race." Sayre claimed to have spent much of his leisure time in the last few years studying and observing women on bicycles and studying the effects of the exercise upon riders.[27]

Dr. Lewis Albert Sayre, no date. He was one of many medical men who advocated for women and bicycles, although he argued the saddles for men and women should be different.

The question of the effect of cycling on the voice, discussed back in 1889, returned when another account was published in August 1897. In a recap of a story that initially appeared in a Chicago newspaper it was pointed out that the results from the article might provide food for thought for Chicago "in the fact that more care should be exercised in talking while riding through the streets." Reportedly the "low-voiced" (that is, quiet) woman was a thing of the past and "no result of the bicycle craze is more conspicuous than that the woman who speaks in quiet, modulated tones had departed, perhaps forever. On the streets, in the yards—everywhere—one hears the shrill, strident tones of the bicycle girl, heard distinctly over the rattle of buggies and the rumble of the trucks, ear-piercing at times, always disquieting to those of a nervous temperament." Even though the person to whom the woman was speaking could be walking or sitting by her side "the bicycle girl addresses her as if she was on the opposite side of the street, and the public at large is kept fully advised of all the gossip of her set." On the boulevards, in the quiet of the evenings, when sound traveled great distances, "the conversation of a couple of bicycle girls as they spin over the smooth roadway can be heard by residents a square distant." Few wheelmen seem to realize the fact that it was unnecessary to raise the voice when speaking to a companion a few feet away "yet all women fall into the habit." Loud talking on the streets, asserted the newsman, "used to be regarded as a token of vulgarity. Today it is a characteristic of wheelwomen. It is unnecessary, as it is grating to the refined sensibilities of people generally." If the female bike riders of Chicago would, he declared, "speak to their companions awheel with the same distinctness they observe in their home parlors and avoid the shrieking they indulge in upon the boulevards—they would make themselves far more attractive to the average man and disarm much of the criticism of wheeling now so prevalent." As had happened in many of the foregoing articles, there was no mention in this piece about male wheelmen and their voices.[28]

In New York City during October 1897 Mrs. Etta Hudders, a lecturer on health and science, had something to say in the way of suggestions to women who rode bicycles. She said the main trouble with them was that they were too automatic when they rode and did not let their bodies sway with the wheel, and consequently they "do not get the exercise they should have in riding, do not exercise enough muscles, do strain themselves—reserve too much exercise of a wrong kind in holding back." She also asserted that women should not indulge in very long bicycle rides "and that women who are given to long rides are almost invariably frail and unhealthy." Hudders argued the best wheeling costume "is a pretty divided skirt, kilt plaited, a wide box plait covering the opening in the front, and a little Eton jacket, low shoes and woolen golf stockings, with thin lisle thread underneath." According to the newspaper, "Mrs. Hudders is an authority on health as it relates to women, and what she had to say here is worthy of consideration."[29]

In the spring of 1898 a newspaper editor remarked that with the return of the cycling season, when century (100 miles) runs by organized clubs were of daily occurrence, the question of women taking part in those long-distance rides was again discussed. It was maintained that such runs had become athletic competitions such as required the utmost physical endurance on the part of the riders "and that constitutionally a woman is not sufficiently strong for such a fatiguing test." According to this editor, "Distinguished medical authorities pronounce the task of covering so great a distance as a hundred miles in a day awheel exceedingly harmful, on account of the prolonged nervous and physical strain involved, for which women rarely possess the requisite physique, and for other reasons that physicians only can properly appreciate."

Even some of the century riders fail to complete the 100 miles sometimes, it was noted, and, "this being true of men, it is by so much the more evident that women should refrain from the practice." He went on to add, "Aside from the injurious physical results that attend century riding by women, the questions present another view even more important, that of the propriety of women engaging in such runs. The example of women attending the ordinary open century run in which the proportion of the participants is rarely less than fifty men to one woman, who rides generally without escort from early morning to late night, in the common ruck, is not calculated to elevate cycling particularly among women. Rather it has a tendency to degrade the sport." As far as this newsman was concerned, "the necessary or usual incidents attending century runs are not conducive to the cultivation of feminine graces and should receive the stamp of disapproval of the cycling public." Concluding his editorial he wrote, "Resolutions condemning the practice are being considered by bicycle organizations. If women lack the good sense and good taste to determine this matter for themselves, the men should determine if for them."[30]

6

1890s—Morality and Propriety

Issues of morality, propriety, and the ethics of women on cycles reached a peak in the 1890s. Initially when few women were to be found on bicycles, as during the velocipede craze of 1868–1870, there was little criticism of those female bikers because there were so few and far between that they could easily be dismissed as odd characters or individual aberrations. Criticism only arrived pervasively after the number of female cyclists grew to some trigger amount. At that point criticism peaked as the patriarchy trembled when its command and control system seemed to be on shaky ground. Later, the number of participants in the activity reached even a higher penetration in the populace and then the criticism faded away as the activity came to be accepted as normal. At that point the patriarchy had accommodated the new fad, or came to no longer see it as a threat.

A young woman wrote to journalist Shirley Dark in September 1890 because she wanted to know if it would be proper for her to ride a bicycle or tricycle alone in Central Park, as she was fond of the exercise but had no one to go with her, i.e., she did not have a male escort. "It is morally certain that most city circles who want to be nice would promptly declare it improper for a young lady to ride anything in the park unattended," replied Dark. "But I am not sure that Mr. Ward McAllister [a famous but self-appointed arbiter of social conventions in New York City at this time], surveying the situation of needed outdoor exercise of the impossibility, in certain wide circles outside his own, of always commanding the escort of a father, a brother, or a groom as escort, and calling on the clear, common sense which makes his decisions, would not tell her to put on a plain gown, go out in the forenoon or early afternoon before the park is filled with riders, and behave like a good girl, attending strictly to her own business. There must be care to preserve these outdoor liberties for women, which mean so much to their health and spirits."

Dark continued by writing, "We can't afford to have our nice middle-class girls hampered by the hallucinations of the upper circle concerning the indispensability of chaperons and escorts if a girl goes out in plain daylight. If we do, the middle-class girls may turn out as badly as some of the upper ones." They might cling to their proprieties—they seemed to need them—for chaperons, escorts, grooms and footmen "don't seem to keep them from coming to grief often. But cycling is so fascinating and needed a sport worth all the gymnastics and gymnasia in the country for development of health and activity, that the good sense of the community or the better part of it should protect women in that and all other needful and gracious liberty." Dark then counseled that one needed to use freedom without abusing it, stating, "You want to dress quietly, not to draw attention, and I do not think the blue striped flannel skirt with cream Zouave jacket covered with gilt buttons depicted by a woman rider in a cycling paper at all ladylike or quiet. It could be seen a mile ahead and would of itself say to any man rider 'follow me.' No wonder the lady rider complained of men racing her wheel in Fairmount Park." Reinforcing her ideas of propriety in female cycling costumes Dark stated, "A cycling habit should be severely plain as a riding habit: all one grave color and not a thread of white trimming or a gilt button about it, and for good taste no jockey cap with its slangy suggestions, but an English gipsy hat, small but shading the face well. In a quiet dress—no nonsense of divided skirt—keeping herself to herself, attending strictly to her own business, a girl is safer on a bicycle than on foot in the park, provided she knows how to ride well."[1]

One month later a question of propriety was submitted to a newspaper. In reply to Mamie E. Hodgkins's question as to the propriety of girls riding safety bicycles the reply was "I for one consider it decidedly proper for them to do so."[2]

The Rev. Alfred Cleveland Coxe, the Episcopal bishop of western New York, had, in June 1891, "discovered a new evil in the world. It is the bicycle-riding habit among young women." In an address to a graduating class of an institution for the education of young women that month, the bishop raised a warning voice against the bicycle. In his address he said he hoped "never to see any of those to whom he spoke astride of this new invention of the enemy." A reporter commented that despite the fact that Washington had more lady bicyclists than any other American city "none of our watchful clergymen nor other guardians of public morals seem to have discovered that the moral tone of the fair riders has become deteriorated because of their indulgence in the joys of the flying wheel." Added the journalist, "There are male natures, it is to be feared, who cannot view an impromptu and informal revelation of wildly disarranged skirts and inverted ankles with that composure which moral and rational beings should ever strive to maintain." Continuing to mock Coxe the newsman declared, "There are in this wicked world eyes that will leer with an unholy light at the sight of snowy underlinen suddenly exposed when an unskillful wheelwoman meets disaster. There are hypocritical and unsympathetic male wretches who, even while they extricate torn skirts from the maws of perverse cogs and aid the distressed fair one to remount, will smile and still be villains." Concluding his analysis the reporter said, "No, Bishop Coxe's objections to female bicycle riding must arise from purely local causes. If he will come to Washington for a while and watch our lady riders as they glide along in grace and beauty, perfect symphonic poems on wheels, he will give them his blessing, and tell the girls of his flock to go and do likewise."[3]

The Reverend Arthur Cleveland Coxe (no date) railed against the female cyclist and described such women as looking like witches on broomsticks.

What Coxe had specifically said, according to another account was that "women on bicycles look like witches on broomsticks." A man in New York City promptly sent a remonstrance to the bishop, in which he mentioned several New York women who had received physical benefit from wheeling. Coxe replied in a letter to that New York man, writing, "It is impossible for me to object to your remonstrance based upon the therapeutic merits of the bicycle. But I am surprised and assured at the comments of the press on some incidental remarks which fell from my lips while addressing a school for girls which is under my care and to which I was commending modesty as indispensable to character in women." Coxe added, "I am still of the opinion that bicycling is grossly immodest as well as ridiculous for women; the exceptional use of it for health does not come under my censure, save only when the crowded thoroughfares of a city are chosen for such exercise."[4]

In another account of Coxe's remarks it was stated that he had turned his erudition and ridicule upon the female bicycle rider. He warned the young women he addressed that they must never indulge in that growing method of transit and recreation. His "climax of depreciation was reached when he likened the young woman on the bicycle to an old woman on a broomstick." The reporter stated, "If it is true that it is unbecoming and not pleasing in masculine eyes for young women to ride the bicycle, the spirit of perversity sometimes alleged of the sex would not have exercise in this way." He went on to say, "But the bishop has perhaps been unfortunate in seeing some ride who were wanting in grace and expertness, or some clumsy or mischievous girl may have run a wheel over his corns. But he displays bad taste or ignorance. On the avenues and some of the streets of this city young women may be seen riding the two-wheeled vehicle almost any evening. They glide along as rapidly and easily as the young men, and there is no suggestion of indelicacy or indecorum." Those who think that legs should be the property of male riders alone "may have their dainty spirits annoyed. But ladies who can ride well should no more hesitate to ride the bicycle in public than to walk, ride horseback or dance." This journalist also mocked Coxe vigorously by saying, "Some cadaverous-visaged old reminiscence of another age is always standing around with up-turned nose, talking about things being indecorous or women being out of their sphere in entering on the new ways the broadening age opens to them. Such people shrug their shoulders and amble away when a woman appears in a role not known to the grandmothers." Concluding his piece the newsman asserted, "A woman may do any reputable thing or fill any position that she has the capacity and aptness for. Whatever she can do well, as a rule, is decorous and becoming for her."[5]

A column that was titled "The Home Corner" appeared in a Texas newspaper in December 1891, which declared, "But if the Home Corner is a little old fashioned in its ideas about the rearing of girls it is in favor of some of the innovations, and one of them is the bicycle girl." The column went on to speak in general about the moral outrage against the cycling woman by noting, "But what storms of opposition assail the bicycle riding girl. People openly tell her that she is coarse, forward, masculine, anything and everything that is objectionable. They hold up their hands in holy horror when they see her, mounted on her safety, go speeding down the street.... There are even mothers who forbid the bicycle on the ground that it is 'tomboyish.'" In conclusion the columnist stated, "The country has [an] urgent need of more tomboys and fewer little women, trained in hypocrisy, rosebuds with a worm at the heart. Wherefore the Home Corner believes that every girl in the land should have a bicycle."[6]

The question of decorum was raised by a columnist in a Utah newspaper in June 1892. He found that in some cities the lady riders then numbered many thousands. Manufacturers of bicycles were giving more attention to ladies' wheels than to any others and it was said they were predicting that in time there would be more female than male riders of the wheel. Those manufacturers declared that women had more time to ride and could do so at any time of the day. According to the columnist he had heard a lady remark that she would like to ride a bicycle but "they make one look so conspicuous." Replied the columnist, "Does not a woman look more graceful and more at home on a drop frame cycle than sitting sidewise on the back of a horse." And, he added, "Many ladies think there will be necessary a special costume for wheeling. This is not so. The true lady will be careful to wear only the most quiet and 'every day' clothes." In conclusion he asserted, "Wheels made for men exclusively are mounted from behind. A ladies wheel is mounted from the side, and ever so much more graceful than the other."[7]

A young woman wrote to a St. Paul, Minnesota, paper in August 1892 inquiring whether, in the newspaper's opinion, it was proper for one of her sex to ride a bicycle. That periodical replied by saying that it saw "no impropriety in the exercise" but offered no other comments.[8]

An account that appeared in January 1893 in San Francisco started by observing that nothing in the form of open-air exercise for women could compare with riding on a safety bicycle. "A few years ago, when it was discerned that several San Francisco ladies had taken to wheeling through Golden Gate Park for health and pleasure combined, that garrulous old dame Madame Grundy threw up her hands in horror and sent post haste for her smelling salts. Then the old lady betook herself to bed and worked herself into a hysterical ecstasy over the shocking impropriety of such a departure." At that time the ordinary or high-wheeler was in vogue and the popular type of safety was just beginning to become known in the East. "As no one had ever seen aught but a tinseled dame of the circus arena make use of a wheel the term 'ladies' bicycle carried with it visions of fair maids and matrons perched high in the air. And Mrs. Grundy groaned." And, it was added, "to think of a woman astride—actually astride—of one of those horrid things! It's too awful for anything. It was a state of affairs which the good old chaperon could not contemplate, and it was little wonder that she was shocked beyond expression." And the public, "the dear, patient public, was content to allow the innovations a fair trial on its merits, and refused to enter into the discussion between Mrs. Grundy and the bicycle enthusiasts." But, said the reporter, "gradually the true form and merits of the lady's wheel became known. It was discerned at once that women could mount and ride with as much ease and facility as they could step in and out of a carriage. The stranger was given a cordial welcome and was invited to stay."[9]

It was reported in August 1893 that Ward McAllister, a self-appointed social arbiter of mores, values, and so forth, had permitted the young women of America to ride tricycles because the Princess of Wales and her daughters rode tricycles but, said Ward, "it is highly improper for young women to use bicycles." A journalist responded, "But if some of our modest, merry, pretty American women who, with the full approval of their parents, husbands or grandmothers, and without a thought of impropriety, flit gracefully through our city parks every day upon bicycles, occasionally taking a long and health bringing tour in the same manner, get hold of Ward McAllister we wouldn't take even chances on him," and "they would tell him, these independent American girls, that immodesty exists in his own toadyish little mind and nowhere else."[10]

Howard Fielding was a satirist who produced an article spoofing societal attitudes toward female cyclists, in September 1893. The subheads of his article included "Effect of the habit on her mental and moral nature," "Her heart soon hardened," and "She will run over pedestrians without remorse." He told a fictional story about a man walking along the street who was knocked over by a female cyclist. That woman was cycling alone and she needed to have her wheel straightened after the accident but she could not do it herself and had to wait for a male biker to appear. When one came along he promptly fixed it. Then Fielding told of two women cyclists approaching him, riding side by side, and he "could not tell whether these were men or women. But the second showed me that one of them was looking at her feet and the other at the constellation of the Great Bear in the heavens behind her. Then I knew that they were women, and I began to hear harps." Fielding continued, "A man will ride recklessly, perhaps, but he'll break his neck to avoid a collision when it comes to the scratch. But a woman moves on like the car of juggernaut." When he asked himself how one could tell a man from a woman cyclist he replied, "If it runs into anybody it's a woman, if it doesn't it's a man.... When you're crossing a street and see something like this bearing down towards you, just say to yourself 'If I live, it's a man, if I die, it's a woman.'" With respect to another woman who was forced to confess to herself that bicycling was unbecoming to her, he wrote, "She cannot get a bicycle costume that does not make her look a 'perfect fright.' Therefore she has been obliged to abandon the exercise" but was jealous of those willowy and athletic women who looked so well on bicycles. In conclusion Fielding wrote, "Those women who think they look so well in their ridiculous bicycle dresses that they can't imagine there is anybody in the world who isn't looking at them. And if there is any such man, they think he deserves to be run over for his lack of appreciation."[11]

According to an October 1894 article, for weeks the columns of a New York City newspaper had teemed with letters from the public about the propriety, impropriety, sanity, insanity, healthfulness and unhealthfulness of bicycling for women. A journalist selected six prominent women and sought their opinion on the subject. The women chosen were Lady Henry Somerset, Miss Frances Willard, Miss Jeanette Gilder, Mrs. John Sherwood, Dr. Grace Peckham, and Katie Field. The latter was the journalist who wrote the piece. Those six returned a unanimous verdict that bicycling by women was not

THE WHEEL WAS NOT HURT.

THE QUESTION OF SEX.

These 1893 sketches spoofed the idea of women riding bicycles. They brought out the usual stereotypes including the one about women being bad drivers, compared to men, before the automobile had arrived.

THE ROUT OF MASCULINITY.

immodest. Willard advocated biking because it helped women to enjoy more outdoor exercise and added, "As to costume, Miss Willard thinks that a simply made street dress, falling to the ankles, meets all requirements." Somerset found it difficult to conceive what arguments could be raised against women's mastery of the bicycle. Gilder stated, "Immodesty lies in intent." Of the many women she had seen mounted on bicycles in America and Europe "she has never met one whose manner or dress seemed to her bold or unladylike." Sherwood was a convert to the new exercise but admitted she was old-fashioned enough "to dread the innovation, because she thinks it dangerous and the dress 'certainly not pretty' but thought cycling was worth a trial." Dr. Murry said that if cycling was healthy for women, it was right. If it wasn't "it was absolutely wrong, modest or immodest. She hails the bicycle as the greatest boon to the many working women who cannot afford the luxury of a horse."[12]

Katie Field declared, "Here is a most important point. There can be no equality of the sexes so long as the men are independent in dress of weather and women are enslaved by skirts the moment rain or snow sets in. Where is sexual equality when man had a dozen pockets and woman struggles with none or one so strangely situated as to require a surgical operation to get into it and then only by standing up?" Field added, "Blessed then be the bicycle, if in its evolution in female dress.... The moment women decide as a sex to be physically strong, that moment fashion will discover a costume combining beauty with perfect physical freedom." With respect to the morality of the activity Field asserted, "To call cycling immodest would be to insult some of the best women in Washington, where the wheel is a universal substitute for the horse. Such a question can only extort laughter in the District of Columbia, the paradise of bicycles." In conclusion, said Field, "women have, as a rule, too much regard for their personal appearance to make hideous spectacles of themselves, and now that pretty girls in Washington and Newport have not only mounted bicycles but have arranged themselves in short skirts and knickerbockers, I almost believe in the dawn of the millennium."[13]

Mrs. Mary Sargent Hopkins gave a lecture on December 21, 1894, at the Professional Women's League in New York City. "Many women have looked askance at cycling because they did not admire the appearance of a woman on a wheel. Those who urge women of taste to ride must not make the wheel conspicuous in any way. Some costumes are picturesque and some are serviceable, and there are some without either beauty or common sense," Hopkins told her audience. "The latter are the creations of a certain class of women who are always rebelling because they are women. They are not content to excel in a womanly way, but want to ape their brothers. There are always women who are willing sacrifices on the altar of reform, but these are women who desire to be conspicuous, and they will invite personal criticism rather than vegetate in obscurity." She went on to say that she did not approve of knickerbockers, because "we need something as an antidote for the absurdity of costume which threatens us. I hope the conservative women, and most women are conservative, will not become disgusted. The wheel is destined to create a revolution in the physical life of women." As a costume Hopkins recommended a combination suit of flannel, equestrian trousers, a short skirt, close-fitting hat, gauntlet gloves, and leggings of leather or cloth reaching to the knee. Hopkins also argued that when women such as Mrs. Mary Livermore (journalist, activist for women's rights) advocate the wheel, when Frances Willard (reformer, suffragist) not only rode but declared the wheel would bring physical benefits to women and when Mrs. Miller ("the apostle of grace and beauty") believed in it heart and soul, and when physicians recommended it, it was time that "the whine about the wheel's being unladylike was stopped." Undoubtedly that adoption of cycling by such prominent women went a long way to ending moral and propriety arguments against the wheel.¹⁴

According to a June 1895 report from College Point in Queens, New York, the teachers in the public schools there, especially those who rode bicycles, were aroused over an order issued by the Board of Education forbidding them to ride their bicycles to school. Those teachers were all women. The Board of Education declared that the minds of the teachers were concentrated more upon their wheels than their work at school. It further declared that "wheeling tends to create immorality." Justice of the Peace William Sutter was the Board of Education member who introduced the resolution at the meeting of the Board. On June 15 he declared, "We, as the trustees, are responsible to the public for the conduct of the schools, and, in a great measure, guardians of the morals of the pupils. I consider that our boys and girls to see their women teachers ride up to the school every day and dismount from a bicycle is conducive to the creation of immoral thoughts, and will sooner or later cause the boys and girls to lose the respect for the teachers and terminate in the complete inability of the young women to maintain discipline." Sutter continued, "In the first place, I don't consider it to be a proper thing for any young woman to ride a bicycle, and in the person of a school teacher it is particularly out of place. As far as the question of riding before or after school hours and when away from the school is concerned we have no authority but we will not permit them to ride bicycles to or from the school. If the teachers ride the scholars will." Dr. A.F.W. Reimer, another member of the board, asserted, "It is not the proper thing for the women to ride the bicycle. They wear skirts, of course, but if we don't stop them now they will want to be in style with the New York women and wear bloomers. Then how would our school rooms look with the women teachers parading about among the boys and girls wearing bloomers? They might just as well wear men's trousers. I suppose it will come to that, but we are determined to stop our teachers before they go that far." Reportedly, after being notified of the order the teachers were "very indignant." According to the reporter who wrote the piece, "The school authorities have also expressed a determination to improve the educational advantages of the schools, the progress of which, they say, has been retarded in recent years by the employment of young girls as teachers."¹⁵

Not all religious figures were opposed to women cyclists. The Rev. J.L. Scudder, of Jersey City, New Jersey, preached on bicycling before 200 members of the Hudson County Wheelmen Association on June 16, 1895. He praised wheeling as beneficial to health. Bloomers though, he said, were unbecoming and would doubtless be replaced by knickerbockers. Fellow cleric the Reverend Dawson of Brooklyn was also there and he prophesized a costume for cycling women that would not only make skirts seem out of style, but even improper on the wheel. Another clergyman from Brooklyn, the Rev.

Dr. R.M. Harrison, compared the lawmakers who hampered bicyclists to the infidels who persecuted Christians.[16]

An article that appeared in print in July 1895 took upon itself the task of generating some don'ts for women cyclists. Most of them were banal, obvious, silly, and so forth. About 102 such don'ts were listed. Examples of these prohibitions were "Don't get lost in the country," "Don't sit on your pocket oil can," "Don't wear laced boots. They are tiresome," and "Don't wear clothes that don't fit." Some of the prohibitions were more serious and/or sexist. They included, "Don't imagine everybody is looking at you," "Don't go out after dark without a male escort," "Don't ask 'What do you think of my bloomers,'" "Don't ride a man's wheel. The time has not come for that as yet," "Don't forget that there is a difference between a lady bicyclist and a bicycle lady," "Don't lift up your skirts suddenly to astonish people by showing them your bloomers underneath," "Don't wear conspicuous colors. In somber hues you will attract enough attention to satisfy even the new woman," and "Don't denounce bloomers as immodest for no better reason than that your parents will not permit you to wear them."[17]

Women often went out for bike rides on Sundays in Los Angeles, in July 1895. Apparently those women all went cycling in groups; that is, there were few if any women who were cycling on their own. Those groups were informal in some cases and formal in other instances, formal in the sense of being members of an organized club. Those groups included no male escorts. The female president of the club declared, "We took the initiative in establishing the custom of making tours without escorts. Crowds have followed in our lead, and it is the thing now for parties of women to go wheeling without a sign of a man." A few members of the club were then said to be reluctant to go on those Sunday rides when a condition for joining the club was that all members would take part in the Sunday runs. One of those women said to the president, "Well, I want to go but it's this way. Our minister said last Sunday that bicycles were demoralizing women and also said a lot of other mean things. While my folks thought he talked in a pretty sensational way, they vetoed Sunday tours for me." One of the other reluctant members added, "My preacher has spoiled my fun, too. He not only preached against it, but he gathered his cycling members together and made a personal appeal to them [to not cycle]." "It's no use for me to repeat what he said. Of course I won't go out on Sunday, but I'm wild to go all the same, and I'm afraid that instead of listening to the sermon tomorrow I will be thinking of you sitting beneath the lovely shade trees of Orange [California]." Remarked the club president, "I know that many preachers are opposed not only to Sunday riding for all cyclists, but are against women riding at any time."[18]

An article that appeared in July 1895 stated, "Cycling having taken such a mighty hold upon the land, it had naturally followed that an etiquette of cycling should be established and that it should be well-defined and rigidly regarded by society." And so this piece set out to establish those rules. The first rule of etiquette stated was that in the first place the correct word for the activity was "cycling" and the "up-to-date young woman does not speak of 'bicycling' nor of 'wheeling.'" Then the article on to produce a "wheel woman's manual." One of those rules stated, "If in town, the early hours of the morning are chosen for a ride through the park. This is on the same principle that it is considered good form for a young woman to drive only in the morning, that is, when she herself is the whip." In the country the rules were not as rigid but the maiden who was a stickler for form did all her cycling "in the hours which come before noon" and "neither is it correct for a young woman to ride unaccompanied." In the matter of chaperons "we are becoming almost as rigid as the French, who do not allow a young girl to cross the street, to say nothing of shopping or calling, without being accompanied by an elder woman, her mother, relative or a friend as a chaperon." Within this rule book "the unmarried woman who cycles must be chaperoned by a married lady—as everyone rides nowadays, this is an affair easily managed. Neither must the married woman ride alone; failing a male escort she is followed by a groom or a maid." The writer of the piece declared, "A woman is very fortunate if among her men or women servants one knows how to ride a bicycle. Ladies occasionally go to the expense of having a servant trained in the art.... If one possesses such a commodity as a brother or a husband he can always be made useful on a cycling excursion."[19]

"In condemning bicycle riding by women and girls as 'mannish' and tending toward immorality, the Women's Rescue League [WRL] of Boston has set itself as a target to be shot at by both sexes," was the opinion given by a journalist in August 1895. Remarking on how differently people looked at such things, the article brought up the example of Elizabeth Cady Stanton, a famed activist and women's right advocate who said, "women are riding to suffrage on the bicycle," and being an ardent suffragist, Stanton wanted more women and more girls to ride bicycles. Said the reporter, "But it is not for this that women and girls are riding wheels. It is because they find bicycling healthful and enjoyable. Many a weak woman is riding a bike to-day on the advice of her physician. Many physicians prescribe the wheel medicine for both men and women." In conclusion the journalist remarked that probably all of those physicians never thought they were doing anything wrong and would have lived in blissful ignorance of their sins "if this Women's Rescue League of Boston had not suddenly discovered that the bicycle is another invention of the devil to lead women into by and forbidden paths."[20]

In Atlanta, Georgia, the Rev. J.B. Hawthorne unleashed a "bitter arraignment of the women cyclists of the south [and it] has had the one effect to be expected—increased the number of fair riders throughout all Dixieland." In

MOURNING CYCLE COSTUME FOR WIDOWS.

ACCOMPANIED BY HER MAID.

WHEN STOPPING TO SPEAK TO A WOMAN.

Illustrations accompanying an 1895 article about the rules for respectable cycling for women, including to have a chaperon. If a chaperon was regularly unavailable the cyclist was advised to have her maid trained to ride and then accompany her mistress.

Hawthorne's hometown of Atlanta the number of female cyclists was said to be steadily on the increase. Hawthorne maintained his attacks on the women despite the fact that other clergymen in Atlanta did not agree with him, and it was reported that "he continues his crusade from his pulpit and through the press, saying very unpleasant things about women who ride wheels, and especially those who wear bloomers." Doctor Hawthorne denounced the drop-frame bicycle as "an invention of the devil." He was a well-known preacher in his time.[21]

JAMES B. HAWTHORNE, D. D.

The Reverend James Boardman Hawthorne, no date, who denounced the woman's drop-frame bicycle as an invention of the devil.

A dispatch from Washington in March 1896 noted that President Grover Cleveland had seldom posed as arbiter for the administration's social affairs and so far had never before been called upon to express his opinion as to what the wives of cabinet members should or should not do. But if that report were correct Cleveland had placed an executive veto upon the cabinet ladies riding bicycles. "Washington is such a paradise for the wheel that the sight of a Senator, a member of the diplomatic corps, a Judge of the Supreme Court or any of the most fashionable girls in the swell set astride a wheel no longer calls for comment," opined a newsman. Recently, though, some of the young members of the "swell set" conceived the idea of getting up a bicycle riding event for charity, and some of the wives of cabinet ministers allowed the use of their names as patrons of the event. It was said that from being passive spectators those ladies manifested a tendency to become active participants in the affair. "This coming to the ears of the President, it is said he plainly placed himself on record as being opposed to women no longer in their first youth riding the bicycle," according to the piece. "He does not object to the new woman or to her riding a bicycle if she is young, but he draws the line when she approaches middle age, and it is for this reason that many of the most prominent women in official circles will not be seen riding for charity."[22]

That report about President Cleveland generated an editorial response from a Virginia newspaper, on the subject of women cyclists. Said the editor, "that he is right on the subject of women bicyclists is patent to most men who have a proper regard and respect for the feminine sex. Many men like to look at women riding on bicycles, but few of them do when their wives, sisters and daughters are the riders."[23]

Elizabeth Cady Stanton ridiculed the idea, in June 1896, that a woman did not look well on a bicycle. "No woman could look worse on a wheel than a man bent at an angle of 45 degrees, and with coat-tails flying," she declared. "As for dress, she does not doubt that in time women will look pretty and graceful in long stockings, knickerbockers, tight-fitting sacks and military capes." Stanton believed in allowing women to ride bikes on Sunday without criticism. "If they prefer a ten-mile ride in the open air to the close[d] atmosphere of a church or to any easy chair at their own fireside perusing the Sunday papers," she said, "go on the wheel, by all means. The Sabbath was made for man and not for the Sabbath. No rational pleasure on that day should be forbidden.'" Stanton concluding by saying, "Young men and women confined in schools and workshops during the week must appreciate a day of freedom in such exhilarating exercise in the open air. The rational idea of Sunday is simply a day of rest and recreation, a change from the regular routine and employments of our everyday working world."[24]

By July 1896 there were a reported 45,000 bicyclists in Washington, D.C., and at least 15,000 of that number were women and girls. Thus, it was said, a sensation was created by the formal declaration of the Women's Rescue League that the bicycle "is a promoter of immorality." At a meeting held by the group on July 2 resolutions were passed as followed: "Whereas, The alarming increase of immorality among young women in the United States is most startling to those who have investigated the subject of disease and vice"; and "Whereas, A great curse has been inflicted upon the people of this country because of the present bicycle craze, and if a halt is not called soon 75 per cent of bicyclists will be an army of invalids within the next ten years"; "Whereas, Disease among young women is most appalling because of imprudent use of the bicycle, by bringing on disease peculiar to women; furthermore, immoderate bicycling by young women is to be deplored because of evil associations and opportunities offered in cycling sports"; "Whereas, Bicycling by young women has helped to swell the ranks of reckless girls who firmly drift into the standing army of outcast women of the United States more than any other medium"; and "Whereas, 'Bicycle run for Christ' by the so-called Christians should be properly termed 'bicycle run for Satan,' for the bicycle is the devil's advance agent, morally and physically, in thousands of instances." Therefore be it "Resolved, That the Women's Rescue League denounce bicycle riding by young women because of producing immoral suggestions and imprudent associations, both in language and dress, which have a tendency to make woman not only unwomanly, but immodest as well"; "Resolved, That married women should not resort to riding the wheel unless they wish to prevent motherhood"; be it further resolved "Resolved, That the Women's Rescue League petition all true women and clergymen to aid in denouncing the present bicycle craze by women as indecent and vulgar"; and be it further "Resolved, That copies of these resolutions be sent where they will do the most effective good for the cause of purity and morality." That document was signed by Charlotte Smith, president of the WRL and by Virginia N. Lount, secretary of the WRL Legislative Committee. The group declared that it intended to begin a national crusade against the use of bicycles by women. The subhead for the article in the newspaper in which it appeared gave its own not-so-subtle editorial by declaring, "Washington female cranks declare war on the riding of wheels by girls."[25]

The WRL called attention to the problem by the issuance of a circular. The timing of the circular had to do with the fact that in the following week there was scheduled to be a bicycle parade in Washington, D.C., in which it was thought that as many as 4,000 cyclists would participate. Of late, group president Charlotte Smith had been giving considerable attention to the increase in wheeling, particularly among women and "she holds that the result of her investigations prove conclusively that women who wheel will be physical wrecks. She also thinks that bicycling for young women is to be deplored, because of the evil associations which may result, and the opportunities for imprudent action which may result therefrom," and "she declares the bicycle the devil's agent, and declares that it has ruined thousands, both morally and physically."[26]

A newspaper in the nation's capital remarked that the anti-bicycling crusade begun by the WRL had revised the discussion of woman and the wheel, "which had apparently been buried under the spread of the craze." In response to the WRL's circular the newspaper sent a reporter out, who interviewed many physicians and clergymen on the subject. "Nine-tenths of the gentlemen seen were decidedly opposed to the stand taken by the League. With a single exception they expressed themselves as favoring the bicycle as a source of innocent amusement and also as a health promoter," detailed the account. "It was argued from a false premise, they were agreed, to claim because a great number of bad women ride bicycles that it follows that all women who ride them are bad, or even had a tendency to be bad." And, it was added, "as a matter of fact it is maintained that as a factor of immorality bicycle riding is not so dangerous a pastime as excursions, buggy riding, picnics and similar amusements." There was another point on which all those who were interviewed agreed, and that was that a person riding a bicycle must have a clear head, and "especially is this so in reference to girls and women, and consequently the indulgence in drink, which is acknowledged the most dangerous step, is of necessity avoided." As to the idea that American women as a class being frail, that idea was derided. It was affirmed that American women of all classes and conditions of life were as strong and healthy and could endure as much as the women of the same class and condition the world over. As to the dress of women cyclists "it was agreed by the physicians to be not only an improvement on the skirts which drag in the mud, but also on account of its looseness adds greatly to comfort and health." Dr. B.B. Adams was one of those interviewed and he said, "Some riders are benefitted while others are not; it all depends on the rider, who must use judgment and not overdo it. It is really not as fatiguing as a sewing machine, but of course all things can be carried to excess. On the whole, it is beneficial to the person because of the loose clothing, and the fresh air exercise." Said Dr. J. Lambert Delaney, "I am an advocate of bicycle riding as a healthy exercise for women. The only trouble is in the overdoing it."[27]

When a newspaper in San Francisco looked at the WRL crusade it declared, "And just now it is making war upon the bicycle as a means of rapid transit or pleasure for women. The league proclaims that immorality is alarmingly on the increase among American women, and all because of the horrid bicycle." With respect to the WRL the editor stated, "It is unfortunate for themselves that they have so little confidence in their sex. It may be, too, that the rescuers are in a measure right when they say that the bicycle promotes immorality, but a mere assertion that it is so does not make it so." Argued the editor, "Undoubtedly the bicycle tends to more familiar association between men and women than some other ways of enjoying companionship, but if the logic of these rescuers is good to apply to bicycle riding it is good to apply to buggy riding or walking. It is the guilty mind that suspicion most troubles." He continued by writing, "No doubt women would be safer if they were kept in seclusion, and they would be safer still if they were in their graves, but there would be no thought of their safety if men were fitted to coffins and the lids nailed down." The editor was of the opinion that "a true woman" did not compromise her modesty anymore on the bicycle that she did riding on a streetcar or in a buggy, for "all things are evil to the evil-minded." He pointed out that a great many women used the bicycle for convenience. They had to go from place to place on legitimate business, and it was quite as proper to go on a bicycle as it was to walk. "It is very true that some women bicycle riders adopt costumes that might be spliced out a little with the same kind of material, but the same is very much more true of some men bicyclists." Concluded the editor, "The fact is, there are just as many good and true women now as there were in those days. The members of the Rescue League might better attend to rescuing their own minds from the many unfounded suspicions which appear to keep them in a state of agitation."[28]

At the end of July 1896 a newspaper in Sacramento, California, remarked that another newspaper, the *Des Moines Register*, had put the case fairly and well in response to the attack by the WRL, stating that "upon all women who ride the bicycle as being immodest, because of the familiarity the riding is supposed to engender." It was reported that the Iowa paper "concedes that the use of the wheel may promote familiar association between men and women that, indeed, in some cases it lets down the bars of conventional restraint which has so long governed women while living more or less in the seclusion of their homes." But, it continued, "these have not necessarily impaired either the modesty or the virtue of women, as the rescuing ladies of the National Capital seem to think and aver. Whether this tendency, which may perhaps be called a 'commoning' tendency, will go any farther remains to be seen. We believe that those women who are modest will be modest still." And, continued the editor, "we are told of a time when a woman would faint if a strange man so much as caught a glimpse of her well-turned ankle, but we have long since passed that stage of civilization.... The modern woman on a bicycle does not faint so easily. She is stronger and more sensible, but no one but another woman, or set of women, leagued under the name of rescuers, would resume to say that she is also more immoral." The response to the WRL circular from a Chicago newspaper contained the following statement: "The alarming pessimistic view of the bicycle question is not justified by the facts.... It is doubtless true that many young women are riding to excess and are laying the foundations of future physical ailments of a grave character, but where one woman is so foolish as to do this a hundred ride the wheel sensibly, decently and healthfully." The Chicago editor went on to say, "It is also doubtless true to the woman of impure life the wheel may offer a convenient means for facilitating the execution of immoral designs, but that the pastime has a tendency to degrade or demoralize is a proposition too absurd for a moment's consideration." And, he added, "a woman who will violate the decencies and proprieties of life while wheeling will violate them upon the occasions when the opportunity is offered. Where one woman rides to destruction on the wheel a thousand ride to good health and maintain all the decorum, modesty and circumspection that characterize the well-bred, self-respecting women from the ideal American homes."[29]

Also in July 1896 a newspaper looked into the attitudes of the clergy to cycling females. The editor noted that the ministers of America received millions of dollars annually in return for the services they rendered as "censors of the public morals." Being conscientious men they felt it was their duty to keep a sharp lookout for any foe that might in any form seek to assail their flocks, as a matter of course from their watchtowers over the gates they espied the approach of the bicycle, "and much to their wonderment and worry they saw a woman mounted thereupon.... Here there was something that demanded a theological diagnosis. The moral or immoral effect of bicycle riding for women must at once be determined, and the degenerating influence of bloomers must be known." But, thought the editor, there were no precedents to guide the clergymen so it was necessary to do a great deal of guessing. "And that is why some ministers have guessed that every woman who dares to ride a wheel with bloomers or with skirts is sure and certain to go to the everlasting bow-bow and no mistake about it, while other ministers say that the wheel is a most wonderful contrivance, and its influence for good is marvelous." In the editor's opinion the entire theological world was then divided by a new line of thought, "and one-half is arrayed against the other half with the innocent, inanimate bicycle between them." Speaking of Hell, the editor concluded, tongue-in-cheek, "It is an awful thing to think that some dear member of a family circle may be forever shut away from the rest of the folks because he or she rode a two-wheeled vehicle to church while the other members of the family rode in a four-wheeled vehicle or walked."[30]

Discrimination against female cyclists took a more tangible form when it was reported in August 1896 that accident insurance companies had decreed that the bicycle girl could not be insured, with the reasoning that "the rule is attributed to the tendency of women to make frivolous claims." In the early stages of bicycling women were insured but "it was found that the claims for trivial and imaginary injuries were made by them so frequently and persistently that the underwriters would be bankrupted if one-half of them were paid. So the companies at a joint meeting made a rule that women bicyclists should be debarred from accident policies." However, not all women were excluded from accident insurance coverage. The report stated, "Those who possess separate estates and who are engaged in business which requires their personal attention and involves travel by rail or steamer are treated as desirable risks. If they are injured while riding a bicycle for health or pleasure they receive the benefits of insurance." (That is to say, women from the upper classes were allowed insurance.) It was said that one-third of all claims recently made for damages under accident policies came from bicycle riders. Those who broke an arm or leg or were otherwise incapacitated from attending to business received $25 a week while they were laid up. The accident insurance policy usually called for payment of $5,000 in case of death and in the case of disability a payment of from $7 to $25 a week, according to the extent of the injuries. The annual premium payment for such insurance ranged from $4 to $20.[31]

In an article that appeared in August 1896 a newspaper wondered whether or not the bicycle had helped the world. "The bicycle has, of late days, been so numerously adopted as a member of the family that it is pertinent or inquire what effect it has had upon the domestic circle which it has [so] largely entered as the welcome guest." This piece believed that three serious considerations existed that affected the machine and its owner—the moral, physical, and the commercial phases. Accordingly the paper held a symposium in which various people gave their opinions. "First, as to the moral aspect of the use of the wheel by women. It has been charged that there has arisen a license in dress and action by the women riders, which needs to be rebuked; and that the use of the wheel is an exercise detrimental to the health of such riders," declared the story. Clergymen were supposedly selected at random to give their opinions on the moral aspects and "their opinions are practically in accord and, as will be seen, form a strong verdict in favor of the bicycle for both men and women. Practically the only point of difference among them is the question of Sunday riding." Said the Rev. George Luccock of the Metropolitan Presbyterian Church in Washington, D.C., "As I ride a wheel myself, I naturally approve of the invention. Of course it can be used to an immoral end, like everything else. Its greatest abuse, to my mind, is using it as a means of desecration of the Sabbath; but this is not the fault of the wheel; it is due to the ungodliness of the riders." The Rev. A.M. Rich, rector of Trinity Episcopal Church in Washington, stated, "If a woman is modest anywhere in her house, on the street, in the drawing room, she can surely be modest on a wheel. On the other hand, if a woman wants to be indecent she has plenty of opportunities besides the bicycle for being so." Rich added, "For years I was opposed to riding by women, but my experience has taught me that so many have been benefitted in health, and in morality, by this kind of exercise that my old prejudice has vanished entirely." And, he added, "but I do not approve of bloomers of any means. If woman must wear bloomers, let her wear them with a skirt over them. A masculine woman loses the chief charm of femininity—modesty, and this, to me, is moral deterioration." With respect to the few "women of prominence" who gave their opinions, they were described as the "warmest proponents" of the woman on the bicycle.[32]

A report in September 1897 originating in a New York City newspaper observed that there was an organization in St. Louis called the Grant and Gravois School Association, which took upon itself the adjustment of all the city's public school difficulties without undue publicity. At its last meeting "it had a fit of violent indignation because it was discovered that one of the women teachers rode a bicycle to school in bloomers. The matter has not been settled yet, either with or without undue publicity and the main question interesting school teachers in St. Louis is whether they must give up their bicycles and bicycle costumes or not." The reporter who presented the story then set off to find out how New York City viewed that "important issue" and to that end he called upon Superintendent Jasper of the city schools. Jasper replied, "The school teachers of New York may wear bicycle costumes without fear of molestation. I have such perfect confidence in their good taste that I

A Sunday Morning Scene of Today.

A sketch of an 1896 Sunday morning bicycle ride that illustrated an article about the moral effects of the cycle.

shall not fear meeting apparitions in bloomers or other sensational attire." He added, "No rule has ever been made in New York schools upon the subject.... The younger teachers are especially discreet and, though they ride their wheels to school, are quite ingenious about their costumes. In all the schools are ladies' rooms where they immediately don long skirts before entering upon their duties. Therefore I see no ground for finding fault with them or making any rules upon the subject." Young women in St. Louis must be behind the times if they could not manage their bicycling without comment, the superintendent thought. Jasper said, "I think the good sense of New York school teachers can be relied upon at all times to dress properly and not attract attention." Charles Buckley Hubbell, president of the New York City Board of Education, declared, "I heartily endorse the custom of women teachers riding their wheels to school." Superintendent Maxwell of the Brooklyn schools was described as warm in his approval of any costumes "that would permit bicycling and not exceed the bounds of decency." When the reporter asked Maxwell if he would make any rule as to the costumes to be worn during school hours he replied by stating, "No, excepting the bloomers. I don't think I like them. Brooklyn women looked very unprepossessing in them a couple of years ago but no one ventured to wear them in schools. However, I guess bloomers have gone out of style, and I guess the women are glad." Maxwell then confided to the reporter, "I will tell you. The ladies have a very clever way in managing their costumes and I can't understand it. When they get off their wheels they are in full-fledged bicycle costumes. Five minutes later they appear in their classes looking exactly the same, only they are not in bicycle costumes. Do you know how they do it? It is an art, I am sure."[33]

In Cincinnati on September 28, 1897, Police Judge Schwab gave indications that he desired to protect the "respectable wheelwomen" in Cincinnati from contamination with fallen women who rode the bicycle. To that end he sentenced a "scarlet woman" to the workhouse for 30 days for no other offense than that of riding a bicycle on the public street. According to the account, "The testimony showed that she was clothed more generously than the majority of wheelwomen, and that she had not conducted herself in an improper way. 'Loitering' was the charge." Said the editor of the newspaper presenting the article, "It's a good thing to keep the scarlet woman from breaking into society, but we think the authorities down at Cincinnati are over-reaching themselves when they fine one for riding a bicycle. If the restriction is good regarding her use of a wheel it must be equally so on foot or in a buggy. No one can with grace excuse this class of woman for being, but the restriction we refer to above is certainly an infringement against the right of personal liberty."[34]

In October 1897 a story declared, "At last a minister comes before the public who has sufficient courage to tell exactly what he thinks of the bicycle skirt, without regard to what the opinion of others may be." He was the Rev. H.S. Place, pastor of the Gordon Avenue Methodist Episcopal Church of Cleveland, who had openly stated in a recently delivered sermon that he saw no reason why "if men were permitted to wear knickerbockers, women should not at least be allowed to wear their skirts several inches above the ankle." However, observed the reporter, Place "is by no means an advocate of the new woman, nor does he declare that a woman should in any degree take the place that nature has apparently allotted to man, but he feels that women should be treated with every possible consideration and that false modesty is in the way as bad as immodesty itself." At the time fashion dictated that short bicycle skirts ended three inches above the ankle.[35]

Later that same month it was reported the General Lew Wallace and the Rev. W.H. Hickman, vice chancellor of DePauw University, "have raised a storm of protests because of highhanded criticisms of the wheel." During an address at the institution Wallace took the occasion to deprecate the use of bicycles, saying that the riders looked more like monkeys than men, and that bicycling was time wasted. However, it remained for Hickman to come out

Who better to give advice to women on what to wear? Why, a minister, of course. And that was what the Reverend Place of Cleveland did in 1898.

"flatfooted in denouncing the use of bicycles for women." He declared, said a journalist, that "it was one of the most baneful agencies every [sic] invented insofar as it concerns the gentler sex. It takes the young woman from her home and home duties; its tendencies are altogether wrong. He also asserts that it affords a means of easy escape from the restrictions of conventionality, and is harmful from a hygienic standpoint."[36]

Writing in 1899 an observer remarked that 48 years earlier—on July 23, 1951—Mrs. Amelia Bloomer first wore her now celebrated costume at a ball at Lowell. Massachusetts. "The storm of wit and ridicule that followed drove the bloomers out of existence within a few months after its invention," it was

The Reverend W.H. Hickman, vice chancellor of DePauw University in 1898, also railed against the machine, declaring, among other things, that it took women away from their home duties.

reported, "only to be revived forty years later in modified form by the advent of the bicycle and athletics among women, and to be hailed as one of the most suitable and useful of female dresses." Mrs. Bloomer, he thought, had been an advocate of what came to known as rational dress. This observer argued for a skirt that reached to nearly halfway between the ankle and the knee, and not quite so full as the present fashion, who added, "If delicacy requires long skirts then why do our ladies a dozen times a day commit the indelicacy of raising their dresses to prevent their dragging in the mud on the street?"[37]

In a May 1894 account of bloomers a reporter wrote that some of the bloomer-wearers "wear [a] loose sailor blouse above the bloomers, and some wear shirt waists and little jackets. None wear a hint of any skirts. Some of the bloomers reach down to the shoe tops and others, the most sensational and yet the most sensible, end at the knee, and leave the stockings and shoes exposed below that point." According to this account, "It is the young women who are breaking the way for their sex with this new movement, but it is noticeable that the other women, who stand on the pavements and look on, nearly all praise the new costumes. Indeed, the reporter has heard no single word of disapproval of it from any woman, though the short bloomers that leave the lower leg fully exposed get a little criticism from the more conservative onlookers. The bloomers are so full that often they look like dresses from a little distance." When a man inquired of a woman in trousers why she wore them she would say, "Because they are the only things to ride a wheel in." Dresses got in the way all the time between the pedals and the feet, and so forth, "but with bloomers on the wildest dream of the women's righters is realized, because a woman is every bit as good as a man. So get out of the way! The bloomers are coming."[38]

A lengthy article in September 1895 discussed the question of bloomers and observed that there was no middle ground of observers and "everybody is either for or against bloomers." The opponents and advocates of bloomers were pretty evenly divided between the sexes and "some of the strongest opponents of bloomers and all they are understood to foreshadow are women and many of them wheelwomen." This journalist argued that the bloomers of 1895 were in no way like the articles worn and made famous by Mrs. Bloomer and that not more than a handful of women ever wore the costume Mrs. Bloomer wanted all women to wear. And, he continued, "it is hard to separate the incident of bloomers from the general subject of bicycling but it will readily be conceded that the spread of the bloomer idea has very materially increased the amount of bicycle[s] among women, and that without bloomers there wouldn't be so many women bicyclists." Also, the slow-but-sure disappearance of the corset from the bicycling girl's costume may be credited fairly to the bloomers. "It is hardly likely that if she hadn't first abandoned skirts she would have been disposed to such a revolution as to abandon corsets."[39]

This reporter went on to add that clergymen of every denomination had expressed emphatic disapproval of the bloomer costume and all that it stood for and for all they thought it pointed to. Quite a crusade against bloomers had been started in St. Louis by the Reverend Father Walsh of St. Bridget's Parish, and he was joined by clergymen of various other Christian sects. Father Walsh positively forbade the young women of his congregation to wear bloomers and even discouraged the riding of a bicycle. But his opposition against bloomers was described as unyielding. He was ably seconded in his crusade by the Rev. W.H. Kern of the Fourth Christian Church of St. Louis. Kern railed, "I stand now and forever against the bloomer." Reportedly, in St. Louis, 85 percent of female bike riders wore bloomers. A few days earlier the Reverend Father Wilson of Terre Haute, Indiana, preached a sermon on the new woman in which "he condemned bloomers without qualifications. He objects to them on physical as well as moral, or spiritual grounds. He declared that he would not even compromise himself by recognizing her [the bloomer wearer] should she speak to him." And then everybody, thought the newsman, remembered Bishop Deane's "bitter remarks about bloomers." However, the most vigorous attack on bloomers was made by the Rev. T.B. Hawthorne of Atlanta. In one of his sermons on the topic Hawthorne declared, "If there is any object on earth which makes jubilee in the realm of unclean spirits, it is a 'society woman' in masculine habiliments, straddling a bicycle, and preparing to make an exhibition of her immodesty on the thoroughfares of a great city." He characterized the custom at length as degrading, as incompatible with true feminine modesty, and the wearers of it as weak creatures who coveted the prerogatives and pleasures of men, and who thereby became despicable in the eyes of all people of virtuous sensibilities. He raged that women were riding to the devil in bloomers, and wound up declaring that he spoke in no unkindness to women who had been beguiled into the unwomanly conduct, but under the force of a divine inspiration compelling him to save them from "the fate of a man who takes a young tiger into his house as a plaything." Hawthorne thought the bloomer craze was born of infidelity and would follow the new woman movement into an utter repudiation of all Christian teachings. Said Hawthorne, "Nine women are against the bicycle fad where there is one in favor of it," and that he knew this to be true from the thousands of letters that had poured into him from all over the United States.[40]

Taking a different position was the Rev. John W. Shorten of the Methodist Church in Mason, Ohio. Controversy broke out at his church when a group of females attended a weeknight church service in bloomers and then when the female organist Miss Ada Coleman, 20, came to play the organ in her bloomers. She rode back and forth to church on her bike and at one service and at one service she parked her bike and went to the organ in her bloomers. Those events scandalized the congregation to such an extent that some of the people in attendance in the congregation got up and stalked out. Before the week was out a dozen new suits of bloomers appeared in the streets of the town. Then the opponents organized their forces and demanded that Shorten denounce from the pulpit the bloomer wearers at the next Sunday sermon. He refused, though, to touch on the topic from the pulpit but did let the opponents know he favored the bloomer, saying he thought bloomers "were a very sensible costume for women to wear when bicycling." Also noted in this article were that various school boards throughout the country had made trouble about bloomers and three or four had positively forbidden the teachers under their jurisdictions from wearing that costume to school "because of the evil effect on the mind of the young." This reporter believed there was "a very strong undercurrent of feeling among women against bloomers" and he thought that got little media attention because "the proportion of women who ride bicycles to the whole population of women is small, and only those directly interested get their views into print. But it is safe to say that, so far, even the great majority of bloomer girls would not favor wearing bloomers except as a part of a bicycling costume." He went on to argue there was even a small opposition to bloomers among bicycling women and those women objected "to bloomers on principle." In his opinion bikes were ridden by thousands of women in skirts of almost ordinary length with thousands more wearing shorter skirts, with some sort of equestrian trousers underneath, "and all of these thousands would view with horror the idea of leaving off skirts altogether." It was safe to say, he believed, that among men who were not wheelmen "there is a very strong opinion against bloomers." A group of young men in Edmeston, New York, had recently formed an anti-bloomer club. The pledge taken by each member went as follows: "I hereby agree to refrain from associating with all young ladies who adopt the bloomer cycling costume, and pledge myself to the use of all honorable means to render such costumes unpopular in the community where I reside." The reporter declared that in many other parts of the country similar organizations had been formed among the young men, however, no details were given. Said Dr. Wood Case of San Francisco, "The danger of the bloomer craze lies in the fact that if the public allows a little lassitude in dress there are those in every community who are disposed to make it disgraceful."[41]

In the last couple of years of the 1800s and into the first couple of years of the 1900s a few items surfaced that showed how women cyclists were treated in some countries. In France a married woman could not ride a bicycle in the public streets or parks without a permit and she could not get the permit from the authorities without the written consent of her husband. In Russia it was even worse for women. Females there were not permitted to possess a bicycle without first obtaining the consent of the government. Few women rode bicycles in Russia and those who did were mostly members of the royal family and the nobility. Women cyclists in St. Petersburg, Russia, were ordered by the police to wear bloomers or rational dress as the wind blew "too capriciously in Russia's capital for skirts to be worn with decency." In Florence, Italy, female cyclists had to carry two bells on their wheels to warn pedestrians of their approach on the machines. Wheelmen were only required to have one bell. In Germany women bikers were obliged to pass an exam before the city police showing that they had perfect control of their bicycles before they could obtain permission to ride in the streets. As well, they had to carry with them their licenses on their cycles. No such rule applied to men. In Vienna, Austria, no wheelwoman was allowed to take her hands from the handlebars while riding in the streets. And, as in all the earlier examples, no such rule applied to wheelmen.[42]

The Rev. W.W. Reynolds, pastor of the Brightwood Methodist Church in Indianapolis, asked Captain Luke P. Colleran of the Chicago Police Department detective headquarters for answers to two questions: "Has the introduction of the bicycle had any effect upon the morals of the women who ride them in Chicago?" and "If so, in what manner has it done so?" Colleran replied, "I must confess that I am not an advocate of the use of the bicycle among women, when viewed from a morality phase. Women of refinement and exquisite moral training, addicted to the use of the wheel, are not infrequently thrown among the uncultivated and degenerate of both sexes, whose coarse, boisterous and immoral conduct is constantly seen while riding along our streets and boulevards. Many there are, doubtless, who escape the contamination, though the contagion be ever present. Again, many of our women bicyclists wear shorter dresses than the laws of morality and decency permit." Colleran continued by stating, "From these facts I must certainly consider the adoption of the bicycle by women as detrimental to the advancement of morality, nay, even its stability. I have always entertained a deep sympathy for the hosts of noble and honorable ladies who, while riding their bicycles, are frequently associated with women whose morality will not stand investigation and whose conversation is coarse."[43]

In response to Colleran's remarks, the editor of a Scranton, Pennsylvania, newspaper recapped the policeman's remarks by saying, "Captain Colleran says the bicycle leads many women to moral ruin; not only that, but every woman who rides a bicycle is unbecomingly spoken of by immoral and depraved men, who may be found loitering on every street corner." He went on to mention a woman who had tried to refute the cop's remarks but dismissed the defense as "flimsy" before adding, "Captain Colleran is a man of wide experience, in police and criminal work, and knows whereof he speaks.

It is true the bicycle is a favorite pastime of the most refined women of our land, but nevertheless they are all exposed to the tongues of immoral and depraved men. Women as bicycle riders are always used as good subjects for slurring jokes behind the footlights. Why is it?" He went on to mention that women were "being insulted daily upon Scranton streets and without cause or provocation." And, he concluded, "the fault, of course, is not with the women who ride bicycles. The fault is with their insulters. But it would become modest women to give as little opportunity for vicious remarks as possible. It is possible to dress for bicycle exercise and to behave while riding so as to nullify all of these criticisms; and the propriety of doing so should be strongly urged."[44]

A report that appeared on August 30, 1899, announced that at the next meeting of the Kenosha, Wisconsin, City Council, an ordinance prepared by City Attorney W.M. Cowell providing for the licensing of women bicyclists would be introduced. That ordinance provided that it would be unlawful for any female to ride a wheel in Kenosha without having first obtained a license for such activity from the Kenosha city clerk. To obtain a license the applicant had to be examined by three experts as to her ability to ride a cycle without endangering the safety and personal rights of others. If the experts put their stamp of approval on the applicant's ability she was then required to file a $300 bond that all damages caused by careless riding or other improper handling or manipulation of the bicycle will be paid by said female if the accident was shown to be resultant from the carelessness of said license. A woman riding a bicycle within the city limits of Kenosha without a license could be arrested and fined $10. All monies collected from such fines, said a reporter, "are to be the compensation of the experts." It was also reported that Chicago authorities were studying the Kenosha ordinance and "The subject is one the police and legal departments have had under consideration for some time. The opinion prevails that women riders enjoy entirely too much freedom, and a disposition is strongly entertained to limit if not to prohibit their indulgence in cycling." Declared Chicago Police Chief Joseph Kipley, "I am deeply impressed with the advantages of the Kenosha ordinance. The inconvenience resulting to the general public from the use of wheels by women and children, admitting they may desire some physical benefit and pleasure from the same, certainly presents a question for council legislation." Kipley added, "I have no doubt many men hastening to and from their daily labors in the city are delayed by women cyclists. Let us clean the boulevards and streets and give men an opportunity to use the bicycle to the greatest advantage. The Kenosha ordinance is certainly worthy of consideration. In its favor it is stated women are invariably mixed up in cycling accidents. I do not doubt this is true, and my argument in favor of a clear right of way for men cyclists is consistent." In conclusion Kipley asserted, "I hope the Kenosha ordinance will pass. In

In 1899 Chicago Police Chief Joseph Kipley (photograph not dated) came out in favor of adopting a by-law that would force women who wanted to ride a bicycle to be required to get a license from city authorities. Men would not have to be licensed.

order that Chicago may have an object lesson in the matter of cycling regulations."[45]

To explain his ordinance Cowell stated, "A woman who starts out on a wheel is a menace to public safety unless she can steer the machine through any crisis." A Boston newspaper editor responded to the ordinance by asserting, "The menace to society ... if there be one at large on any wheel, is the male scorcher [speeder]." Also responding to the Cowell proposal was an editor with a Sacramento, California, paper, who stated, "Let women ride and ride at will. It does her good and it fills the landscape with motion and color. If she neglects her home—if the biscuit be soggy, the children unwashed, the husband ungroomed, that is another matter. But no examination, no discrimination."[46]

7

1890s—Fashion

While some media attention was devoted to the relationship between health and cycling by women and to the question of propriety, morals and ethics and the woman biker, the greatest amount of attention was devoted to what the woman bicycle rider wore, could wear, must wear, should wear, and so forth. Part of the battle women waged for equality involved achieving the right to wear reasonable, or rational dress. And much of that battle took place with the cycle in the foreground. Women started this period by wearing ordinary, everyday walking clothing, the sort of costume a woman wore when she went out to the store, and so on. And that meant a skirt that reached, and often touched, the ground, and of course, a corset. These ordinary clothes were anywhere from impossible to impractical to wear while riding a bike. Impossible, for example, to wear while trying to ride a high-wheeler. By the end of this period when the bike was rapidly on its way to being a forgotten fad, women had managed to evolve a great deal toward rational clothing. They had not made the jump to wearing pants, or trousers, but they had moved a considerable distance toward that goal. As the number of women riding wheels increased so did the attention devoted to cycling costumes. While much of the media attention was devoted to the evolution and emancipation of women's clothing much of it was simply the advertising industry trying to sell more clothing to women. The nascent advertising industry was busy in this period trying to convince women they needed to buy all sorts of new items before they could ride a wheel. Some of these items were simply more of the same with news articles being little more than advertising masquerading as news items, though some of the items did represent forward steps toward clothing emancipation.

That tendency to sell extra stuff could be seen in an article that was published in May 1890 in which it was declared, "The growing predilection of young women for all manner of outdoor sports and occupations necessitates

An ordinary walking dress of 1890 (top left), 1894 (top right), and 1899 (right). A woman going out in the daytime to shop, visit friends, go to the library, and so forth, would wear a dress like these.

special costumes for different pursuits; and we present to our readers this week two novelties of this kind, which have just been perfected by Redfern from his own artistic designs." Redfern Ltd. was a famous British couture and tailoring establishment. The first of those items was a "pedestrian" costume suitable for a day's tramp on country roads. "The second novelty is rather more startling, for it is nothing less than a Redfern bicycle habit. The girls have learned that it is good fun to belong to a wheelman's club and that the exercise is not only productive of much enjoyment, but is also highly conducive to health and therefore to rosy cheeks and brilliant eyes." It was also noted in this account, "But the wheel [tricycle] intended for feminine use is heavy and ungraceful and makes too great demands on the muscles, so here and there an unconventional demoiselle is following the lead of a certain well-known lady and is adopting the bicycle for her use." And it was for those women that Redfern had designed its bicycle gown. "The skirt, of plaited tweed, is divided, but the pleats are so lapped that this is not perceptible, except in the increased ease and grace of the wearer. The bodice, with its wide, notched lapels, opens to the waist over an embroidered pique waistcoat, above which appears a small portion of white linen shirt with high collar. A peaked cap of the gown material completes the costume."[1]

A reporter writing in June 1890 noted the progression of riding machines from the velocipede to the bicycle to the high-wheeler and finally to the safety bike but "still something seemed lacking to make the enjoyment complete, and, strange to say, the last triumph is due to the reformer who invented the divided skirt.... No sooner had it made its appearance, than a ladies riding school was opened in Minneapolis and met with great success, the young ladies of the flour city adopted with equal favor the twin skirt and the safety bicycle." In conclusion, said the account, "Now that womankind has taken them to her heart and adopted them as the proper thing, there is no doubt but what for a few years at least the wheel will be the favorite amusement for both sexes."[2]

As early as August 1891 the textile industry was attempting to take advantage of the interest in bicycling by pitching clothing to women that had nothing to do with emancipation and little to do with ease of cycling. A prize-winning costume was featured that was designed by Mrs. William Ritson of Gorse Bank, Cheshire, England. The unspecified prize was

A Redfern bicycle habit, 1890.

offered and awarded by an English periodical. Soft gray or fawn serge was the material recommended. While the article pointed out its characteristics it went on to conclude, "All these things sound very practical, but the costume has a square, ungraceful look which does not promise well for its popularity."[3]

In that same month the *Ladies' Home Journal* declared that there were two conditions needed for a "girl's perfect bicycle costume." Those conditions were looseness (to permit free action to the muscles) and a dark color. "A plain skirt is a matter of course.... The under or foundation skirt should never be less than two and a half yards wide." A blouse waist was "not absolutely necessary; unless it is especially becoming, it looks mannish, or else slovenly on a rider when at full speed. Of course you ride in very loose corsets or a corset-waist, which is better." As a final bit of advice to the reader the article said, "Many riders like, as an undergarment, the divided skirt. Still others veto it. It is a matter of personal comfort or discomfort. Dress warmly and yet beware of getting overheated."[4]

When a New York City paper surveyed the situation in November 1891 it began its story by declaring, "One of the rarest, raciest products of the wave of modern progress is the bicycle girl. She sits her steel horse precisely as her brother sits his, and established thereby the long-for equality of the sexes which the women's clubs have argued themselves black in the face to bring about, but in vain. She wears a more hygienic garb than the dress reformers have ever dreamed of in their most inspired moments." Reportedly, except in the coldest weather, no petticoat was needed and when worn it had to be of warm twill and had to be scant, but not divided, for "the dual skirt is clumsy and cumbersome worn underneath and neither desirable no picturesque on the outside." There was said to be great disagreement among the experts on the question of corsets. While the reporter admitted that the corset was better abolished, it still had to be worn. "Still if, as many contend, they cannot ride without it, let it be a riding corset, cut entirely away on the hips, with a low bust, not too closely boned and, above all, worn loosely." And, finally, "now, last and least of all in importance is the gown, which is of habit cloth, just long enough to clear the ground, just full enough to allow perfectly free motion of the legs."[5]

A piece that appeared in January 1892 began by discussing the physical education of girls, which included cycling. Soon, though, the piece moved on to clothing. "Whether it be bicycling or tricycling for which one 'goes in,' it should be a recognized fact that the amusement requires a suitable costume equally with riding, shooting, bathing or gymnastics," said the account. "Half the opposition to ladies and girls indulging in this excellent amusement, which has one great advantage over many other pastimes, in that it can be pursued winter or summer, spring or autumn, provided the weather be but reasonably fine, arises no doubt from the fact that nine-tenths of the women and girls one sees 'wheeling,' either from their unsuitable attire, their want of knowledge, or from their looking ill at ease, act as potent arguments against the practice." In dealing with the bicycle costume the journalist pointed out that while many different propositions for the proper bicycle costume had emerged during the previous six to eight years, a really sensible costume had not yet evolved, a costume "which is neither open to the objections of the one advocated by the 'advanced school,' who would have put ladies and girls who cycle into frilled knickerbockers, a blouse, and a skirt the length of that worn in the gymnasium, nor of that brought forward by their less advanced sister, which was in reality the bloomer dress redivivus." Concluding the article the journalist declared, "Many mothers would, I think, allow their daughters to indulge in what is undoubtedly a splendid form of exercise, could they but see them properly attired in a dress such as that described, and mounted on a suitable machine."[6]

Also worried about fashion issues was a newsman with a Minnesota newspaper who gloomily declared in July 1892, "So long as the eyesight of most women is good, and the common sense of a few women who ride the bicycle is so uncommonly lacking, it is to be feared that the ranks of feminine 'cyclists' will increase but slowly. It must be confessed that nine out of ten of the women who ride a wheel present an appearance which is sure to give a spectator positive chills of horrors. And it is so unnecessary." He went on to argue that some women must have thought they were biking in a vacuum, for "they are apparently in blissful ignorance of the effect which a stiff breeze has upon such stuff as gingham and thin silk. They do not know that any critical bystander could guess their weight to a pound." He went on to outline an "ideal bicycle ensemble." In the first place her gown was made of a heavy dark blue serge, so wide that four yards only were required for the entire suit. The skirt was lined with a lighter weight serge of the same color so that the wind did not catch it and inflate it into a "generous and irrepressible balloon." Next, a divided skirt made of a still lighter weight serge was worn under the dress, and black tights under the skirt. Those three pieces "cling to each other with a truly commendable loyalty, so that the dress is prevented from creeping up and making a liberal display of ankle." And, to finish off the outfit, "the waist is a plain, tight-fitting habit waist, with reverse collar, inside of which a chemisette and neat cravat are worn.... For summer new gloves have been introduced which combine coolness with durability."[7]

Doctor Richardson spoke highly of cycling for females, in December 1892, and said, "I have no hesitation in saying that the young woman who is about to learn the art of cycling will do best by choosing the bicycle from the first. Women sit more gracefully on the bicycle than on the tricycle; they work at less labor and all things considered, they work at less risk." He remarked that women were "hampered by their dress" in that activity "but he does not make so strong a point of this as he might do. The ordinary female skirt is quite unsuited for bicycling, though it may pass on the tricycle." In conclusion the reporter noted, "If a costume like that in which Herr Stempel has induced many ladies of social position, pupils of his gymnasium to give public displays were introduced by the women members of some good cycling club for wear in that exercise, it would be perceived to be so superior in point of modesty as well as of grace and safety, and to attract so little notice after being once seen, that it would be quickly adopted generally."[8]

An account that appeared in January 1893 observed, "Bicycling has become such a fashionable pastime that dressmakers have now devoted a department to the making of bicycle gowns, just the same as tennis costumes, or ballroom dresses for that matter.... An attempt was made last summer to introduce the divided skirt ... but the attempt met with no success."[9]

Several months later in 1893 another story detailed, "All women bicyclists wear short plain skirts, which in the case of a conventional bicycle dress turns under and gathers itself, trousers fashion just below the knee." And, he continued, "good taste, however, directs in bicycle riding as in most other things, that the least conspicuous is the most acceptable attire. It is still something of a shock to many persons to see a woman mounted on the tandem wheels, and the less she can add to it by her dress the better."[10]

"We saw a few days ago a pretty girl dressed in a pretty suit riding a bicycle," explained a journalist in July 1893. "There was nothing unusual about this fact, except that the girl wore Turkish trousers and black gaiters to the knee, instead of the flapping skirts which wheelmen commonly deem it necessary to put on, and which always make their wheeling ridiculous." He added that her movements were graceful and if people looked at her a little more than they should it was to admire and commend her. "There was certainly nothing about the young lady's appearance or demeanor which was not modest and seemly," he argued. "Why not replace skirts altogether in the riding, walking and other active out of door exercises which women, with the full approval and unanimous applause of their brethren, are engaging in more and more? There is no valid reason why it should not be done, except stupid prejudice."[11]

Reportedly, a young woman entered a newspaper office in an eastern American city and gave those in that office an impromptu discourse on bicycling for women, with particular attention to the costumes for that activity. She had been a cyclist for eight years and exclaimed that dress had a great deal to do with making bicycling popular with women, for "bicycling is a pastime that any woman may indulge in with perfect propriety, and yet a good many women are prejudiced against it because of the ill-looking attire that many women wear." She remarked that there was a good deal of reform agitation going on about bicycle dress for women and that in Boston the females were urged to wear the Syrian trousers, "but that is too radical. Now, the way I dress is this; I wear no petticoats, but instead what are called equestrian trousers. What are equestrian trousers? Why they are tights, plain tights, closely knitted and warm." The outer gown, she continued, was "of the walking gown pattern." As to the problem of how to keep a dress in order when the wind was blowing briskly she explained that she used a line of tape, about one inch in width, sewed along the bottom of the gown in front and at the sides. It gave enough added weight to keep the dress from blowing upward. "You see this attire does not depart much from the conventional style of any neat walking attire."[12]

Another fashion article emerged in August 1893. This account began by declaring, "When a few of our independent and sensible women decided that the bicycle was altogether too fine a thing to be monopolized by the sterner sex great was the consternation and numerous the comments from their more conservative sisters." Continued the story, "But in a short time these reposeful creatures found that the bicyclists were decidedly robust and healthy, the head of the house having incidentally commented upon their bright eyes and rosy cheeks. And then, too, they had lost none of that modesty of demeanor and were as altogether charming as their less daring and confident critics." Decidedly, thought the journalist, the French fashions for the bicyclists would not appeal to the sedate. The old-fashioned stuck to the tradition of their grandmother's class but he doubted if the young girls found much to approve of in those standards. "Still, one will have to admit that these costumes are much more comfortable than the skirts worn by the American bicyclist, which are apt to get entangled in the wheel and throw the rider. The first appearance would be a little trying. Uncomplimentary remarks would be made. The wearer would be credited with a love for notoriety, a desire to attract attention with a quiet, disregard for other people's opinions," thought the writer of the piece. But those French women bikers might confer a lasting benefit upon the supposed American women's desire "to make themselves at all conspicuous. For would we not in time become accustomed to the knee breeches and short skirts and consider them as lady-like and proper as we thought the first maiden's appearance on the wheel unladylike and improper? Any striking color or daring contrast of colors could be avoided, and would be by a lady." The French woman, it was said, delighted in the admiring glances that a striking costume called forth from the crowds that thronged the boulevard and was not at all annoyed if many eyes followed her as she rode along. Those French female cyclists mostly wore knee breeches, something taboo at that time in America. With respect to those French women, said the account, "Everyone, regardless of age, wears the knee breeches, but some wear longer skirts than others."[13]

A Mannish Coat.

The Joy of Short Skirts.

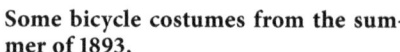

Some bicycle costumes from the summer of 1893.

A Blonde in Satin Breeches.

One reporter in September 1893 observed, "If things keep on as they have been of late, the dress reformers will have to look to women bicyclists as their leaders. From all sides come rumors of strange garments seen in a flash as a wheel woman spins past." One woman wrote the following description of a cyclist she saw on a country road: "Gray was the color of her. Coat over blouse to begin with and continuations that looked like Turkish trousers. Let me add that the sole impropriety about the costume is in my description of it."[14]

The power of the advertising industry could be seen in this account that appeared in September 1893, albeit that it was early in that industry's life: "The woman who objected to being hanged because she had no hanging dress was within her rights. To most women a dress for an occasion is coequal with an occasion for dress. It is sentiments like this that make the wheels of commerce move." Among garments of "special import" were those for riding, boating, yachting, lawn tennis, the bicycle, climbing, hunting, and now golf. "Let no one conceive that these costumes are interchangeable, except perhaps a lawn tennis outfit may take part in golf. On the contrary, each has some special distinguishable quality fondly conceived to be essential." This account also mentioned the French cyclists by observing, "Parisians have adopted bicycling in a much more thorough way than our American women. The French girl who rides a bicycle does not attempt to retain the long skirt, but she wears a stylish knickerbocker suit of some kind, and women riders have become so numerous on the broad, smooth avenues of the outskirts of Paris that no one pays any particular attention to them."[15]

ON THE WING.

In 1893 many women cyclists still rode around in very long skirts.

A report that appeared in March 1894 and originated in a New York City newspaper was probably designed to shock, or at least deliver unsettling information. It started by noting that during Quebec City's recent winter carnival "thousands, perhaps tens of thousands of Canadian women now wear trousers during the Canadian winters." That caused an unidentified woman to say, "Well, that tends to show that trousers may be going to become a common general garment peculiar to neither sex." She went on to say that she had two pairs herself and her daughter also owned a pair. In Switzerland, she continued, "Within the past two or more years, full trousers, like the Turkish ones, are worn for mountain exercises by English, French and German women. The same trousers are worn in the Scotch highlands by the English, and of late a movement has begun for the adoption of trousers and long tailed coats for equestrianism." The leading English fashion papers had published pictures of the dress worn by these "new votaries of the bifurcated garment of the master sex, and the costume has been seen to be pretty. As many as half a dozen women have appeared simultaneously in Hyde Park in this new dress." Still, such women were rarely seen in New York City, for "it is only now and then that a woman so dressed is seen in Central or Prospect parks or the streets that lead to those parks, yet some are seen every now and then, and in the smaller cities of New England, New York and New Jersey they multiply rapidly, so that in certain of these towns no one turns a head for a second glance at a woman in that dress." It was predicted herein that trousers would be adopted by female cyclists.[16]

A month later it was reported, "The fair weather has developed the bicycle girl with the divided skirt. This garment isn't as chic as it might be, inasmuch as its Turkish dimensions do not especially distinguish it from the full skirt, concealing with prudish chariness the beautiful lines of the leg. But that it is pantalooned is evinced by the daylight beneath the seat which a front or back view discloses."[17]

One want supplied made half a dozen more, grumbled one reporter in April 1894. No sooner was a bicycle for women invented than necessity arose for a special hat, gown and shoe for the rider to wear. "The bicycle is an immense weight in the conventional dress reformer's side of the scale, for it is impossible to ride a wheel to advantage in long skirts, and a great many persons will make a sacrifice to pleasure that they will not make for duty's sake. No doubt a large number of women now believe in short skirts who would have scorned the idea of them before the advent of the bicycle," declared the journalist. "The long skirt is an undesirable hindrance in all active amusements and particularly in bicycling." This article also mentioned the French women and commented that Parisian women soon discarded the long skirt for bicycle wear and "have not abandoned the skirt altogether, appearing in short tight trousers similar to those worn by men. It is doubtful if women on this side of the water will follow fashion as far as that. Indeed it is not at all necessary to go entirely without skirts, as a scant one falling just below the knees is no burden, does not interfere with freedom of movement and runs no chance of catching in the gearing when the wheel is in motion—a fruitful source of accidents." According to this story, "These short skirts are commonly seen now. Full trousers of the same material are worn under them in place of a petticoat and cloth or leather leggings buttoning them to the knee." Good colors were said to be drab gray, brown, dark green navy blue, and black "and all noticeable kinds of decoration should be strictly avoided." Illustrated was an example of that type of costume; it had navy blue cloth, cloth leggings, an Eton jacket, and had an outing shirt with a four-in-hand tie.[18]

An article from June 1894 noted the proliferation of female cyclists in

New York City, in particular in Central Park and went on to declare, "The New York woman bicyclist has not the courage of her Parisian sister and only during the past few months the divided skirts have begun to displace the clinging and cumbersome street dress. The few dress-reform bicyclists who dare venture beyond the walls of the bicycle academies are, however, objects of much curiosity and comment on the boulevard." He went on to report that a slight but athletic young lady "who doubtless considered it far less immodest to ride a bicycle in divided skirts than with skirts a-flying in the wind, created a mild sensation a few evenings ago." It seemed that her costume "consisted of a shirtwaist, rather narrow fawn-colored divided skirts reaching a few inches below her knees, and a pair of fawn-colored leggings buttoning up on the outside." It all caused this correspondent to conclude, "While the divided skirt and knickerbockers are now startling and regarded as freaks of fashion, there is no doubt that under the growing influence of woman's rights, woman suffrage and dress reform the picturesque female bicyclist will soon be one of the staple sights of our streets."[19]

In July 1894 journalist Earle Eaton remarked, "The bicycle girl is very much in evidence nowadays. The English girl is as fond of her wheel as she is of the platitudes of *Punch*, the American girl loves her 'silent steed' as ardently as the Arab loves his prancing steed of the desert, and the French girl—well, Miss Paris has simply gone cycling mad." He added, "A few years ago the wheelwoman was almost an unknown quantity. The ordinary or high wheel was then in vogue, and it was not only a dangerous wheel to ride, but it is also a wheel that did not recommend itself to a woman who was particular about the proprieties. With the advent of the safety or low wheel came woman's opportunity. The safety was easy to mount, was not at all dangerous and was, in fact, just the wheel unemancipated women had been praying for." Clad in conventional skirts, she was soon a familiar figure on city streets and country roads. "Today the bicycle girl is happy in the possession of her wheel, but her mind is wrestling with a great

A daringly short skirt, in 1894.

problem—She does not shriek for woman's rights. She little cares for suffrage bloomers. With her the question of the hour is, 'Shall I wear the bloomers?'" Eaton said that for more and more women the answer was yes, because more and more were wearing bloomers. "The bloomers, it is true, are of as many types as there were colors, in Joseph's famous coat, but they are all the badges of emancipation—they are bloomers. Many of the costumes are so full and balloonlike that they closely resemble the conventional skirt and are as modest and as inconspicuous as that familiar article of woman's apparel. Other women, however, have emancipated themselves into men's tight knickerbockers at a single bound, a proceeding that is as yet somewhat startling to the uneducated public." As far as Eaton was concerned the "bloomerized" woman had come to stay and declared, "The bloomer craze is not a fad with her. It is a necessity. She cannot ride a wheel without risking her precious neck if she wears skirts, for skirts persist in getting tangled up in her bicycle to the utter demoralization of her equilibrium. Clad in bloomers, she is free and untrammeled. She does not fear a fall."[20]

H. Strugnell of New York City, who designed a costume for the New York bloomer girl, told Earle Eaton that at least 200 women in Brooklyn and New York City "were wearing the rational bicycle costume." Strugnell added, "Last season the bloomer girls were few and far between, and the pioneers who first wore the rational costume on the streets were greeted with such rude cries as, 'Take off them pants,' 'Does mama know you've got 'em on, Mamie?' and other remarks that were not particularly encouraging to the plucky dress reformers." This year, however, the bloomer girls were reported to be so numerous and so really inconspicuous when mounted on their wheels that unkind comment had been silenced. For the benefit of carping critics who perhaps had never seen a bloomer girl, declared Eaton, "it may be said that the best type of the rational bicycling costume—the type worn by the New York Girl—is not in the least mannish or immodest. The trousers are very full and reach to the knee, where they are drawn in by elastic and where the fullness falls

The New York City bloomer girl and her bike, in 1894.

downward, concealing at least six inches of the limb below. The baggy character of the trousers also causes them to fold together much like divided skirts, so that when the bloomer girl is on her wheel only a close observer can tell whether she belongs to the emancipated or the unemancipated ranks of womankind." Below the knee the ankle had concealed 12-button leggings of the same color as the jacket and bloomers. Tailor-made bicycle costumes ranged in price from $12 to $40 "and the only truly mannish things about them are the cunning little jackets." One feature of the ideal bloomer costume described as sensible was the detachable skirt that went with it "and that can be donned in a second after the fair rider dismounts. Thus equipped, the bloomer girl becomes conventionally dressed the instant she leaves her wheel, and she may walk up and down the street before all men perfectly at her ease and as inconspicuous as any other skirted but bloomerless woman in sight. The detachable skirt is very light and may be rolled up in a tiny bundle and carried on the wheel." In New York City, reported Eaton, many women devotees of the rational costume "are riding men's diamond framed wheels in preference to the lower and less speedy loop framed bicycles. The bicycles for men are so much higher that a skirted woman cannot easily mount them, but the bloomer girl has no difficulty, whatever in reaching the more lofty seat, and her costume leaves her so free and untrammeled that the wheel no longer needs the unsightly dress guard."[21]

"Although the bloomer costume and divided skirt seem to closely resemble one another, the latter is a failure on the wheel, I am told," declared Eaton. "It is so much fuller than the bloomers that it draws up and collects in an

The Paris bloomer girl and her Chicago counterpart in 1894.

unsightly wad at the seat of the wheel when the rider mounts." Mentioned in the story was Mrs. J.E. McWilliams of Chicago who took "her first step to emancipation" one night when her bike had a flat tire and was useless. On that occasion she donned her husband's knickerbockers, appropriated his bicycle, and took a spin through the streets that night. "This form of costume, however, is rather extreme and hardly meets the approval of the majority of bloomer girls," said Eaton. "The same statement may also apply to the knickerbockers worn by Mrs. Neta Jean Boardman, the pioneer bloomerized young woman of New York. She began riding in rather tight knickerbockers about a year ago and was at first followed by crowds. Today she attracts very little attention, but her costume is almost too conspicuous to be adopted by many women." Mrs. Boardman at first rode her wheel in conventional attire, but one day her skirt caught in a pedal, and she was thrown in front of a Broadway cable car. At that point she was determined to wear knickerbockers rather than run such a risk again. Eaton observed that in France the women cyclists had willfully taken to the rational costume and "with women the world over the wheel seems to be the thing, and judging from the rapidly increasing popularity of the rational wheeling costumes among the fair sex of the earth the bicycle is the best card in the whole dress reform pack." Eaton concluded, "When Frances E. Willard not only urges all womankind to ride a wheel, but to ride a wheel in bloomers, the spirit of emancipations is indeed stalking across the earth in bifurcated garments.... In these fin de siècle days, however, the true 'end of the century' woman cyclist seems to be the brave bicycle girl with the baggy bloomers."[22]

As of the end of August 1894 Lady Henry Somerset and Miss Frances Willard had organized a big society in England and proposed to duplicate that group in the United States, the purpose of which was the popularizing of bicycle riding among women. But, stated a reporter, "the real object of these two eminent reformers, however, is to bring about dress reform among women, through the medium of sport." In the opinion of this newsman, "Every former effort to get women to wear bloomers and breeches in public has failed, and it has been decided to devote attention to bicycling solely." Bicycle rides had been established by the organization with the towns along the way having been laid out "so that women accompanied by men can go from one bicycling station to another, and everything is done for the convenience of the riders. The only condition is that they shall wear breeches or bloomers, and English women have accepted this condition with great alacrity." According to the article, "Lady Henry declares that the movement is the entering wedge of real dress reform."[23]

An article by Ada Cone that appeared in August 1894 described bathing and bicycling dress for women in France and Europe where, generally speaking, "the French feminine world seems to have taken to the bicycle with an ardor all the more fervid for being late, and the Paris dressmakers have had the problem thrust upon them of a suitable dress for this exercise also." The French cycle woman stood forth, therefore, "in trousers undisguised. The significant part of the matter is that the pretext is seized by a considerable number of women to promenade on foot in trousers, and a common sight in Paris of late is women in groups of twos and threes on the boulevards without any machine at all. Nobody stares any more. It is a bicycle woman, they reflect, and there is a machine somewhere; at home perhaps, but no matter; a reason is comprehended for the dress, and so it is felt to be justified." Cone continued, "Thus another wheel of woman's chariot is turned, quietly, irrevocably, and without rolling over any corpses of hostile thought. Years ago Mrs. Bloomer tried a revolution which ended in jeers; today a more radical dress is accepted with complaisance. This it is to interpret and not precede a demand." According to Cone, "In a great store in Paris I came the other day upon the section of a woman's bicycle dress, and I thought I had got into the men's department. There were piles on piles of trousers all alike and stacks of jackets and gaiters."[24]

When a lengthy article was published in a New York City newspaper in September 1894 it began by observing that the question "Shall women ride the bicycle?" was no longer open for discussion, because "she has settled it for herself—affirmatively. And all that men can find to say against it will not affect the result one whit, except perhaps, in strengthening her determination—that being the general effect of opposition upon the feminine mind." The account went on to add, "Only a few years ago, in this country, the wearing of trousers, even under a long riding skirt, was denounced by many foolish persons—especially those who were not riders—as indecent. But women quickly found that

A French bicycle costume, 1894.

the trousers were not only safer and more comfortable than skirts, but were very often conservative of modesty, and to-day no one even notices a lady going by to or from a riding school in conspicuously evident trousers and with her riding skirt conveniently thrown over her arm." A tilting saddle was devised for women to make mounting a bicycle easier and to prevent the pointed end of the saddle from contacting the point of a woman's spine and causing injury. Also noted was the fact that a woman's bike was not as strong as a man's, due to its U shape, and weaker frame. "Every consideration of precedence, decency and good taste, then is on the side of radical reforms in woman's dress for what has become and must continue [as] one of the main enjoyments of her outdoor life," asserted the article. "The French, who admittedly lead in matters of fashion, having adopted the bicycle with enthusiasm, have naturally exhibited much artistic taste, even genius, is designing costumes for it." Several female cycling costumes were described in the article and, said the reporter, and "not one of them violates the nicest modesty prescribed by good sense. Nevertheless many women in this country will hesitate to adopt the new substitutes for skirts, though conscious of their great desirability, simply from fear of inviting the reprehensive remarks of prudes, or the unwelcome notice of yahoos. General adoption of the new style will double come in time."[25]

Also in September 1894 it was noted, "One of the sights of Central Park on pleasant afternoons is to see the procession of women bicyclists who ride in bloomers and seem to rejoice in their emancipation from skirts. They have ceased to excite astonishment and almost comment, and certainly demonstrate the common sense and appropriateness of a dress that is not only cool, sensible and comfortable, but modest and becoming." The latest bicycles for women were then being made without the drop frame, it was reported, "and we may expect to be able to discriminate between the sexes when on wheels only by the fullness of the trousers and character of the back hair." An "authority on the subject" told a journalist "the majority of women will always prefer the drop bar as being more distinctive and feminine, even though they weigh considerably more and have drawbacks in other ways." In the concluding remarks the reporter asserted, "The rapid spread of the bicycle habit among women is really amazing, and all classes and conditions of them are to be found on the road."[26]

A brief report from Paris in October 1894 declared, "What is called the rational cycling costume for women is in danger of going out of existence in Paris, for the prefect has caused letters to be written to some well-known women cyclists, cautioning them that they are infringing the law in wearing men's clothes."[27]

In a general article about various pastimes, in October 1894, the reporter declared, "The sudden craze for bicycling among women is one of those pecu-

IN ORDINARY COSTUME.

SKIRTS THAT ARE OUT OF THE WAY.

A WOMAN'S BICYCLE

A GOOD DESIGN FROM "VOGUE."

A lengthy article in 1894 in a New York City newspaper discussed the topic of women and cycling and illustrated the piece with these four sketches.

liar and sensible developments which no man can account for. For some years there have been women riders, but it is only recently that the sport has taken possession of the sex in the shape of a fashionable fad." With respect to the costume they would wear in the coming months he speculated they would wear loose gowns like riding habits and gaiters, unless "they imitate our cousins across the water and wear breeches. Some of these breeches have penetrated to this country, and a few women were seen wearing them at the summer resorts, but in

Europe they are not uncommon." The coat of the costume was like a man's frock coat, and reached nearly to the knee. In addition, "it is double breasted, and fits close to the figure. Any sort of man's hat is worn. The breeches are simply loose knickerbockers. Gaiters come from the shoe up to the knee." According to this account, "There is a law in most cities against a woman wearing man's apparel, but it can safely be said [it is] not to apply to the bicycle costume, which is made expressly for women; but there is no reason visible to the naked eye why a woman bicycle rider should not borrow her brother's knickerbockers, if he has a pair, or why he should not borrow hers. So far as one can judge, both garments are the same." Also addressed was the idea of women riding alone. "Simultaneously with the appearance of bicycle riding among society women of the city it can be confidently predicted that there will be bicycle parties given, for no one expects girls to go riding alone, and it is a sure thing that there will be plenty of men who are ready to accompany them."[28]

When the women of France took up bicycling, said one newsman in August 1894, "it was not to be supposed that if French women accepted the wheel they would accept with it the costumes designed by English and American women. And they didn't. They designed new costumes that were advanced." And, he asserted, "every former effort to get women to wear bloomers or knickerbockers or divided skirts has failed.... Less than a year ago a woman dressed in such a costume attracted unpleasant attention when she went out on her wheel. If nature intended her for [to wear] such a costume she may attract admiration now, but there is no leering with it."[29]

A very brief article appeared in December 1894 that was about fashion only and featured a cycling costume brought out by Alfred Day, the well-known tailor. It was a tweed outfit in colors of chestnut brown and gray.[30]

In the same month, an article that originated from London, England,

This 1894 costume came from Alfred Day, the well-known tailor, and accompanied one of an increasing number of articles that were solely concerned with selling fashion items to women while using cycling as a backdrop.

remarked that in France, and Paris especially, "knickerbockered women on bicycles can be seen by the hundreds on Sunday afternoons. Probably if they could see the ridiculous appearance they present, with their baggy knickers and spindle shanks, they would discard the new costume forever, but the fact remains that, while foreign women cyclists have universally adopted the Zouave style of lower garment, most English women who go cycling prefer the older fashioned and more graceful manner of raiment." The journalist also felt it was worthy of remark that the few who donned the knickerbockers invariably "carry a little bundle tied behind them which looks suspiciously like a spare skirt. Very likely the extra costume is for use in cases of emergency, such as when a strict landlady refuses to acknowledge the right of the wearer of baggy attire to a seat in the dining room unless the knickers are hidden from sight."[31]

Ike Johnston was said to be a cycling authority in New York City and taught many of the females in the elite group the Four Hundred to ride bicycles. In another December 1894 article Johnston claimed that petticoats "in no way interfere with swift, safe and graceful cycling. He does not believe in bloomers or bifurcated skirts; he pronounced the conventional costume 'all right,' simply requesting his pupils to wear plain walking dresses when learning to ride." He taught in two large academies "where smart women" were found everyday learning to ride. "There is never a knickerbocker to be seen about the place. Popular pictures showing girls and matrons in trousers are a libel upon the genuine society woman," continued Johnston. "She has never for an instant contemplated such garb, and would scorn to be seen without her wide French skirt—untrimmed, it is true, but with a silk petticoat beneath—and ready at a moment's notice to step down and out upon Broadway." Johnston added, "The idea that the bicycle is to revolutionize female attire is an utterly exploded idea. Unless women of wealth and position agree to adopt a dress reform there is not the smallest chance of its winning success. Just at first these recognized sartorial leaders were uncertain as to what the cycle might demand of them; but having mastered the wheel they unhesitating[ly] pronounce 'reform' as both ungraceful and unnecessary." Pupils, Johnston said, needed five one-hour lessons to be expert cyclists and "Except at sunrise in the park, one seldom sees a fashionable woman on her wheel in New York City. As a rule they avoid all publicity, and depend upon country lanes and high roads for cycling."[32]

Still in December 1894 a reporter posed the question as to what kind of costume women should wear when riding bicycles. "This question is being widely debated within and without the family circles of the fair riders. The divided skirt, which was first adopted by the women riders, has become unpopular because it is considered cumbersome. There are, however, even more objections to the bloomer costume. It is not only clumsy and trouble-

A LESSON IN MOUNTING.

A LESSON IN DISMOUNTING.

Illustrations from 1895 showing how women were taught to ride a bicycle in a New York City academy.

A LESSON WITH THE STRAP.

some, but it seemed ugly as well, and is not only strongly objected to by the fathers, brothers and male friends of the fair riders, but of the women themselves." He continued by noting, "Having one and all of them concluded that a woman, no matter who she may be, can look only a fright in the horrid bloomers, they have pronounced their edict against that particular style of costume in strong terms, and the consequence is it must go." However, that meant the question remained as to what would replace bloomers, "granted that the above styles of costumes are to be banished." In response to that query he wrote, "According to the bicycle costume makers and the teachers of bicycle riding in this city, there are now two styles of dress which have adherents among the women riders. One is composed of neat-fitting knickerbockers, with a short skirt, a single or double breasted sack-coat, and suitable hose and shoes.... Henry Strugnell, the cyclists' outfitter, is of the opinion that the costume will be the one generally worn in the future." Another style of bicycle dress advocated by O.D. Bartlett of the Gormully and Jeffery Bicycle School—which he told the reporter was coming into fashion with a considerable number of the pupils—"Consists of tights, a skirt not too long, weighed at the bottom and lined with silk, and single or double breasted coats."[33]

In April 1895 fashion writer Ellen Osborn observed, "There are as many cycle outfits [and] tailor-bicycle costumes in the shops this spring as there are tea gowns. The ready-made suits are in two pieces—blazer and bloomers. The women who have their bicycle suits made get them sometimes in three pieces and sometimes in two, which means that there are always bloomers, and that there may or may not be skirts also." She argued the discourse was said to be mainly upon skirts because knickerbockers "have no longer the fascination of faddism." Knickers had become so proper that the fin de siècle girl, who cared only for that thing that was a trifle risqué, didn't have to wear them. "They will stand on their own legs in the future, to be worn or not to be worn, as they prove or fail to prove themselves the most practicable garments for cycling." Osborn felt the woman who was able to pay from $60 to $80 for a thoroughly up-to-date and conventional wheeling dress was out on the boulevards that spring in a pepper and salt melton skirt, made to open on the sides instead of in the back, and coming down to the top of the shoes. That skirt was scant or full, according to the rider's figure and was lined with a very heavy silk or with farmer's satin. Under it she wore bloomers or, very possibly, equestrian tights, buttoned just below the knees. A single button cutaway coat, with a shirt waist or a silk blouse gave her "the smart look so necessary to her peace of mind." Osborn said the girl she was talking about got her fashions from London while the girl from Paris "rides in a very much shorter skirt.... Bicycle riders adhere to a very righteous code that, if skirts are not to be long enough to be skirts, it is really more in accord with the proprieties to drop them frankly, stand upon the necessities of the occasion, and come out bravely in knickers."[34]

The knickers of 1895 were, wrote Ellen Osborn, numerous and varied, and "the full knickers, like the divided skirts, are hideous and not especially convenient. They're not worth the cost of a revolution in society. There are times when compromises won't work. This is one of them. It's a choice between the conventional and the radical—skirts and fairly close-fitting knickers. There's no good foothold on any middle ground." Ready-made cycling suits testified to the popularity of the activity and all the big shops were said to be full of them with the cost of such costumes ranging from $12 to $112. "The cheapest ones are as hideous as ready-made bathing suits, but the shop girl who spends her spare change to hire a machine will soon teach the shop to treat her better." In Osborn's opinion the bloomers had come to stay and that meant the question arose as to where to draw the line. She said she heard of a landlady with a boarder who wore her bicycling costume (bloomers) around the house. The landlady said to her, "I won't have it. It's all right to wear 'em bicycling, if the others do, I 'spose, but you can't wear 'em in my house." The boarder replied that there was nobody else in the house to see them. Said Osborn, "But, after all, the landlady was right, and the boarder wasn't. Just as soon as the mysterious 'they' wear bloomers in ballrooms, or rings in their noses, it will be quite right for one lone woman to do so, and not much before. For there's luck in odd numbers, only when the numbers are so large that they have ceased to be odd." Still, argued Osborn, "a considerable extension of what we may call the bloomer principle has proved possible. Obviously bifurcated unmasculine specimens of the genus homo were observed skating in Central Park last winter, and in more authoritative London. Bloomers are recognized as suitable for walking trips, shooting tramps—few of these are taken by women in the country." Concluded Osborn, "Perhaps the landlady will be less obdurate by and by, and perhaps she won't. There is only one safe rule in matters of fashion, and that is that one never can tell."[35]

The women of Orlando, Florida, were reportedly all excited over the bloomer question, in May 1895. Some two months earlier the women in that city formed a bicycle club and at a recent regular monthly meeting the question of adopting a costume came up. One woman at that meeting introduced a resolution requiring members to adopt "the bloomer costume." That resolution led to a heated debate with the main opposition coming from half a dozen young women who were all engaged to be married. "Their lovers objected to their riding bicycles," said the reporter, "and that if they appeared in bloomers they were sure their lovers would abandon them altogether." Some of the matrons in the club were also bitterly against the resolution, declaring that they would quit the club before they would disgrace themselves by appearing in such "heathenish" garb. However, the advocates of bloomers were in a majority and carried the resolution. In response to that the opponents of bloomers immediately withdrew from the club saying that they would also boycott socially the women who appeared in such costume. As well, they threatened to go before the town council and secure the passage of an ordinance forbidding women to appear on the street in bloomers. Everybody in the town had taken sides in the controversy and the feeling between the bloomer and anti-bloomer factions was described as "warm." Meanwhile, in Victoria, British Columbia, Canada, the police had declared themselves against bloomers and would not allow them to be worn on the streets, and the city fathers of Westport, Missouri, had commenced a crusade against them, which the reporter thought was likely to succeed. In contrast this rational garb was reported to being very popular in some of the higher education institutions for women—notably at Ann Arbor, Michigan, where many of the 600 students had adopted bloomers for daily wear. The young women cyclists of Grand Rapids, Michigan, had also decided to adopt the bloomer costume.[36]

In a June 1895 piece that appeared originally in a New York City newspaper an unnamed woman doctor was cited as saying, "As regards the matter of costume, I think the long skirt is bound to go. It looks out of place on a bicycle, and is certainly much in the way. The truth of the matter is that no costume which can be devised is going to make women appear at their very best on a bicycle." She continued by declaring, "The very position that they assume and the constant movement of the limbs up and down prohibit a graceful appearance. The delight of the exercise, however, more than compensates for any drawback of this kind, and most wheel-women are willing enough to look even awkward in order the enjoy the sport." The impression seemed to prevail, she argued, that for a woman bicyclist to decry skirts was to proclaim herself unfeminine, and somewhat more immodest than her conventional sisters. The physician said that such was not the case, but rather, "in my opinion, for a woman to ride in bloomers, with a skirt over them, which is continually blowing up and showing the bloomers beneath, is far more indelicate than for the bloomers to be in evidence from the start." The wearing of the skirt suggested that there was something to conceal and where the bloomers only were worn it was a frank intimation that the rider recognized the nature of her undertaking and had dressed herself appropriately. With respect to the display of a woman's ankle, she declared, "I do not see why it is more vulgar than to show her arms and part of her spinal column in evening dress. There would be nothing vulgar in a woman's sitting with her foot up, if she had on a divided skirt gathered at the knee, or even bloomers, but when she has on an ordinary flowing skirt and elevates her foot ever so little, the aspect is entirely different." Continuing, she stated, "I fail to see where the long skirt worn when riding a bicycle conveys an idea of modesty. In the first place, the motion of the limbs, which it is intended to conceal, it shows much more plainly than the bloomers or full trousers. As a woman sits on a bicycle the plain front breadths of the skirt fit smoothly over the knees; no other skirt is usually worn beneath it, and the peddling up and down of the limbs looks anything like graceful."[37]

This unnamed physician did, though, like the divided skirt, because "these divided skirts are made very long, are gathered at the knee and fall over so many inches that the effect around the bottom is plain and smooth like the edge of a skirt. They are very wide, and the extreme fullness entirely obviates any suggestion of the vulgar." A reporter then asked the doctor about what sort of costume the stout woman could wear. "Alas, there is no way of making a stout woman look well on a wheel. If she wears a long skirt she is in danger of sudden death, and if she wears bloomers she is in danger of adverse criticism, even more deserved than that vouchsafed to her slim sisters. The riding will benefit her so much, however, that it behooves her to make the venture and enjoy herself, whether she looks well or not." Next, the reporter asked another woman, also unnamed, what she thought about bloomers for bicycle wear. That woman, described as one "whose opinions are much sought after," replied, "I think they are atrocious. The idea of a woman in trousers, modified or unmodified, is particularly repugnant to me. If women can't engage in a certain species of amusement without making targets of themselves and raising all this hubbub of criticism I say let them leave it alone and confine themselves to gentler pastimes." This prominent woman wondered how a woman could enjoy any amusement, however charming, when she knew that everyone was staring at her. "If women can't ride the bicycle in skirts, let the bicycle go. The skirts are a long-established institution, a badge of woman's dignity and reserve and feminine grace." That woman concluded by declaring, "The bicycle is a new diversion, and it seems to me an enormity that for it woman must nearly fling aside all traditional distinctiveness of garb and much else besides, for when the skirts go a number of abstract attributes of recognized excellence will go with them. I am an advocate of everything that makes woman healthful, but she should hang on to her femininity first and last."[38]

In a historical article that appeared in June 1895 its journalist remarked that about 30 years earlier a stage production called *The Black Crook* was produced at Niblo's Garden in New York City and the occasion was a notable one. "For the first time on the American stage, women appeared in public in silk tights and without skirts. The sensation produced by this entirely unprecedented display of the feminine form seems strange to us of a later generation, who have been accustomed to Amazonian marches, skirt dancers, living pictures and all the other devices for the exhibition of legs." Clergymen denounced the play from the pulpit and respectable newspapers in more than one instances preached against it editorially, and refused its advertisements, said the newsman. For months the playhouse on Broadway was packed night after night with audiences that consisted largely of men, all anxious to see the "splendid display of undraped beauty." Then when interest began to pall, one or two "variety theater managers of the lower order" gave plays in which cancan dancing was a prominent feature. "In these playhouses the principal attraction was a display of legs, for the most part of ample proportions, attired in underclothes and stockings of the fashion of the day. At a critical moment in the performance a strong light was thrown on the stage and the women lifted their skirts well above their knees and performed a clumsy cancan, which was at best a vulgar and inartistic imitation of the real Parisian article, to be seen now and then at the French and Arion balls." This journalist added that from the time of *The Black Crook* the struggle for the emancipation of women's legs from "the thralldom of skirts" had been going on, but it was not until about one year earlier that old-fashioned prejudice was overcome to such an extent that on the stages of reputable theaters and even on the public highways in 1895 the public was treated to exhibitions of feminine curves which would have been impossible a decade earlier. "The stage and the bicycle are responsible for this, and news that women of social position are not afraid to show themselves in Central Park with their lover limbs encased in close-fitting knickerbockers and stockings, some of the philosophers of the town are beginning to wonder how much further the custom will be carried." Miss Georgie Parker was a popular entertainer in the vaudeville houses for a "great many years" and she spoke about the new order—how changes in bicycle costumes led to responses on the stage—by saying, "When a man can go out in Central Park and see a dozen pairs of well-shaped legs in tight-fitting knickerbockers for nothing, he won't pay to go to the theater unless he can see a great deal more." And, she continued, "as for this talk about such displays being immodest, that is merely a matter of public opinion, and public opinion regarding matters of this sort has changed a great many times." The author of this piece concluded, "Just how far this end-of-the-century fashion will be carried it is difficult to tell, but there are some who affirm that before the present year is over New York will see women in pink tights walking and bicycling through the open streets."[39]

The Knickerbocker Cycling Club of Chicago had reportedly attained prominence in June 1895 as an organization of women who had discarded skirts when riding bicycles and adopted knickerbockers and leggings instead. There were about 50 members in the club, which to that date demanded no fees nor dues and boasted no officers. The president was Mrs. K.B. Cornell, at whose home the club was first organized with about 20 members. Said Cornell, "I have always ridden in knickerbockers because I consider them much more suitable and modest than a skirt which blows about. When I am out for a run I wear a full suit of woolen underwear, gaiters and knickerbock-

Nine ideas for bicycle costumes submitted to a Chicago newspaper by its readers in 1895.

ers of men's suiting, a loose blouse and a jacket." She added that she wished to make it known to the reporter and to the people of Chicago that "there are literally no 'bloomers' worn on bicycles. Bloomers are drawn in at the ankle. So are Turkish trousers, but knickerbockers, loose or tight fitting, come only to the knee." Cornell declared, "It is curious that the disagreeable remarks made to us [when the group was out cycling] are not from men, but from boys and women." Remarks hurled their way included "How scandalous." Concluded Cornell, "Of course the members of the Knickerbocker club use their wheels for amusement and want to ride in the most comfortable fashion.... We are by no means a collection of eccentrics, but simply women who want a good time with the fewest drawbacks."[40]

In that same month an Englishman was said to have invented a cycling gown designed along new lines. It was a convertible costume, suitable for the promenade or for cycling, golfing and even mountaineering. Off the bicycle it represented itself as a full-length skirt, adapted for home wear. Knickerbockers were worn beneath it, and gaiters, if desired. The skirt was made to button on either side and when the woman mounted her cycle she simply unfastened a few of the buttons on the sides of the skirt and the garment fell loosely about her figure.[41]

"Should women wear bloomers?" was the question posed in the headline of an article that appeared in July 1895. A letter had been mailed out by the newspaper to a "selected list of ladies." It read, in part, "Bloomers have been made the subject of many flippant references by the professional paragrapher and those opposed to the garb on principle have made virulent attacks against its use. However, bicycling is now recognized as a healthful and pleasurable pastime by many who formerly ridiculed it. The subject of what a woman should wear when bicycling is an important one." The letter then asked its recipients their opinions of the query "Should women wear bloomers?" A number of the replies received by the paper were printed. One woman, noted, with respect to bloomers, "They may be objectionable, but surely they are the least objectionable of any style of dress yet tried. Men find the narrow legs of their trousers of sufficient danger to justify them in wearing patent fastenings to hold the trousers close around the ankle; surely this danger cannot be compared to that of a flowing dress skirt." She continued, "No danger in a short skirt? Well, perhaps not; but any kind of a skirt compels a woman to ride a drop frame machine. Approve of diamond frame for ladies? Yes, a diamond frame and bloomers." Said Mrs. Frank Wiggins, "Every man who rides a bicycle for pleasure, business or health tries to get the lightest machine he can possible get. No drop frame can possible be made as light as a diamond frame; and if the light frames are preferable for men they certainly are for women."[42]

Another example of the attempt to join the fashion industry to cycling

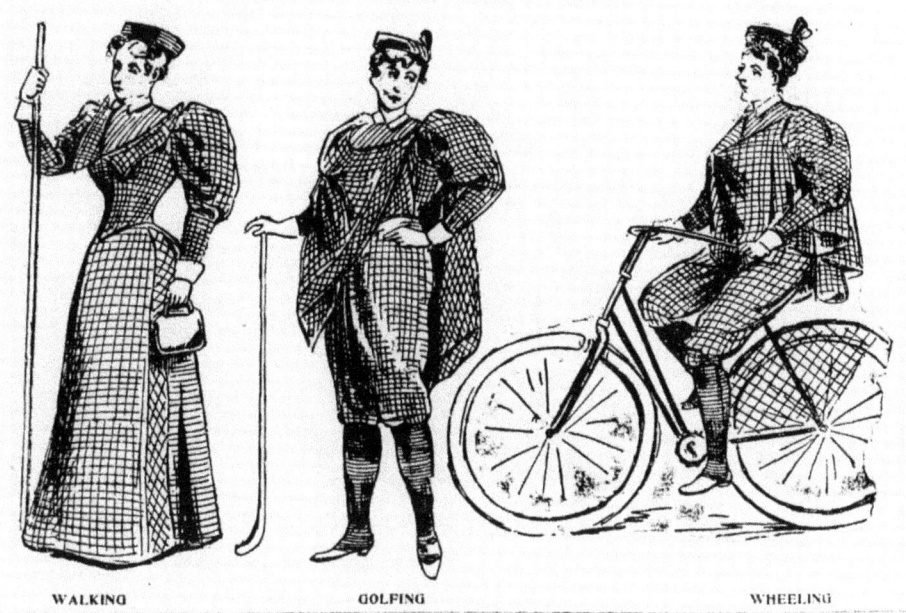

THE NEW CONVERTIBLE COSTUME

WALKING — GOLFING — WHEELING

HAVE NO USE FOR SKIRTS

A Chicago Club Dresses in Knickerbockers When Out Wheeling

TALKS WITH THE OFFICERS

They Tell Why the Club Prefers the New Style of Dress and Also Relate Some of Their Experiences

Walking, golfing and wheeling outfits for women who had no use for skirts, 1895.

women could be seen in an article that was published in August 1895. It featured an illustration of six designs of bicycle costumes that had been produced by "well-known tailors and all have been tried and found to be as practicable as they are becoming." The sketches were reproduced through the courtesy of Stephens and Hickok, the local (Los Angeles) agents of the Columbia Bicycle Company. Costume number one was designed and worn by Mrs. Jenness-

The magazine *Puck* looked at the bicycle as the great dress reformer of the 19th century, 1895.

Miller who had named her creation "Columbia." It consisted of trousers "designed to look as much like a divided skirt as possible.... The trousers are gathered to a band at the knee." Number two was by Redfern of New York and London, "consisting of a short skirt worn over knickerbockers of the same material." Costume number three was designed and worn by Georgia Cayvan and consisted of Zouave trousers and an Eton jacket. Number four was another design from Redfern and was said to be the costume for bicycling most favored in France; it consisted of bloomers with a Norfolk coat. Costume five was a design by Gosta Kraemer of New York City and featured a medium plain skirt and a modification of the Eton jacket. Number six was a second design by Gosta Kraemer and consisted of trousers that were very full and gathered to a band buttoning at the knee.[43]

"If a woman will follow the pursuits of a man, will become an equal in work and ambitions, she must have a practical costume." said Mrs. Russell Sage, in August 1895. "She cannot wait to grasp her skirts if; she must grasp a particular car railing; she cannot wait for her skirts if she must be at the office in time to begin work with her brother. The women of leisure need take no part in the demand for reform dress, only inasmuch as she chooses to assist her working sister." Margaret Sage was a famous philanthropist of this era. In 1869 she married famed robber baron Russell Sage. She continued,

These six designs for bicycle outfits were submitted in 1895 to a newspaper by well-known designers.

"But as a street or walking dress we need a uniform which can be worn till worn out on every outdoor occasion. This need not embrace coat, vest, necktie, etc., but should essentially contain all—but only all—it calls for—a comfortable, practical walking costume, whether bloomer, divided skirt or pantalets, with any feminine variations of which it will reasonable admit." She concluded, "On a bicycle, of course, I cannot see how a woman would attempt to ride without the bloomer."[44]

An article from August 1895 predicted the coming of the bloomer girl in the coming year with subheads that included "Corsets and leggings have been discarded" and "Bloomers are also rapidly shrinking and soon will dwindle into plain close-fitting knickerbockers." Speculating on the future of bloomers the reporter declared, "A year ago women who blushed at the mere mention of bloomers now wear them baldly, defiantly and gracefully. True, the bloomers are almost as voluminous as skirts, but at any place frequented by women cyclists about the metropolitan district, it is quite apparent that the bloomers are shrinking slowly but surely." Soon, it was predicted, "the bloomer will have shrunk into tightly-fitting knickerbockers." The journalist also stated, "It is easy to see that the general downfall of the corset is near at hand. Bicyclers will not only discard it when wheeling, but also in ordinary street wear. Women who are not wheelers will also eventually come to the knowledge that they can get along without it, just as surely as shorter skirts and bloomers will be universally worn a few years hence." He went on to point out that the French costume was well ahead of that worn in the United States, and commented, "There is an exaggerated idea that all the French bicycle costumes are dreadfully indelicate. From the accompanying illustrations it can be seen that they are not so terrible after all." The bloomers worn by the Parisian female were very full, "giving no indication of what is enclosed.

A trio of Parisienne cyclists in 1895.

They fasten at the knee with straps, but from the knee down to the instep the leg is exposed boldly." In conclusion the article said, "It is claimed that the circumference of the bloomer will rapidly decrease until it fits the leg snugly. Cold matter-of-fact common sense is the one rule governing cyclists' costumes these days, no attention whatever being paid to precedent or conventionality. This will make the life of the full bloomer of short duration."[45]

Also in August 1895 the city council of White Pigeon, Michigan, was petitioned, wrote a reporter, "by a considerable body of the citizens" therein to prohibit women from wearing bloomers on the street. Part of the petition alleged that horses were scared by the bloomer apparitions. It was also noted that in Coldwater, Michigan, some of the women cyclists had recently moved out of the bloomer stage and took to "men's knickerbockers and gold stockings."[46]

A journalist mentioned a reporter, in August 1895, in another newspaper "who feels some concern less the female woman commonly referred to as the new woman, may invade the sacred domain of man and appropriate his trousers" and was therefore moved to ask the question that also formed the headline of his piece, "What is male attire?" He then cited the fact that from early times in Europe and America, it had been considered "the height of impropriety for the sex[es] to exchange costumes," but was grieved to see that the bloomer and knickerbocker women bicyclists were then unsettling the question. He viewed with alarm the encroachments of the new woman. He had seen her appropriate the hat, collar, shirt front and vest, as well as the coat, of the sterner sex, and now, with the hope the line may be drawn at the trousers, "he cries aloud against the bloomer." A second part of that article claimed there was a great deal of trouble in the Toronto School Board over the "bloomer outbreak." One of its members had recently made a motion that the school inspectors be required to report to the board the names of all women teachers who rode bicycles "in male attire, commonly called bloomers." He insisted that they were immodest and unbecoming and furnished a bad example to the young girls who were attending the public schools. However, that motion lost when it was tabled after the board discovered a statute that barred women from wearing men's clothing. It was somehow hoped that the by-law would solve the problem. That is, the buck was passed. Concluded the reporter, "In a number of cities there are ordinances which prohibit the men and women from wearing the garments of the opposite sex and this appears to be the most effectual way to check the advance of the bloomer. However, if the law should hold that the bloomer was invented by a woman for women, 'where are we at?'"[47]

In an article the following month a composite illustration featured some of the latest styles in cyclists' bloomers then being worn by female bikers at Golden Gate Park in San Francisco.[48]

An ad for women's bikes that appeared in September 1895 displayed one made for women who preferred to wear knickerbockers "rather than cumbersome skirts." However, from the illustration it looked like a regular man's bicycle.[49]

According to a story in September 1895, "The bicycle girl who has been in doubt as to the propriety and modesty of the bloomer garb need have no further quiverings of conscience as far as this matter is concerned, for the Fellowship of Ethical Research has set its stamp of approval upon the much discussed garment, which some cycling women wear, and others wish to don, but lack the courage." The question of the moral influence of the bicycle formed the subject of an address that Dr. Isaac Hull Platt of Lakewood, New Jersey, delivered before the Fellowship of Ethical Research in Philadelphia. Platt said the bicycle and the bloomer were all right, "so that settled it." The wheel was heralded by Platt as "the emancipator of feminine thralldom" and he was especially favorable in his commendation of bicycling for women and in "her espousal of a rational dress." Platt did not allow himself to be drawn off into a discussion of the relative merits of divided skirts, the compromise of short skirt and leggings, out-and-out bloomers, or the extreme of costumes

SOME OF THE LATEST STYLES IN BLOOMERS AT THE PARK.
[Sketched by a "Call" artist.]

A collection of sketches of various types of bloomers worn by female bikers in 1895 in San Francisco's Golden Gate Park.

as exemplified in Mary Walker trousers. Instead, the article said, "He confined his attacks to the unwieldy skirts, which shackle the limbs of women in general and the bicycle woman in particular 'as a ball and chain on a prisoner's ankle,' and discreetly left the mooted question of trousers or compromise skirts for after consideration." Reportedly, Platt was consistent, and "he clothed his facts as plainly as he would have the bicycle woman cloth herself. When he meant leg he did not say limb. It was a point in his remarks that when society ceased to insist that women moved about on wheels, and conceded that they were bipeds, half the victory for rational dress was achieved." Said Platt, "I believe that there is no single influence at work which is doing so much for the emancipation of woman as her use of the bicycle. Insomuch as

An 1895 ad for a woman's bicycle specially designed for females who wore knickerbockers.

she uses it, it takes her from the maddening monotony of the continual journey from the cook stove to the sink.... It gives her self-confidence and independence and, what is by no means of the least importance, it promises to give her a rational costume by at last relegating the skirt into innocuous desuetude." He continued, "That a reasonable human being should ever adopt a long skirt as an article of daily apparel is incredible. It must have been forced upon women in some prehistoric age of her lord and master to mark her servitude, and to act as a shackle to hamper her movements and prevent her from getting away, as a ball and chain are attached to the ankle of a prisoner. Imagine a man going about his daily avocation in a long skirt." Platt added, "I suppose that every individual over the age of 2 years and not an idiot is aware of the fact that a normal woman has two legs, and yet for some reason, utterly unaccountable, it has been the convention for countless ages for her to go through the shallow farce of pretending that she has none." Concluded Platt, "Now that she has learned to ride a bicycle she finds the skirt more inconvenient than ever before, besides being dangerous and immodest. In a fit of desperation she is discarding it, and it would seem that before long she will stand before the world as the equal of man, a free and acknowledged biped. If the bicy-cle should have no other moral influence than this, it would be far from little."[50]

A month later, in October 1895, a report that originated in a New York City newspaper declared that the "all absorbing problem of the hour, the woman's bicycle suit, is not yet resolved." To be convinced of that conclusion it was only necessary to stroll along any thoroughfare frequented by women bicyclists, as "many are the attempts that have been made to solve the problem, but so far all have failed. Skirted, or bloomered, or knickerbockered, or whatever she be, it is rare indeed to encounter a feminine figure that presents a graceful appearance on a bicycle." At first glance, continued the piece, "it would seem that no woman with the fatal gift of beauty had taken to the wheel; but the conclusion is almost wholly due to clothes, not to the woman. Comfort, as well as good looks, is still an unknown quantity in woman's bicy-cle costume." No matter the price of the costume, he concluded, "it is sure either to flap too much or to be too scant; it either drags or it bags; and, worst of all, if it is a skirt, it invariably 'rides up.'"[51]

Because Miss Alice Graeme "wore bloomers that looked nice on her shapely figure and rode a man's wheel the doors of the Bowman Riding Academy in New York have been shut against her," stated a reporter in February 1896. Management of the facility claimed to have found no fault with Graeme or her costume but declared that the ladies of the exclusive Michaux Club "were properly shocked," according to the story and "for this reason the young woman's bloomers ceased to bloom." Graeme was an actor rehearsing for a part in a bicycle play. Her part required her to ride a bicycle and so she went to the Bowman school for instruction. At certain hours at that academy the Michaux Club members frequented the same academy, where the women cycled around to the music of an orchestra. There was a rumor that Graeme's bloomers were "not as baggy as they might have been." According to the manager at the Bowman school, "Miss Graeme conducted herself in an extremely modest and ladylike manner but that the Michaux girls drew the line at bloomers in the academy."[52]

A wordy ad appeared in March 1896 that featured the Rambler bikes for

An 1896 sketch that ran along with an article about a woman who had been chastised for wearing bloomers at a bicycle academy.

women. Note the very long dress depicted on the rider. The bicycle in the advertisement cost $100 and was said to weigh just 25 pounds, which was quite light for the time period and much lighter than bikes that were just a few years older.[53]

Several ads appeared in different newspapers in March 1896 and each illustrated the fashionable aspects of cycling. One ad for the department store Le Bon Marché touted ladies' bicycle costumes, with the prices running from $6 to $18. Those suits came with caps, leggings, and other accessories. A second ad featured bicycle shoes, leggings, and other items while the third ad hyped a "practical demonstration of a ladies bicycle suit." A bicycle celebrity would be in a department store in person at a certain time to "demonstrate the suit."[54]

It was reported in May 1896 that another novelty introduced recently was a small leather bag intended to be suspended from a woman's belt. Its

This wordy ad in 1896 featured a Rambler bicycle for women. Note the very long dress, still being worn by some, despite the danger of the skirt getting caught in the machine.

Ladies' Bicycle Suits

And Outfits.

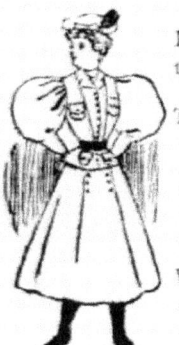 

We show a most complete line of Ladies' Bicycle outfits at perhaps the lowest prices in the city:

THE CUTS represent "The Star" style of Bicycle Suits, made in correct divided-skirt style, with flap that folds back—no bloomers necessary.

WE SHOW regular Bloomer Suits with skirts in a variety of styles, with belts and without. No catching up of skirt.

Prices range from **$6** to **$18** in fine all-wool cloth, in checks, plaids, etc.; also in linen, duck, etc. Suits made to measure; no extra charge. Prices of Suits include Leggings.

SEPARATE SKIRTS IN ALL STYLES.

| Caps and Hats —TO— Match Suits, $1.50. | LARGE LINE of Leggings in leather, canvas, corduroy, cloth and duck, 50c to $2.00. | All-Wool Sweaters, In Black, Navy, White, Red, and Tan, $2.98 up. |

We handle everything accessory to a complete costumer, such as tights, belts, etc.

BON MARCHE,
Ladies' Outfitters,
314-316 Seventh Street.

Above and the following two pages: A series of three items from 1896 about the marketing of extraneous items to the bicycling women as marketers and admen tried to take advantage of what was clearly an increasing trend of females adopting the wheel.

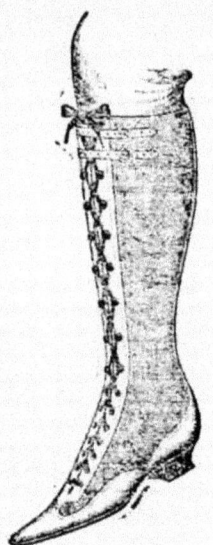

job was to hold change, tickets, and other little odds and ends that a man could store in his pockets but a woman, having no pockets, could not. New bicycle boots had also appeared on the market. They reached up to the knee and did away with the necessity of wearing gaiters. "As bicycling grows in popularity among women, tailor and dressmakers have combined all their

The Ladies Are Invited

TO ATTEND A PUBLIC DEMONSTRATION OF THE PRACTICABILITY AND UTILITY OF THE LATEST AND BEST

LADIES' BICYCLE SUIT,
WITH PATENTED SKIRT.

Miss Tanner, from the Madison Square Garden 'Cycle Show
AND LATER THE WASHINGTON 'CYCLE SHOW.

will be in attendance on our Second Floor each day during the week from 10 to 12 A. M. and 1 to 4 P. M.--dressed in the complete suit--and give exhibitions of mounting and dismounting from the wheel, showing you in the most convincing manner how superior this Suit is to all others.

At the conclusion of the exhibition at the store Miss Tanner will take a spin on the different roads radiating from Richmond, wearing this most popular skirt. Monday's run will be to the Lakeside Club-House.

The wheel Miss Tanner rides is one of the "Saks 'Cycle"--fully equal to the best $75 machine--and sold by us, with 12 months' guarantee, for $48.50.

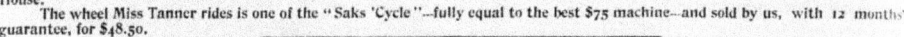

A. SAKS & COMPANY,
Eleventh and Main Streets.

efforts to evolve costumes, both suitable and comfortable for riders. That they have admirably succeeded, the happy, comfortable well satisfied appearance of this season's bicycle women seems to prove. The question of how to dress for the wheel no longer seems an insoluble one," declared a reporter. "A year ago 'to be or not to be,' as regards the bloomer, seemed to be the uppermost puzzle in all feminine bicycledom." Declared the newsman, "And now it seems to be satisfactorily decided that the bloomer will never become popular in this country. They are too ugly both on and off the wheel.... The modified divided skirt, which is so adroitly arranged that one can notice no singularity in its construction, is now universally adopted by women riders of all classes." It was made with a apron-front effect beneath, which fell upon the two divided skirts in such a way that when on the wheel the rider presented the same appearance as if she was wearing the ordinary skirt. The great advantage of that skirt arrangement was said to be that it permitted a woman to ride "the diamond frame without any inconvenience or ungraceful effect." Among other novelties introduced for the female biker was a bicycling glove that was a modification of the driving glove with the palm made of strong leather to wear much better than ordinary gloves, which wore out quickly.[55]

Dr. R.L. Dickinson, a well-known gynecologist in his time, considered at length in June 1896 costumes for women bicyclists, with his views first to health, second to grace, third to fashion, and fourth to comfort, although the fourth category ran through all the other considerations. In his view there were four costumes: (1) the full knickerbocker, (2) the fuller long bloomer, (3) the short skirt with leggings, and (4) the skirt to the top of the toe. "The last is decreed by fashion for the thin woman and leisurely rider on level roads, and for the shy woman it is a suitable garment," he thought. "One in this costume can step off the wheel into the house or shop in proper walking dress. But if the skirt is no more than two and half to three yards it is liable to catch in the rear sprocket. It is uncomfortable at the knee, as it has to lift up and forward half the weight of the skirt, and in a wind is difficult to manage." Dickinson felt the best combination for comfort was the separate jacket, skirt and shirt waist, for the body covering that could be taken off in hot rides was hygienically very desirable. He noted there were many devices for changing the long skirt into the short skirt and for converting the skirt into bloomers by means of tapes running through eyes and "the bloomer falling to the top of the calf, well hung, moderately full, with either leggings or stockings is modest and well adapted to the need." For the right woman, rightly designed, the doctor held it to be the

THE BLOOMER GIRL'S CONQUEROR

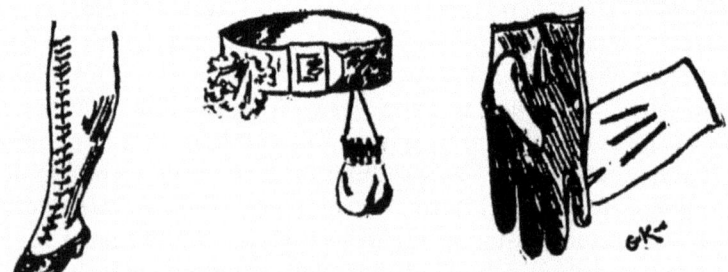

SOME ADJUNCTS OF THE BICYCLE GIRL

An outlandish costume for biking from 1896 along with a drawing of other necessary items.

most becoming costume. Also, it was reported, "the doctor holds that with the decline of prudery the closer fitting clothes for arduous work or for play will at no distant day find their natural place. Baggy sleeves have no place on the wheel; the Eton jacket is not ungraceful, but the longer jacket fitted at the back and loose in front is every way better." As for headgear, the doctor insisted on protection for the eyes. The "bicycle face," so-called was mainly "sun-scowl" and any hat should, therefore, have a sufficient visor, for "the usual feminine street hat, all feathers and flowers, is all out of place on the wheel." It was also noted that at a meeting of prominent medical specialists at the New York Academy of Medicine, in the discussion of bicycling for women by men who rode bikes themselves, each speaker had words of strong commendation for the exercise, "but each emphatically added a warning against riding in corsets and tight clothing."[56]

A writer grumbled in a June 1896 piece that women complained that no one had yet invented suitable underclothing for outdoor sports. Writers paid much attention to the length of outer skirts, the question of whether to wear bloomers or skirts, but nobody dealt with the question of unseen articles of clothing for bikers. "It has been established beyond controversy that a woman cannot wear the same underclothing while bicycling or enjoying other athletic sports that she finds suitable for her ordinary avocations," noted the newsman. "She may wear a set of garments while shopping, visiting, or even dancing, with comfort, that would be restrictive and awkward for bicycling." To begin with, the reporter stated, "the wheelwoman doesn't want muslin underwear. She has found that the delicate linens and embroideries and laces will not stand the wear and tear of hard riding ... this kind of underwear is heating and bulky, and causes discomfort in a dozen different ways." He thought there had been many attempts to persuade wheelwomen to wear tights, generally black, but the women did not like them because "they cling tightly and are too warm. What is needed is something loose-fitting, so that there shall be nothing to impede the free movement of the limbs. The silk knickerbockers that are wore next to the skin are the same shape as the bloomers outside, but not so full." When it came time for the wheelwoman to select a corset the greatest care had to be used. Under the corset was worn a little silk vest. A new bicycle corset was described as "only about eight inches from top to bottom, thus allowing free movement and escaping danger of being itself broken. Many women makeshift when they begin to ride the wheel by resurrecting a pair of half-worn corsets and allowing them to take the place of some specially made. But most of the corsets designed for ordinary use are too long for comfort in riding, besides being too heavily boned about the hip and stomach."[57]

An article that originally appeared in *Scribner's Magazine* and then was reprinted in newspapers in July 1896 discussed the role of the bicycle in female dress reform. It began by declaring, "It really begins to be debatable whether anything has happened to the human race since the first locomotive drew the first train of cars that will affect it so materially as the bicycle." Continuing on the piece stated, "Consider its effect on women. Within two years it has given to all American womankind the liberty of dress for which the reformers have been sighing for generations. The dress reform movement never seemed to affect any considerable number of women, or to modify women's clothes to any noticeable degree," and "the bicycle has not put many women into trousers—nothing will do that in this country—but it has given all women practical liberty to wear trousers if they want to, and, indeed, to get themselves into any sort of decent raiment which they find convenient for whatever enterprise they have in mind."[58]

One newsman claimed to have discerned the difference between wheelwomen in Chicago and wheelwomen in New York City, with respect to clothing. He said that in New York the girls who wore bloomers all wore leggings with them while in Chicago there was not one female bicyclist in 200 who wore leggings. They all went out in their stockings alone. Supposedly that reporter, based in Chicago, walked two blocks in his home city one afternoon and counted 22 young women cyclists who were dressed in bloomers "and not a single one of them had anything over their calves except stockings."[59]

An article that appeared in August 1896 said that Jeannette Gilder (a pioneer for United States women in journalism) was then in Paris and wrote to an eastern paper in America that she had been "much shocked by the boldness with which French women go in for startling eccentricity in costume, especially the cyclists." Said Gilder, "Every woman rode a man's wheel and every woman wore bloomers. Anything uglier than their costumes you cannot imagine." She added, "Bare legs were the worst. The most advanced women bicyclists wear low shoes, socks and the legs bare from the top of the sock to just below the knee. The only reason for such an exposure is vulgarity. Fancy a woman riding up Fifth Avenue with her legs bare from the knee down. How quickly she would be run in by a policeman."[60]

In September 1896 from London, England, author Marie Corelli wrote, "I do not ride a bicycle, have not invented a bicycle costume and entirely abhor bicycle riding for women. Men look sufficiently hideous and undignified on a bicycle, and women are worse than hideous, they are immodest." Corelli added, "The poet's idea of exquisite womanhood is utterly destroyed by the sight of these perspiring, red-faced, lank objects working their legs, treadmill fashion, in mere blatant feminine vulgarity."[61]

A brief fashion-only piece appeared in print in October 1896 praising a striped bicycle dress made of tweed. The piece contained much hyperbole and not much else as it touted a ridiculous costume.[62]

According to one reporter, writing in October 1896, "In Paris the bicycle girl is devoted to her bloomers. She has no use for a skirt. The fact is that the cycling woman of the French capital is apt to be somewhat daring in regard to her costume. At present she is not only riding in bloomers, but she has given up wearing long stockings, and has adopted socks. The socks she wears with low shoes. Thus a goodly portion of her bare leg is visible to the motley throng. But she doesn't seem to mind it in the least." And, the writer con-

This drawing was published in 1922 and showed a century of changes in cycling women from the hobby horse of 1819 to the modern rider of 1920, although there were hardly any women so engaged in that later year.

cluded, "this new fashion, however, is a little too Frenchy for the American girl, for, according to all accounts, she is still showing her old-time interest in bicycling hose."[63]

In the opinion of one journalist in January 1897, "The charm of a womanly woman is a real power. Her gentleness, her delicacy, her modesty are real forces. The girl who dresses like a man, who swaggers, who talks loudly, discusses risqué books and smokes cigarettes is like a soldier who has thrown away his weapons before he goes into battle." He went on to assert, "Her bicycle, for example, may be a good, useful thing, but she will not induce the public to approve of bicycles for women by appearing on it as an offensive caricature of a man. She will not win the world to her cause, however just, by disgusting it with herself. Why should any of our girls throw away the weapons which God has given them?" All this came after the article headline exclaimed, "Don't do it!"[64]

Another fashion-only article appeared in May 1897, in a New York City newspaper. It was very extensive and very commercial. The piece read like a paid plant of advertisements that was posing as news.[65]

An article that appeared on July 1897 carried the provocative title "Women may wear pants." The journalist announced that in the city of Washington, D.C., it was not a misdemeanor for women to wear men's clothes or any such part of "the manly garb that suits their fancy. There is nothing in the law defining any limit in the intricate matter of what women wear or may choose to wear, from high theater hats and puffed sleeves to the color of their stockings, and the unlimited fancy of woman may stray as much toward trousers and silk hats and high collars as it sees fit." The journalist explained the above as the opinion of Major William C. Moore, Washington police chief. A woman had been arrested in Baltimore a few days earlier because she wore the clothes usually known as men's apparel. The police authorities of Baltimore could find no law against her action and she was released. That incident led to an investigation of the law in the District of Columbia, which led to the reporter calling on Moore on July 6. The reporter received the following statement from Moore: "It may be the general opinion that it is a misdemeanor for one sex to wear the clothes of another but such is not the fact. We would not arrest a woman or a man in Washington for doing it if nothing else were in the case. Sometimes men and women masquerade with some criminal object in view, and in such a case we would arrest them, but the charge would not be wearing unseemly clothing." Moore went on to explain, "Dr. Mary Walker always wears male garments, so called, and I believe there are other instances here and in other cities. Dr. Walker, you know, goes all over the United States and is not molested [i.e. persecuted]. On one or two occasions she has been arrested by a policeman under the mistaken impression that she was doing something wrong, but she has always been set free."

7. 1890s—Fashion

LINEN BICYCLE SUIT AT WANAMAKER'S.

BICYCLE COSTUMES SKETCHED AT B. ALTMAN & CO.'S.

BICYCLE SUIT, CLOTH JACKET AND VELVETEEN SKIRT DESIGNED BY MCCREERY, ELEVENTH ST.

BICYCLE COSTUME DESIGNED BY MATTHEWS, BROOKLYN.

This collection of 1897 sketches was solely concerned with the fashion aspects of bicycling and to hype different types of costumes for the consumer to purchase.

The reporter explained to Moore that there was a general impression that Walker obtained a permit from the police to wear a man's suit and silk hat and that if anyone else should desire to do the same thing a permit would be necessary in every case. Moore replied that such was not the case and "there has not been a woman arrested in Washington for thirty years for wearing trousers, I am sure, and perhaps not ever." As evidence of what Moore said must be true, the reporter cited stage performances wherein women actors donned men's clothing but were never persecuted. He added, "Washington, the home of the bicycle and the mecca of the reformer, is perhaps more acutely interested in this question than any other city. The law of the land is not against freedom from skirts. The other laws which govern women in this

WOMEN MAY WEAR PANTS

Major Moore Says It Is Not Against the Law.

NOT LIMITED TO SKIRTS

Bloomers, Knickers or Regulation Trousers of the Prevailing Mode Adorning Feminine Legs Will Not Subject Wearers to Arrest.—Theater and Bicycle as Emancipators.

Washington, D.C., Police Chief William Moore announced in 1897 that it was legal in his city for women to wear pants. There apparently had been some question as to the legality of such activity. Cited was local and notorious cross-dresser Mary Edwards Walker.

regard certainly are moderating gradually. Anyone may note this." In conclusion he declared, "Any evening on the Avenue [there] may be seen divided skirts and bloomers, with the accompanying show of pretty ankle and calf."[66]

According to a September 1897 article, two years earlier the bifurcated garment was the fashion, "but many women did not adopt it, although its use brought the wheel before the public prominently and nearly every woman in the land who did not already ride began learning. With the decline of bloomers a rational costume became universal, and today women who rise [to] the wheel have a freedom of action they did not formerly possess." This observer declared, "The popular costume of today is a short skirt, coming

More fashion hype from 1897.

just below the knees, with loose fitting knickerbockers of the same kind of fabric, and jacket to match. Either leggings or gold stockings are worn. For the head a plain hat or neat cap is the thing."[67]

By the last year or two of the 1890s the number of articles that dealt with the female cycling costume were more or less gone. Articles that were printed dealt just with the fashion-only aspect of the costume; that is, there were commercial-only items designed to get people to buy more stuff. One such article appeared in March 1898 that dealt mostly with styles and what the coming trends in bicycle fashion would be for the 1898 bicycle girl. "The skirts of the new cycling costumes are divided at the back only, or are circular and the fullness set into godet flutes in the back," the reporter declared. "Those divided in the back have the front and sides flat and smooth over the front and sides."[68]

Still more fashion hype, from 1898 this time.

CORRECT CYCLING DRESS FOR MISS 1898

She Is to Wear Trimmed Hats, Red Coats and Vests, Silk Hose and All the Becoming Accessories Possible

Fashion and accessories were on display in 1898 as the reader was advised on the correct cycling dress.

Another long, flowery piece about the "correct cycling dress for Miss 1898" and all the "becoming accessories," was published in May 1898. "Once upon a time the feminine cyclist was a woman of no importance now ... the leading firms vie with each other in providing her with smart costumes, and altogether she is made so much of that it must be difficult for her to remember that society once was not quite sure whether it would not be advisable to pass her by on the other side. Now, if society does pass by, she is on her

This page and the following two pages: These drawings from 1899 carried the fashion touting a step further by offering bicycle costumes for specific seasons of the year, such as spring, summer, and so on, with a final sketch of "the 1899 bicycle girl."

own wheel and wears a stunning costume built by a tailor and a hat which is not very much less trimmed than her walking hat," enthused the story. It went on to observe, "The divided skirts are a thing of the past. The circular skirt has taken its place and is much more convenient. It is also modest when properly cut." For wear beneath the circular cycling skirt was, said the reporter, "a novelty which will, we predict, meet with delighted acceptance. It is a combination of knickerbockers and underskirt. To a very deep fitted yoke is added a modestly full pair of bloomers drawn in below the knee by an elastic. Above these, and added at the same seam is a full divided skirt,

A SUBURBAN MEETING AT WHICH BICYCLE SKIRTS AND BOOTS ARE COMPARED AND ADMIRED.

THREE GOOD CYCLING SUITS FOR JANUARY BUILT TO DEFY WIND AND COLD.

THE BICYCLE GIRL WILL BE VERY EXPERT THIS SEASON, AND WILL WEAR MANY NEW AND PRETTY BICYCLE COSTUMES.

open on the outside to the hip and edged by a narrow ruffle. This new garment is called the cythere."[69]

Style articles appeared often in 1898 and 1899 with a tendency to become even more specialized and even more narrowly focused. A piece that appeared in May 1898 declared, "The bicycle dress was the rule and the long skirt the exception.... The bloomer bicycle girl is almost gone; but not quite. You still see her. She wears very large bloomers which are so arranged that when she stands you would scarcely notice that they were not skirts. Indeed, you would hardly notice that fact when she rides." An article early in 1899 focused on costumes for women for winter bicycling. A few months after that a similar piece was published with little in evidence except touting commercial interest. That one focused on spring costumes for the female bikers.[70]

THE BICYCLE GIRL OF '99.

This photograph presented the fashion industry's idea of what that 1899 bicycle girl should wear.

A couple more fashion-only stories appeared in the spring of 1899 and remained solely concerned with styles and text of a superficial and vacuous nature. But by then, well into 1899 the cycling craze, for men and women, was on the way out and rapidly crashing to nothing but a memory by five or so years later. Although, however, in the middle of 1899 that was likely not very obvious.[71]

Chapter Notes

Chapter 1

1. "Origin of the bicycle." *Memphis Appeal* (TN), November 8, 1884.
2. "The divided skirt." *St. Paul Globe*, June 29, 1890.
3. "Items." *Orangeburg News* (SC), November 28, 1867; No title. *Evening Star* (Washington), September 29, 1868; "News of the day." *Charleston Daily News* (SC), November 12, 1868.
4. "Velocipeding by ladies." *Edgefield Advertiser* (SC), November 25, 1868.
5. "The human wheel and its rival—the velocipede mania." *Ottawa Free Trader* (IL), January 16, 1869.
6. *Ibid.*
7. No title. *Evening Argus* (Rock Island, IL), February 9, 1869.
8. "Scraps and facts." *Yorkville Enquirer* (SC), February 18, 1869.
9. "The velocipede." *Bolivar Bulletin* (TN), February 27, 1869.
10. "Velocipediana." *Evansville Journal* (IN), March 4, 1869.
11. "City intelligence." *New York Herald*, March 25, 1869.
12. "Velocipede exhibition." *Evansville Journal* (IN), March 31, 1869.
13. "City topics." *New Orleans Crescent*, April 2, 1869; "City topics." *New Orleans Crescent*, April 4, 1869.
14. "The Empire City Rink." *New York Herald*, April 14, 1869.
15. "Interesting exhibitions." *Evening Argus* (Rock Island, IL), May 20 1869.
16. "Velocipede notes." *New York Herald*, April 4, 1869.
17. "Late telegrams." Evening Star (Washington), April 3, 1869.
18. No title. *Evening Star* (Washington), April 17, 1869.
19. "The velocipede." *Home Journal* (Winchester, TN), May 13, 1869.
20. "Women on the velocipede." *Marshall County Republican* (Plymouth, IN), May 20, 1869.
21. "Foreign items." *Charleston Daily News* (SC), July 27, 1869.
22. No title. *Wheeling Daily Intelligencer* (WV), March 16, 1879.
23. "The cyclers paradise." *Evening Star* (Washington), August 16, 1884.

Chapter 2

1. No title. *Opelousas Courier* (LA), September 25, 1880.
2. "Tricycling women." *Cairo Bulletin* (IL), July 21, 1881.

3. "Tricycling in England." *Evening Star* (Washington), May 27, 1882.
4. "Sunbeams." *Sun* (New York), May 26, 1883.
5. "Breezes from the summer resorts." *Indiana State Journal* (Indianapolis), July 11, 1883.
6. No title. *New York Tribune*, August 29, 1883.
7. "Tricycles for ladies." *New York Tribune*, December 17, 1883.
8. "The tricycle's popularity." *Evening Critic* (Washington), July 15, 1884.
9. "Men and women on wheels." *Evening Star* (Washington), July 16, 1887.
10. "Belva Lockwood." *Daily Times* (Richmond, VA), May 27, 1888.
11. "The cyclers paradise." *Evening Star* (Washington), August 16, 1884.
12. "The close of the watering place season." *Evening Star* (Washington), September 6, 1884.
13. "News and notes for women." *Abbeville Press and Banner* (SC), September 17, 1884.
14. "Women on wheels." *Evening Star* (Washington), September 27, 1884.
15. *Ibid.*
16. "The steel steed." *Memphis Daily Appeal* (TN), October 18, 1884.
17. "Notes of the wheel." *Memphis Daily Appeal* (TN), October 31, 1884.
18. "The girl who rides a tricycle." *Phillipsburg Herald* (KS), February 21, 1885.
19. "End of the season." *St. Paul Globe*, May 31, 1885.
20. "Tricycles." *Iron County Register* (Ironton, MO), July 16, 1885.
21. "Ladies on tricycles." *St. Paul Globe*, August 16, 1885.
22. "Women on the tricycle." *Evening Star* (Washington), September 12, 1885.
23. "A girls' tricycle cub." *Ottawa Free Trader* (IL), June 12, 1886.
24. "Letter from Washington." *Pascagoula Democrat-Star* (MS), July 2, 1886.
25. "Tricycling for women." *Salt Lake Herald*, July 11, 1886.
26. "Women on wheels." *Iron County Register* (Ironton, MO), September 2, 1886.
27. "A tricycle at the White House." *St. Paul Globe*, November 3, 1886.
28. "The tricycle for women." *United Opinion* (Bradford, VT), April 29 1887.
29. "Men and women on wheels." *Evening Star* (Washington), July 16, 1887.
30. Ad. *Springfield Daily Republican* (OH), August 6, 1887.
31. "Women on the wheel." *Omaha Daily Bee*, August 7, 1887.
32. "Beauty on wheels." *Sun* (NY), October 2, 1887.
33. "New York women on tricycles." *Evening World* (NY), November 9, 1887.
34. "Women on tricycles." *Abbeville Press and Banner* (SC), February 1, 1888.
35. "Philadelphia's expert tricycle women." *Sun* (NY), February26, 1888.
36. "Women who ride tricycles." *Indianapolis Journal*, May 26, 1888.
37. "Lady tricyclers." *Somerset Herald* (PA), May 30, 1888.
38. "Girl and bicycle." *Coconino Weekly Sun* (Flagstaff, AZ), August 10, 1893.

Chapter 3

1. "History of the bicycle." Wikipedia, accessed May 25, 2016.
2. "Personal and otherwise." *New Orleans Daily Democrat*, March 13, 1879.
3. Ad. *Jackson Standard* (OH), October 7, 1880.
4. Ad. *Clarksville Weekly Chronicle* (TN), September 9, 1882; Ad. *Hocking Sentinel* (Logan, OH), May 1, 1884.
5. "Louise Armaindo." *San Antonio Light*, February 10, 1885.
6. "Bicycling." *Sacramento Record-Union* (CA), June 1, 1882.
7. "General and personal." *San Antonio Light*, May 26, 1883.
8. "Noted two-wheel flyers." *Evening Star* (Washington), December 26, 1883.
9. "The cyclers paradise." *Evening Star* (Washington), August 16, 1884.
10. "Lady bicyclers." *St. Paul Globe*, August 23, 1885.
11. "The silent steed." *St. Paul Globe*, November 22, 1885.

12. "Washington on wheels." *Washington Critic*, April 16, 1886.
13. Sarah King. "A bicycle show." *Helena Weekly Herald* (MT), May 27, 1886.
14. "First bicycle made in capital city." *Washington Times*, March 17, 1902.
15. "A few years ago manufacturers were afraid to make wheel for women." *Los Angeles Herald*, June 30, 1895.
16. "The American bicycle." *Anderson Intelligencer* (SC), August 1, 1894.
17. "Cycling trade history." *Omaha Daily Bee*, February 28, 1897.
18. "Men and women on wheels." *Evening Star* (Washington), July 16, 1887.
19. "The boon of the bicycle." *Los Angeles Herald*, February 14, 1897.
20. "Riding for ladies." *Los Angeles Herald*, September 12, 1897.
21. "Bicycles for ladies." *St. Paul Globe*, March 2, 1888.
22. "Bicycles for women." *Sacramento Record-Union* (CA), May 10, 1888.
23. "Women on bicycles." *Evening Star* (Washington), March 17, 1888.
24. *Ibid.*
25. "The local lounger." *Ottawa Free Trader* (IL), April 21, 1888.
26. "Lady tricyclers." *Somerset Herald* (PA), May 30, 1888.
27. "Bicycles now for women." *Sun* (NY), June 10, 1888.
28. *Ibid.*
29. "How she mounts a bicycle." *St. Paul Globe*, September 30, 1888.
30. "A cycling prima donna." *Evening World* (NY), November 29, 1888.
31. "Ladies on the wheel." *Indianapolis Journal*, December 25, 1888.
32. "The novel female bicyclists' race." *Evening World* (NY), February 12, 1889.
33. Robert Graves. "Washington's wheels." *Austin Weekly Statesman* (TX), May 16, 1889.
34. "Astride the wheel." *Salt Lake Herald*, May 19, 1889.
35. "Women on the wheel." *Los Angeles Herald*, May 31, 1889.
36. "A female bicyclist." *Los Angeles Herald*, June 19, 1889.
37. Bessie Bramble. "Belles with muscle." *Pittsburgh Dispatch*, September 22, 1889.
38. Robert Graves. "The Washington girl." *Wichita Daily Eagle* (KS), September 29, 1889.
39. Ad. *Seattle Post-Intelligencer*, October 16, 1889.

Chapter 4

1. "Ladies bicycle riding school." *St. Paul Globe*, May 16, 1890; Ad. "Ladies bicycle school" *St. Paul Globe*, June 8, 1890.
2. "Fair bicyclists." *St. Paul Globe*, May 25, 1890.
3. "City for bicyclists." *Wichita Daily Eagle* (KS), September 21, 1890.
4. "First feminine bicyclist." *Los Angeles Herald*, November 28, 1890.
5. "Woman on the wheel." *Evening Star* (Washington), Dec 6, 1890.
6. John L. Heaton. "They all ride now." *Salt Lake Herald*, April 26, 1891.
7. *Ibid.*
8. "Wheels and riders." *St. Paul Globe*, April 26, 1891.
9. G.W. Weippiert. "The queen of sports." *Perrysburg Journal* (OH), October 3, 1891.
10. "The physical education of girls." *Juniata Sentinel and Republican* (Mifflintown, PA), January 6, 1892.
11. "Great endurance on the bicycles." *San Francisco Call*, January 17, 1892.
12. "Women who like the wheel." *Sun* (NY), January 31, 1892.
13. "In social circles." *Evening Capital Journal* (Salem, OR), March 26, 1892.
14. "More ladies' wheels sold." *Evening Star* (Washington), May 21, 1892.
15. "Hackensack's bicycle riders." *Sun* (NY), August 28, 1892.
16. "Women wheelers." *San Francisco Call*, January 8, 1893.
17. "Graceful women riders." *Burlington Free Press* (VT), August 24, 1893.
18. Isabella Proctor. "Cycling for women." *Roanoke Times* (VA), August 18, 1893.
19. "Greenhorns on bicycles" *Sun* (NY), May 20, 1894.

20. "A novelty in bicycles." *Sun* (NY), June 16, 1894.
21. *Ibid.*
22. No title. *New York Tribune*, June 23, 1894.
23. "Here and there." *Times* (Richmond, VA), October 14, 1894.
24. "Society." *St. Paul Globe*, October 21, 1894.
25. "Women cyclists." *San Francisco Call*, November 10, 1894.
26. Pauline Pry. "Women on bicycles." *Evening Star* (Washington), November 24, 1894.
27. "Rise of the bicycle." *New York Tribune*, December 30, 1894.
28. *Ibid.*
29. "Scenes at a bicycle school." *New York Tribune*, February 3, 1895.
30. "Ladies on wheels." *St. Paul Globe*, April 14, 1895.
31. "An army on wheels." *Sun* (NY), April 28, 1895.
32. "Types of feminine bicyclers seen on Riverside Drive yesterday." *Evening World* (NY), May 6, 1895.
33. Ad. *Courier* (Lincoln, NE), May 11, 1895.
34. "The bicycle epidemic." *Courier* (Lincoln, NE), June 15, 1895.
35. "The overshadowing fad." *Omaha Daily Bee*, June 16, 1895.
36. Lillian Russell. "Miss Russell on bicycling." *Los Angeles Herald*, July 21, 1895.
37. "At the theaters." *St. Paul Globe*, January 20, 1896; No title. *Hutchinson Gazette* (KS), April 9, 1896.
38. Ad. *Alexandria Gazette* (VA), May 21, 1896.
39. "Wheels and riders." *St. Paul Globe*, May 10 1896.
40. "The new woman." *Times* (Richmond, VA), May 10, 1896.
41. "Phenomenal growth of the bicycle trade." *Record-Union* (Sacramento, CA), May 24, 1896.
42. "Calvé and Melba on wheels." *St. Paul Globe*, June 8, 1896.
43. Millicent Arrowpoint. "Bicycle tennis." *Omaha Daily Bee*, June 21, 1896.
44. "The bicycle girl and her last season's wheel." *San Francisco Call*, November 15, 1896.
45. "Girl's jewelry." *Hartford Republican* (KY), November 20, 1896.
46. "False prophecies." *Omaha Daily Bee*, January 17, 1897.
47. "For women cyclists." *Evening Star* (Washington), February 6, 1897.
48. Amos J. Cummings. "Heaven of bicycles." *St. Paul Globe*, July 18, 1897.
49. Charlotte L. Bolton. "Women should ride." *Los Angeles Herald*, September 12, 1897.
50. "Fun on the bicycle." *Willmar Tribune* (MN), September 14, 1897.
51. Mrs. Grey Canfield. "A bicycle school run by girls." *Los Angeles Herald*, January 2, 1898.
52. "Sports of the day." *Los Angeles Herald*, February 7, 1898.
53. "Bicycle day supplement." *New York Tribune*, February 22, 1898.
54. Lillian Russell. "How I preserve my youth." *Evening World* (NY), July 26, 1901.
55. "The bicycle girl." *Seattle Republican*, August 9, 1901.
56. "Here is the auto-car which promises to be a dangerous rival of the bike." *San Francisco Call*, February 28, 1897.
57. "Bicycle girls all gone." *Spokane Press*, October 31, 1906.
58. "The auto craze." *Los Angeles Herald*, June 16, 1907.

Chapter 5

1. "Astride the wheel." *Salt Lake Herald*, March 10, 1889.
2. "Effect of cycling upon the voice." *Indianapolis Journal*, December 22, 1889.
3. "A real summer girl." *San Saba News* (TX), July 15, 1892.
4. "Is bicycling safe?" *St. Paul Globe*, August 8, 1892.
5. "Bicycling." *Salt Lake Herald*, May 28, 1893.
6. "Women and bicycles." *Saturday Morning Courier* (Lincoln, NE), August 5, 1893.

7. Isabella Proctor. "Cycling for women." *Roanoke Times* (VA), August 18, 1893.
8. "Desultory musings." *Guthrie Daily Leader* (OK), October 15, 1893.
9. "Women bicyclists." *Capital Journal* (Salem, OR), August 28, 1894.
10. "Scientific notes." *Washington Times*, October 17, 1894.
11. "Bicycling for women." *Sun* (NY), December 22, 1894.
12. Dr. Mary T. Bissell. "The bicycle for women." *Advocate* (Topeka, KS), January 9, 1895.
13. "Ladies awheel." *San Francisco Call*, May 18, 1895.
14. "Woman and her bicycle." *Sun* (NY), May 23, 1895.
15. "A distressing view." *Record-Union* (Sacramento, CA), June 8, 1895.
16. "A possible reformer." *Record-Union* (Sacramento), August 30, 1895.
17. *Ibid.*
18. "Ride a bike, say doctors." *Sun* (NY), October 6, 1895.
19. "Women and the wheel." *Yakima Herald* (WA), January 30, 1896.
20. "Cycle circles." *Evening Bulletin* (Maysville, KY), July 11, 1896.
21. "Woe for the bicycle girl." *Morning Times* (Washington), January 10, 1897.
22. *Ibid.*
23. "Wheeling and dancing." *Evening Times* (Washington), March 18, 1897.
24. "Bicycles and tuberculosis in women." *Progress* (Shreveport, LA), May 8, 1897.
25. "Does the bicycle make women cruel?" *Los Angeles Herald*, June 13, 1897.
26. *Ibid.*
27. "Did bicycles save women?" *Wichita Daily Eagle* (KS), July 4, 1897.
28. "The bicycle voice." *Times* (Washington), August 22, 1897.
29. "Is bicycle riding by women injurious." *Norfolk Virginian*, October 16, 1897.
30. No title. *St. Johns Herald* (AZ), May 28, 1898.

Chapter 6

1. Shirley Dark. "Women on bicycles." *Evening Star* (Washington), September 6, 1890.
2. "The bicycle question." *National Tribune* (Washington), October 16, 1890.
3. No title. *Sunday Herald Weekly National Intelligencer* (Washington), June 28, 1891.
4. "Women and bicycles." *Sun* (NY), July 5, 1891.
5. "They may ride." *St. Paul Globe*, July 13, 1891.
6. "The Home Corner." *Austin Weekly Statesman* (TX), December 17, 1891.
7. "Ah, there!" *Salt Lake Herald*, June 12, 1892.
8. "Is bicycling safe?" *St. Paul Globe*, August 8, 1892.
9. "Women wheelers." *San Francisco Call*, January 8, 1893.
10. "Girl and bicycle." *Coconino Weekly Sun* (Flagstaff, AZ), August 10, 1893.
11. "A woman on wheels." *St. Paul Globe*, September 17, 1893.
12. Katie Field. "Six women agree." *Lafayette Advertiser* (LA), October 20, 1894.
13. *Ibid.*
14. "Bicycling for women." *Sun* (NY), December 22, 1894.
15. "Mustn't ride wheels to school." *Sun* (NY), June 15, 1895.
16. "Preachers don't like bloomers." *Evening World* (NY), June 17, 1895.
17. "Some don'ts for women cyclists." *Los Angeles Herald*, July 14, 1895.
18. "As to wheeling on Sunday." *Los Angeles Herald*, July 14, 1895.
19. "Cycle of our modern time." *Omaha Daily Bee*, July 28, 1895.
20. "Women and the wheel." *Record-Union* (Sacramento, CA), August 10, 1895.
21. "Army of the common wheel." *Omaha Daily Bee*, September 1, 1895.
22. "An arbiter of fashion." *San Francisco Call*, March 13, 1896.
23. No title. *Alexandria Gazette* (VA), March 13, 1896.
24. "Backs the bicycle girl." *Evening Times* (Washington), June 9, 1896.
25. "Devil's advance agent." *Wichita Eagle*, July 3, 1896.
26. "War on the bike." *Los Angeles Herald*, July 3, 1896.

27. "Defend the women riders." *Morning Times* (Washington), July 4, 1896.
28. "Women bicycle riders." *San Francisco Call*, July 9, 1896.
29. "Women, League, wheel and press." *Record-Union* (Sacramento, CA), July 27, 1896.
30. "Cycle circles." *Evening Bulletin* (Maysville, KY), July 11, 1896.
31. "Will not insure women profs." *St. Paul Globe*, August 23, 1896; "Bicycle girls not insurable." *Progress* (Shreveport, LA), October 3, 1896.
32. "Has the bicycle helped the world?" *Morning Times* (Washington), August 9, 1896.
33. "Teacher as bicyclists." *Wichita Daily Eagle*, September 19, 1897.
34. "Scarlet women." *Marietta Daily Ledger* (OH), September 30, 1897.
35. "A minister writes of bicycle skirts." *Los Angeles Herald*, October 17, 1897.
36. No title. *Gulf Coast Breeze* (Crawfordville, FL), October 22, 1897.
37. "Amelia Bloomer's suit." *Evening Star* (Washington), August 15, 1899.
38. "Greenhorns on bicycles." *Sun* (NY), May 20, 1894.
39. "What shall the new woman wear, skirts or bloomers?" *Los Angeles Herald*, September 15, 1895.
40. Ibid.
41. Ibid.
42. "Of interest to cyclists." *Record-Union* (Sacramento, CA), September 3, 1898; "Must wear bloomers." *St. Johns Herald* (AZ), July 1, 1899; "Wheelwomen in Europe." *Banner-Democrat* (Lake Providence, LA), November 3, 1900; "Rules for cyclists." *Star* (Reynoldsville, PA), September 13, 1905.
43. "Bicycles and morality." *Sun* (NY), May 19, 1899.
44. "The bicycle." *Scranton Tribune* (PA), May 20, 1899.
45. "Women bicyclists will be licensed." *San Francisco Call*, August 31, 1899.
46. "Of scorchers." *Record-Union* (Sacramento, CA), September 11, 1899.

Chapter 7

1. "Redfern ideas." *San Francisco Call*, May 2, 1890.
2. "The divided skirt." *St. Paul Globe*, June 29, 1890.
3. No title. *Pittsburgh Dispatch*, August 1, 1891.
4. "The girl on a wheel." *Washington Bee* (D.C.), August 22, 1891.
5. "The bicycle girl." *Sun* (NY), November 15, 1891.
6. "The physical education of girls." *Juniata Sentinel and Republican* (Mifflintown, PA), January 6, 1892.
7. "Cycle and buskin." *St. Paul Globe*, July 17, 1892.
8. "Bicycling for girls." *Daily Herald* (Brownsville, TX), December 8, 1892.
9. "Women wheelers." *San Francisco Call*, January 8, 1893.
10. "Out door sports." *Salt Lake Herald*, May 28, 1893.
11. "How women may ride bicycles." *Los Angeles Herald*, July 10, 1893.
12. "Bicycle exercise." *Saturday Morning Courier* (Lincoln, NE), July 22, 1893.
13. "Style in bicycle garb." *Princeton Union* (MN), August 10, 1893.
14. "Bicycle dress." *Los Angeles Herald*, September 17, 1893.
15. "Athletics and fashion." *St. Paul Globe*, September 17, 1893.
16. "Trousers for women." *Helena Independent* (MT), March 2, 1894.
17. "The girl with the divided skirts." *St. Paul Globe*, April 8, 1894.
18. "Dresses for Daisy Bell." *Weekly Tribune* (Great Falls, MT), April 20, 1894.
19. "Bicyclists of the boulevard." *Sun* (NY), June 24, 1894.
20. Earle Eaton. "Daisy's new bloomers." *Roanoke Times* (VA), July 15, 1894.
21. Ibid.
22. Ibid.
23. No title. *Vermont Phoenix* (Brattleboro, VT), August 31, 1894.
24. Ada Cone. "Feminine trousers." *Richmond Dispatch* (VA), August 26, 1894.

25. "Woman and the bicycle." *New York Tribune*, September 17, 1894.
26. "Many women on wheels." *Hartford Republican* (KY), September 28, 1894.
27. "Women life savers." Daily Ardmoreite (Ardmore, OK), October 17, 1894.
28. "Society's pastimes." *Evening Star* (Washington), October 27, 1894.
29. "Cyclists in bloomers." *Sun* (NY), August 5, 1894.
30. "For a bicycle rider." *Evening World* (NY), December 4, 1894.
31. "The bloomer question abroad." *Advocate* (Topeka, KS), December 5, 1894.
32. Mary L. Bisland. "Smart cycling." *Salt Lake Herald*, December 16, 1894.
33. "Bicycle costumes for women." *New York Tribune*, December 17, 1894.
34. Ellen Osborn. "Chic dresses for wheelwomen." *Washington Times*, April 21, 1895.
35. *Ibid.*
36. "Battle of the bloomers." *Courier* (Lincoln, NE), May 25, 1895.
37. "A distressing view." *Record-Union* (Sacramento, CA), June 8, 1895.
38. *Ibid.*
39. "Skirtless women now." *Los Angeles Herald*, June 9, 1895.
40. "Have no use for skirts." *Los Angeles Herald*, June 30, 1895.
41. "Convertible costume." *Los Angeles Herald*, June 30, 1895.
42. "Should women wear bloomers." *Los Angeles Herald*, July 28, 1895.
43. "Practical costumes these." *Los Angeles Herald*, August 25, 1895.
44. "Mrs. Sage says bloomers." *Los Angeles Herald*, August 25, 1895.
45. "Bloomer girl of next year." *Salt Lake Herald*, August 26, 1895.
46. "Bloomers scare the horses." *Norfolk Virginian*, August 30, 1895.
47. "What is male attire." Norfolk Virginian, August 31, 1895.
48. "Women as wheel pupils." *San Francisco Call*, September 9, 1895.
49. Ad. *Bismarck Weekly Tribune* (ND), September 20, 1895.
50. "Bloomer and the bicycle." *Omaha Daily Bee*, September 29, 1895.
51. "On a bicycle." *Morning Times* (Washington), October 19, 1895.
52. "Are they immodest." *Houston Daily Post*, February 23, 1896.
53. Ad. *Morning Times* (Washington), March 8, 1896.
54. Ad. *Morning Times* (Washington), March 26, 1896; Ad. *Morning Times* (Washington), March 26, 1896; Ad. *Richmond Dispatch* (VA), March 29, 1896.
55. "Women and the wheel in 1896." *Los Angeles Herald*, May 10, 1896.
56. "Wheelwomen's costumes." *Record-Union* (Sacramento, CA), June 7, 1896.
57. "For wheelwomen." *St. Paul Globe*, June 21, 1896.
58. "The bicycle the chief of dress reformers." *North Platte Semi-Weekly* (NE), July 3, 1896.
59. "Simply stockings." *Roanoke Daily Times* (VA), August 1, 1896.
60. "Bare-legged women cyclers." *Salt Lake Herald*, August 16, 1896.
61. "Worse than hideous." *Record-Union* (Sacramento, CA), September 20, 1896.
62. "Cycle suit of tweed." *Morning Times* (Washington), October 13, 1896.
63. "Gossip of the wheel." *St. Paul Globe*, October 25, 1896.
64. "Don't do it!" *Lincoln County Leader* (Toledo, OR), January 7, 1897.
65. "Fashion and fancy." *New York Tribune*, May 23, 1897.
66. "Women may wear pants." *Times* (Washington), July 7, 1897.
67. "Riding for ladies." *Los Angeles Herald*, September 12, 1897.
68. "The 1898 bicycle girl." *St. Paul Globe*, March 6, 1898.
69. "Correct cycling dress for Miss 1898." *Los Angeles Herald*, May 1, 1898.
70. "Bicycle girls and their summer road gowns." *San Francisco Call*, May 29, 1898; "Suits for winter wheeling." *St. Paul Globe*, January 8, 1899; "A first glimpse of the spring bicycle girl." *St. Paul Globe*, March 12, 1899; "The 1899 bicycle girl." *Richmond Dispatch* (VA), March 19, 1899.
71. "The athletic summer girl." *San Francisco Call*, May 21, 1899; Daisy May. "Bicycle maid of '99." *Wichita Daily Eagle*, June 11, 1899.

Bibliography

Ad. *Alexandria Gazette* (VA), May 21, 1896.
Ad. *Bismarck Weekly Tribune* (ND), September 20, 1895.
Ad. *Clarksville Weekly Chronicle* (TN), September 9, 1882.
Ad. *Courier* (Lincoln, NE), May 11, 1895.
Ad. *Hocking Sentinel* (Logan, OH), May 1, 1884.
Ad. *Jackson Standard* (OH), October 7, 1880.
Ad. *Morning Times* (Washington), March 8, 1896.
Ad. *Morning Times* (Washington), March 26, 1896.
Ad. *Richmond Dispatch* (VA), March 29, 1896.
Ad. *Sacramento Record-Union* (CA), September 19, 1883.
Ad. *Seattle Post-Intelligencer,* October 16, 1889.
Ad. *Springfield Daily Republican* (OH), August 6, 1887.
"Ah there!" *Salt Lake Herald,* June 12, 1892.
"Amelia Bloomer's suit." *Evening Star* (Washington), August 15, 1899.
"The American bicycle." *Anderson Intelligencer* (SC), August 1, 1894.
"An arbiter of fashion." *San Francisco Call,* March 13, 1896.
"Are they immodest." *Houston Daily Post,* February 23 1896.
"Army of the common wheel." *Omaha Daily Bee,* September 1, 1895.
"An army on wheels." *Sun* (NY), April 28, 1895.
Arrowpoint, Millicent. "Bicycle tennis." *Omaha Daily Bee,* June 21, 1896.
"As to wheeling on Sunday." *Los Angeles Herald,* July 14, 1895.
"Astride the wheel." *Salt Lake Herald,* March 10, 1889.
"Astride the wheel." *Salt Lake Herald,* May 19, 1889.
"The athletic summer girl." *San Francisco Call,* May 21, 1899.
"Athletics and fashion." *St. Paul Globe,* September 17, 1893.
"At the theaters." *St. Paul Globe,* January 20, 1896.
"The auto craze." *Los Angeles Herald,* June 16, 1907.
"Backs the bicycle." *Evening Times* (Washington), June 9, 1896.
"Bare-legged women cyclers." *Salt Lake Herald,* August 16, 1896.
"Battle of the bloomers." *Courier* (Lincoln, NE), May 25, 1895.
"Beauty on wheels." *Iola Register* (KS), February 27, 1891.
"Beauty on wheels." *Sun* (NY), October 2, 1887.
"Belva Lockwood." *Daily Times* (Richmond, VA), May 27, 1888.
"Bicycle costumes for women." *New York Tribune,* December 17, 1894.
"Bicycle day supplement." *New York Tribune,* February 22, 1898.
"Bicycle dress." *Los Angeles Herald,* September 17, 1893.
"The bicycle epidemic." *Courier* (Lincoln, NE), June 15, 1895.

"Bicycle exercise." *Saturday Morning Courier* (Lincoln, NE0, July 22, 1893.
"The bicycle girl." *Seattle Republican,* August 9, 1901.
"The bicycle girl." *Sun* (NY), November 15, 1891.
"The bicycle girl and her last season's wheel." *San Francisco Call,* November 15, 1896.
"Bicycle girls and their summer road gowns." *San Francisco Call,* May 29, 1898.
"Bicycle girls all gone." *Spokane Press* (Washington), October 31, 1906.
"Bicycle girls not insurable." *Progress* (Shreveport, LA), October 3, 1896.
"The bicycle question." *National Tribune* (Washington), October 16, 1890.
"The bicycle." *Scranton Tribune* (PA), May 20, 1899.
"The bicycle: the chief of dress reformers." *North Platte Semi-Weekly Tribune* (NE), July 3, 1896.
"The bicycle voice." *Times* (Washington), August 22, 1897.
"Bicycles and morality." *Sun* (NY), May 19, 1899.
"Bicycles and tuberculosis in women." *Progress* (Shreveport, LA), May 8, 1897.
"Bicycles for ladies." *St. Paul Globe,* March 2, 1888.
"Bicycles for women." *Sacramento Record-Union* (CA), May 10, 1888.
"Bicycles." *Intermountain Catholic* (Salt Lake City), September 4, 1909.
"Bicycles now for women." *Sun* (NY), June 10, 1888.
"Bicycling for girls." *Daily Herald* (Brownsville, TX), December 8, 1892.
"Bicycling for women." *Sun* (NY), December 22, 1894.
"Bicycling." *Sacramento Record-Union* (CA), June 1, 1882.
"Bicycling." *Salt Lake Herald,* May 28, 1893.
"Bicyclists of the boulevard." *Sun* (NY), June 24, 1894.
Bisland, Mary L. "Smart cycling." *Salt Lake Herald,* December 16, 1894.
Bissell, Mary T. "The bicycle for women." *Advocate* (Topeka, KS), January 9, 1895.
"Bloomer and the bicycle." *Omaha Daily Bee,* September 29, 1895.
"Bloomer girl of next year." *Salt Lake Review,* August 26, 1895.
"The bloomer question abroad." *Advocate* (Topeka, KS), December 5, 1894.
"Bloomers scare the horses." *Norfolk Virginian,* August 30, 1895.
Bolton, Charlotte L. "Women should ride." *Los Angeles Herald,* September 12, 1897.
"The boon of the bicycle." *Los Angeles Herald,* February 14, 1897.
Bramble, Bessie. "Belles with muscle." *Pittsburgh Dispatch,* September 22, 1889.
"Breezes from the summer resorts." *Indiana State Journal* (Indianapolis), July 11, 1883.
"Calve and Melba on wheels." *St. Paul Globe,* June 8, 1896.
Canfield, Mrs. Grey. "A bicycle school run by girls." *Los Angeles Herald,* January 2, 1898.
"Can you recall this bit of old Philadelphia." *Evening Public Ledger* (Philadelphia), February 28, 1922.
"City for bicyclists." *Wichita Daily Eagle* (KS), September 21, 1890.
"City intelligence." *New York Herald,* March 25, 1869.
"City topics." *New Orleans Crescent,* April 2, 1869.
"City topics." *New Orleans Crescent,* April 4, 1869.
"The close of the watering place season." *Evening Star* (Washington), September 6, 1884.
Cone, Ada. "Feminine trousers. *Richmond Dispatch* (VA), August 26, 1894.
"Convertible costume." *Los Angeles Herald,* June 30, 1895.
"Correct cycling dress for Miss 1898." *Los Angeles Herald,* May 1, 1898.
Cummings, Amos J. "Heaven of bicycles." *St. Paul Globe,* July 18, 1897.
"Cycle and buskin." *St. Paul Globe,* July 17, 1892.
"Cycle circles." *Evening Bulletin* (Maysville, KY), July 11, 1896.
"Cycle of our modern time." *Omaha Daily Bee,* July 28, 1895.
"Cycle suit of tweed." *Morning Times* (Washington), October 13, 1896.
"The cyclers paradise." *Evening Star* (Washington), August 16, 1884.
"A cycling prima donna." *Evening World* (NY), November 29, 1888.
"Cycling trade history." *Omaha Daily Bee,* February 28, 1897.
"Cyclists in bloomers." *Sun* (NY), August 5, 1894.

Dark, Shirley. "Women on bicycles." *Evening Star* (Washington), September 6, 1890.
"Defend the women riders." *Morning Times* (Washington), July 4, 1896.
"Desultory musings." *Guthrie Daily Leader* (OK), October 15, 1893.
"Devil's advance agent." *Wichita Daily Eagle*, July 3, 1896.
"Did bicycles save women?" *Wichita Daily Eagle* (KS), July 4, 1897.
"A distressing view." *Record-Union* (Sacramento, CA), June 8, 1895.
"The divided skirt." *St. Paul Globe*, June 29, 1890.
"Does the bicycle make women cruel?" *Los Angeles Herald*, June 13, 1897.
"Don't do it!" *Lincoln County Leader* (Toledo, OR), January 7, 1897.
"Dresses for Daisy Bell." *Weekly Tribune* (Great Falls, MT), April 20, 1894.
Eaton, Earle. "Daisy's new bloomers." *Roanoke Times* (VA), July 15, 1894.
"Effect of cycling upon the voice." *Indianapolis Journal*, December 22, 1889.
"The 1898 bicycle girl." *St. Paul Globe*, March 6, 1898.
"The 1899 bicycle girl." *Richmond Dispatch* (VA), March 19, 1899.
"The Empire City rink." *New York Herald*, April 14, 1869.
"End of the season." *St. Paul Globe*, May 31, 1885.
"Fair bicyclists." *St. Paul Globe*, May 25, 1890.
"False prophecies." *Omaha Daily Bee*, January 17, 1897.
"Fashion and fancy." *New York Tribune*, May 23, 1897.
"A female bicyclist." *Los Angeles Herald*, June 19, 1889.
"A few years ago manufacturers were afraid to make wheels for women." *Los Angeles Herald*, June 30, 1895.
Field, Katie. "Six women agree." *Lafayette Advertiser* (LA), October 20, 1894.
"First bicycle made in capital city." *Washington Times*, March 17, 1902.
"First feminine bicyclist." *Los Angeles Herald*, November 28, 1890.
"A first glimpse of the spring bicycle girl." *St. Paul Globe*, March 12, 1899.
"For a bicycle rider." *Evening World* (NY), December 4, 1894.
"Foreign items." *Charleston Daily News* (SC), July 27, 1869.
"For wheelwomen." *St. Paul Globe*, June 21, 1896.
"For women cyclists." *Evening Star* (Washington), February 6, 1897.
"Fun on the bicycle." *Willmar Tribune* (MN), September 14, 1897.
"General and personal." *San Antonio Light*, May 26, 1883.
"Girl and bicycle." *Coconino Weekly Sun* (Flagstaff, AZ), August 10, 1893.
"The girl on a wheel." *Washington Bee* (Washington), August 22, 1891.
"The girl who rides a tricycle." *Phillipsburg Herald* (KS), February 21, 1885.
"The girl with the divided skirts." *St. Paul Globe*, April 8, 1894.
"Girl's jewelry." *Hartford Republican* (KY), November 20, 1896.
"A girls' tricycle club." *Ottawa Free Trader* (IL), June 12, 1886.
"Gossip of the wheel." *St. Paul Globe*, October 25, 1896.
"Graceful women riders." *Burlington Free Press* (VT), august 24, 1893.
Graves, Robert. "The Washington girl." *Wichita Daily Eagle* (KS), September 29, 1889.
Graves, Robert. "Washington's wheels." *Austin Weekly Statesman* (TX), May 16, 1889.
"Great endurance on the bicycles." *San Francisco Call*, January 17, 1892.
"Greenhorns on bicycles." *Sun* (NY), May 20, 1894.
"Hackensack's bicycle riders." *Sun* (NY), August 28, 1892.
"Has the bicycle helped the world?" *Morning Times* (Washington), August 9, 1896.
"Have no use for skirts." *Los Angeles Herald*, June 30, 1895.
Heaton, John L. "They all ride now." *Salt Lake Herald*, April 26, 1891.
"Here and there." *Times* (Richmond, VA), October 14, 1894.
"Here is the auto-car which promises to be a dangerous rival of the bike." *San Francisco Call*, Feb. 28, 1897.
"The home corner." *Austin Weekly Statesman* (TX), December 17, 1891.
"How she mounts a bicycle." *St. Paul Globe*, September 30, 1888.
"How women may ride bicycles." *Los Angeles Herald*, July 10, 1893.

"The human wheel and its rival—the velocipede mania." *Ottawa Free Trader* (IL), January 16, 1869.
"In social circles." *Evening Capital Journal* (Salem, OR), March 26, 1892.
"Interesting exhibitions." *Evening Argus* (Rock Island, IL), May 20, 1869.
"Is bicycle riding by women injurious." *Norfolk Virginian*, October 16, 1897.
"Is bicycling safe?" *St. Paul Globe*, August 8, 1892.
"Items." *Orangeburg News* (SC), November 28, 1867.
King, Sarah. "A bicycle show." *Helena Weekly Herald* (MT), May 27, 1886.
"Ladies awheel." *San Francisco Call*, May 18, 1895.
"Ladies bicycle riding school." *St. Paul Globe*, May 16, 1890.
"Ladies bicycle school." *St. Paul Globe*, June 8, 1890.
"Ladies on the wheel." *Indianapolis Journal*, December 25, 1888.
"Ladies on tricycles." *St. Paul Globe*, August 16, 1885.
"Ladies on wheels." *St. Paul Globe*, April 14, 1895.
"Lady bicyclers." *St. Paul Globe*, August 23, 1885.
"Lady tricyclers." *Somerset Herald* (PA), May 30, 1888.
"Late telegrams." *Evening Star* (Washington), April 3, 1869.
"Letter from Washington." *Pascagoula Democrat-Star* (MS), July 2, 1886.
"The local lounger." *Ottawa Free Trader* (IL), April 21, 1888.
"Louise Armaindo." *San Antonio Light*, February 10, 1885.
"Many women on wheels." *Hartford Republican* (KY), September 28, 1894.
May, Daisy. "Bicycle maid of '99." *Wichita Daily Eagle* (KS), June 11, 1899.
"Men and women on wheels." *Evening Star* (Washington), July 16, 1887.
"A minister writes of bicycle skirts." *Los Angeles Herald*, October 17, 1897.
"More ladies' wheels sold." *Evening Star* (Washington), May 21, 1892.
"Mrs. Sage says bloomers." *Los Angeles Herald*, August 25, 1895.
"Musn't ride wheels to school." *Sun* (NY), June 15, 1895.
"Must wear bloomers." *St. Johns Herald* (AZ), July 1, 1899.
"The new woman." *Times* (Richmond, VA), May 10, 1896.
"News and notes for women." *Abbeville Press and Banner* (SC), September 17, 1884.
"News of the day." *Charleston Daily News* (SC), November 12, 1868.
"New York women on tricycles." *Evening World* (NY), November 9, 1887.
"Noted, two-wheel flyers." *Evening Star* (Washington), December 26, 1883.
"Notes of the wheel." *Memphis Daily Appeal* (TN), October 31, 1884.
No title. *Alexandria Gazette* (VA), March 13, 1896.
No title. *Evening Argus* (Rock Island, IL), February 9, 1869.
No title. *Evening Star* (Washington), September 29, 1868.
No title. *Evening Star* (Washington), April 17, 1869.
No title. *Gulf Coast Breeze* (Crawfordville, FL), October 22, 1897.
No title. *Hutchinson Gazette* (KS), April 9, 1896.
No title. *New York Tribune*, August 29, 1883.
No title. *New York Tribune*, June 23, 1894.
No title. *Opelousas Courier* (LA), September 25, 1880.
No title. *Pittsburgh Dispatch*, August 1, 1891.
No title. *St. Johns Herald* (AZ), May 28, 1898.
No title. *Sunday Herald and Weekly National Intelligencer* (Washington), June 28, 1891.
No title. *Vermont Phoenix* (Brattleboro, VT), August 31, 1894.
No title. *Wheeling Daily Intelligencer* (WV), March 16, 1870.
"The novel female bicyclists' race." *Evening World* (NY), February 12, 1889.
"A novelty in bicycles." *Sun* (NY), June 16, 1894.
"Of interest to cyclists." *Record-Union* (Sacramento, CA), September 3, 1898.
"Of scorchers." *Record-Union* (Sacramento, CA), September 11, 1899.
"On a bicycle." *Morning Times* (Washington), October 19, 1895
"Origin of the bicycle." *Memphis Appeal* (TN), November 8, 1884.

Osborn, Ellen. "Chic dresses for wheelwomen." *Washington Times*, April 21, 1895.
"Outdoor sports." *Salt Lake Herald*, May 28, 1893.
"The overshadowing fad." *Omaha Daily Bee*, June 16, 1895.
"Personal and otherwise." *New Orleans Daily Democrat*, March 13, 1879.
"Phenomenal growth of the bicycle trade." *Record-Union* (Sacramento, CA), May 24, 1896.
"Philadelphia's expert tricycle women." *Sun* (NY), February 26, 1888.
"The physical education of girls." *Juniata Sentinel and Republican* (Mifflintown, PA), January 6, 1892.
"A possible reformer." *Record-Union* (Sacramento, CA), August 30, 1895.
"Practical costumes these." *Los Angeles Herald*, August 25, 1895.
"Preachers don't like bloomers." *Evening World* (NY), June 17, 1895.
Proctor, Isabella. "Cycling for women." *Roanoke Times* (VA), August 18, 1893.
Pry, Pauline. "Women on bicycles." *Evening Star* (Washington), November 24, 1894.
"A real summer girl." *San Saba News* (San Saba, TX), July 15, 1892.
"Redfern ideas." *San Francisco Call*, May 2, 1890.
"Ride a bike, say doctors." *Sun* (NY), October 6, 1895.
"Riding for ladies." *Los Angeles Herald*, September 12, 1897.
"Rise of the bicycle." *New York Tribune*, December 30, 1894.
"Rules for cyclists." *Star* (Reynoldsville, PA), September 13, 1905.
Russell, Lillian. "How I preserve my youth." *Evening World* (NY), July 26, 1901.
Russell, Lillian. "Miss Russell on bicycling." *Los Angeles Herald*, July 21, 1895.
"Scarlet women." *Marietta Daily Ledger* (OH), September 30, 1897.
"Scenes at a bicycle school." *New York Tribune*, February 3, 1895.
"Scientific notes." *Washington Times*, October 17, 1894.
"Scraps and facts." *Yorkville Enquirer* (SC), February 18, 1869.
"Should women wear bloomers." *Los Angeles Herald*, July 28, 1895.
"The silent steed." *St. Paul Globe*, November 22, 1885.
"Simply stockings." *Roanoke Daily Times* (VA), August 1, 1896.
"Skirtless women now." *Los Angeles Herald*, June 9, 1895.
"Society." *St. Paul Globe*, October 21, 1894.
"Society's pastimes." *Evening Star* (Washington), October 27, 1894.
"Some don'ts for women cyclists." *Los Angeles Herald*, July 14, 1895.
"Sports of the day." *Los Angeles Herald*, February 7, 1898.
"The steel steed." *Memphis Daily Appeal* (TN), October 18, 1884.
"Style in bicycle garb." *Princeton Union* (MN), August 10, 1893.
"Suits for winter wheeling." *St. Paul Globe*, January 8, 1899.
"Sunbeams." *Sun* (NY), September 19, 1882.
"Teacher as bicyclists." *Wichita Daily Eagle* (KS), September 19, 1897.
"They may ride." *St. Paul Globe*, July 13, 1891.
"A tricycle at the White House." *St. Paul Globe*, November 3, 1886.
"The tricycle for women." *United Opinion* (Bradford, VT), April 29, 1887.
"Tricycles for ladies." *New York Tribune*, December 17, 1883.
"Tricycles." *Iron County Register* (Ironton, MO), July 16, 1885.
"The tricycle's popularity." *Evening Critic* (Washington), July 15, 1884.
"Tricycling for women." *Salt Lake Herald*, July 11, 1886.
"Tricycling in England." *Evening Star* (Washington), May 27, 1882.
"Tricycling women." *Cairo Bulletin* (IL), July 21, 1881.
"Trousers for women." *Helena Independent* (MT), March 2, 1894.
"Types of feminine bicyclers seen on Riverside Drive yesterday." *Evening World* (NY), May 6, 1895.
"The velocipede." *Bolivar Bulletin* (TN), February 27, 1869.
"The velocipede." *Home Journal* (Winchester, TN), May 13, 1869.
"Velocipede exhibition." *Evansville Journal* (IN), March 31, 1869.
"Velocipede notes." *New York Herald*, April 4, 1869.

"Velocipediana." *Evansville Journal* (IN), March 4, 1869.
"Velocipeding by ladies." *Edgefield Advertiser* (SC), November 25, 1868.
"War on the bike." *Los Angeles Herald,* July 3, 1896.
"Washington on wheels." *Washington Critic,* April 16, 1886.
Weippiert, G.W. "The queen of sports." *Perrysburg Journal* (OH), October 3, 1891.
"What is male attire." *Norfolk Virginian,* August 31, 1895.
"What shall the new woman wear, skirts or bloomers?" *Los Angeles Herald,* September 15, 1895.
"Wheeling and dancing." *Evening Times* (Washington), March 18, 1897.
"Wheels and riders." *St. Paul Globe,* April 26, 1891.
"Wheels and riders." *St. Paul Globe,* May 10, 1896.
"Wheelwomen in Europe." *Banner-Democrat* (Lake Providence, LA), November 3, 1900.
"Wheelwomen's costumes." *Record-Union* (Sacramento, CA), June 7, 1896.
"Will not insure women profs." *St. Paul Globe,* August 23, 1896.
"Woe for the bicycle girl." *Morning Times* (Washington), January 10, 1897.
"Woman and her bicycle." *Sun* (NY), May 23, 1895.
"Woman and the bicycle." *New York Tribune,* September 17, 1894.
"Woman on the wheel." *Evening Star* (Washington), December 6, 1890.
"A woman on wheels." *St. Paul Globe,* September 17, 1893.
"Women and bicycles." *Saturday Morning Courier* (Lincoln, NE), August 5, 1893.
"Women and bicycles." *Sun* (NY), July 5, 1891.
"Women and the wheel in 1896." *Los Angeles Herald,* May 10, 1896.
"Women and the wheel." *Record-Union* (Sacramento, CA), August 10, 1895.
"Women and the wheel." *Yakima Herald* (WA), January 30, 1896.
"Women as wheel pupils." *San Francisco Call,* September 9, 1895.
"Women bicycle riders." *San Francisco Call,* July 9, 1896.
"Women bicyclists." *Capital Journal* (Salem, OR), August 28, 1894.
"Women bicyclists will be licensed." *San Francisco Call,* August 31, 1899.
"Women cyclists." *San Francisco Call,* November 10, 1894.
"Women, league, wheel and press." *Record-Union* (Sacramento, CA), July 27, 1896.
"Women life savers." *Daily Ardmoreite* (Ardmore, OK), October 17, 1894.
"Women may wear pants." *Times* (Washington), July 7, 1897.
"Women on bicycles." *Evening Star* (Washington), March 17, 1888.
"Women on the tricycle." *Evening Star* (Washington), September 12, 1885.
"Women on the velocipede." *Marshall County Republican* (Plymouth, IN), May 20, 1869.
"Women on the wheel." *Los Angeles Herald,* May 31, 1889.
"Women on the wheel." *Omaha Daily Bee,* August 7, 1887.
"Women on tricycles." *Abbeville Press and Banner* (SC), February 1, 1888.
"Women on wheels." *Evening Star* (Washington), September 27, 1884.
"Women on wheels." *Iron County Register* (Ironton, MO), September 2, 1886.
"Women wheelers." *San Francisco Call,* January 8, 1893.
"Women who like the wheel." *Sun* (NY), January 31, 1892.
"Women who ride tricycles." *Indianapolis Journal,* May 26, 1888.
"Worse than hideous." *Record-Union* (Sacramento, CA), September 20, 1896.

Index

Abbott, S.W. 117
acceptance by women 45, 68
accessories 92; clothing 185–189
accidents 50
Adams, B.B. 138
advertising 99–101; cycle outfits 184–188; fashion 181; industry 151, 158–159; tie-ins 10, 82, 85–86
advice, costume 171
ages, of riders 64
Alameda Bicycle and Athletic Club 73
ankles, exposed 139
annex, club, women 73
anxiety 109
Armaindo, Louise 38
arrests 194
astride, riding style 7
athleticism 15–16, 21
athletics, and women 58–60
attire: male 180–181; most popular 82; suitable 50, 66, 77–79, 97, 108, 110–111, 121, 124, 130, 145, 155
automobiles 101–104

Bartlett, O.D. 171
Beecher, Henry Ward 9
Berkeley Ladies Athletic Club (NYC) 109
Bernhardt, Sarah 91
bicycle craze: begins 47–48; 1890s 62–65
The Bicycle Girl, 1896 85
bicycle girl: (1883) 40; (1889) 60; (1894) 81; evolution 161–162
bicycle gown 153
bicycle habit 152
bicycle leg 114–115
bicycle suit, as fashion 184
bicycle tennis 91–92
bicycles: accommodated 82; death of 101–104
bicycling dress, France 164–165
bifurcated garments 9, 22, 53, 197
bigotry 106

Bissell, Mary 109–110
The Black Crook 174
Bloomer, Amelia 144–145, 165
bloomers 24, 46–47, 74, 82, 89, 91, 97, 131, 141, 142–143, 144–147, 162, 166, 172, 173–174, 176, 179–180, 189, 201; against 169–170; class issues 184; costume 163; day vs. night 80; fashion styles 181; favored 173; France 179–180; horses scared by 180; male objections 172; Michigan 173; Orlando FL 172; Paris 193; police opposed 172; St. Louis 146; and teachers 181; Victoria, BC, Canada 172; Westport Missouri 172
Boardman, Neta Jean 164
Bolton, Charlotte L. 46–47, 95–96
boneshakers 5, 36
Boston 32, 58
Bowman Riding Academy (NYC) 184
Bramble, Bessie 58–60
brands, of bikes 87
British Medical Journal 109
Brooklyn 32, 74, 142–143
business usage 40, 46, 51, 57
bustles 23, 53
buyers, male 87
bystanders, outraged 46

California 72
Calve, Emma 89–91
cancan dancing 174
Capital Bicycle Club 40
carnivals 38
Case, Wood 147
Cayvan, Georgia 178
celebrity endorsements 85
Central Park, NYC 32
century runs (100 miles) 69–70, 121–122; condemned 121–122; morality of 122
Chantilly, Eugenie 117
chaperons 12, 83–84, 123–124, 133
Chicago 53, 69, 91

219

Cincinnati 143
circuses 38
class (social) 15, 16, 25, 26, 31, 32, 35, 38, 67, 78–79, 80, 130–131, 143
clergymen 141; attitudes 139–140; and bloomers 146
Cleveland, Grover 135
Cleveland, Mrs. Grover 29
clocks 92
clothing: consideration 151–200; fashionable 166–168; male, appropriated 181; specialized 152, 154–155; subdued 127
clubs: admission of women 53, 58; anti-bloomer 147; discrimination 26, 73, 97–98; female 73; New York City 32; statistics 40, 46
Cole, Carlotta 65
Coleman, Ada 146–147
Colleran, Luke P. 148
colors 108
Columbia Bicycle Company 66–67
commercialization 10–12, 92
commuting 57; Washington 95
Cone, Ada 164–165
conservatism 80–81
Corelli, Marie 192
Cornell, Mrs. K.B. 175
corsets 94, 111–112, 120, 145, 154, 179
costs 46, 51, 68, 80–81, 89; prohibitive 36
costumes: bicycle 154, 155–158, 162–163, 166; design 153–154; 1896, types 189–191; special 152; suitable 155; worn 168–171, 192
Cowell, W.M. 149–150
Coxe, Alfred Cleveland 124–126; mocked 126
craze: demise of 101–104; driven by the wealthy 67; 1895 83; reasons for 66
criticisms 72
cross dressing 181
cruelty, from cycling: female 117–119; male 118–119
crusade against 136–139
Cullen, Thomas J. 72–73
Cummings, Amos 94–95
cycles: speeds 40; cycles, statistics 41 (Denver 83; manufacturing 44; Minneapolis 68; United States 66; Washington 46, 50–51, 52, 55–56); weights 48, 77
cycling: cause of insanity in women 117–119; costumes 151, 198–201; and dancing 114–117; in public 70; suits, ready-made 171
cyclists: demographics 81, 95; numbers, Washington 136; statistics 51, 81 (Philadelphia 53; San Francisco 72; Washington 48)

dancing ability: female 114–117; male 115–117
dandy horse 5
Dark, Shirley 123–124
Day, Alfred 168
Dazell, Gavin 5
dealers: bike 47–48; Washington 70–71

decorum 126–127
defiance 46
deliveries using cycles 51
demoralization 132
Denver 40, 83
depravity 124
descriptions, hyperbolic 30–31
Detroit 38
diamond frame 36, 189; demand, by women 94
Dickinson, R.L. 189–191
discrimination 9, 43, 58, 77, 112, 114–119, 140
disease: rates, male vs. female 117; and vice 136–139
distance riding 121
Dorcas societies 72
dress: inconspicuous 124; rational 22, 76, 94, 145, 151, 197; reform 47, 58–60, 112, 130, 154–156, 164, 166 (and the bicycle 192; class controlled 169)
driving wheel 44
drop frame 7, 46, 94; devil's invention 133–135; vs. diamond frame 49–50, 176; and fashion 36–37; as unisex 74
Dunham, Carroll 81

Eaton, Earle 161–164
elevated trains 82
emancipation 94, 112, 181–183
Empire City Rink (NYC) 11
England 15, 18, 27, 32, 40, 192
equal rights 9, 130
escorts, male 5, 12, 19, 26, 31, 41, 46, 49, 65, 110–111, 120, 123–124, 132
ethics 123–150
etiquette 132–133
Europe 42, 68
evil 124; associations 137
evolution, bicycle 5–14
excitement, effects 70
exercise: benefits 105–122; excessive 109; lacking 107; outdoor 46, 69–70, 111
exhibitions 10–12; traveling 38–39

fainting 109, 139
family disputes 110
fashion 151–200; concerns 160; and cycling 176–178; designers 168; impediment 9, 18; selling of 159
fatigue 111
feet: exposure 52; use of 107–108
Fellowship of Ethical Research 181
femininity 174
ferries 82
Field, Kate 73, 128–130
Fielding, Howard 128
fitness, physical 15–16
Florence, Italy 147
foreign attitudes 147–148
foreign influences 7

Fournier, Mme. Henry 117
France 7, 10, 147, 157, 168–169, 179–180, 192
freedom 94
gaiters 168
gamblers 70
garages, for bikes 83

Garrigues, Henry J. 113
Germany 147
Gilder, Jeannette 128–130, 192
girls, young 111–112
gloves, cycling 189
Gormully and Jeffrey Bicycle School 171
Gould, Marjorie 102
gracefulness 65
gracelessness 14, 18, 108, 116, 173
Graeme, Alice 184
Grant and Gravois School Association 141
Graves, Robert 60
Gray, Langdon Carter 112–113
Gross, Carrie 110
Grundy, Mrs. 105–106, 127
gymkhana 97
gymnastic events, on bikes 97

Hackensack NJ 71–72
Hall, Pauline 53
harassment 46, 157; street 65, 72, 126, 162, 176
Harberton, Frances 22
Hardcastle, Delia 64
Harrison, Louis 85
Harrison, R.M. 131–132
Hart, George S. 53–54
Hawthorne. J.B. 133–135, 146
headgear 191
headlights 8
health benefits 105; critics 107–108, 112–113
health effects 105–122; debate 113
Heaton, John 66–67
Hickman, W.H. 143–144
high wheeler 7, 35–36, 47, 55; athleticism 7; limitations 7; mounting 35
Hill, L.D. 73
hill climbing 9, 16, 33–34
hobby horse 5
Hodgkins, Mamie E. 124
Hogg, Douglas 109
Hopkins, Mary Sargent 109, 130–131
horse riding 23, 70; sidesaddle 16
Howland, William B. 29–30
Hubbell, Charles Buckley 142
Hudders, Etta 121
hygiene 109–110, 144

ideal woman 87
imitating men 47, 78, 110, 130, 194
immodesty 181

immorality 25–26, 133, 136–139
impropriety 131
income level, riders 31–32
inconspicuousness 130
independence 94
injuries 107
insanity, from biking, women 117–119
insomnia 109
instruction 53–54, 72–73, 80
instruction, belt and rope 81
instructors, female 81, 83–84, 97
insults, street, to women bikers 149
insurance, accident 7, 140

Jardine, Felice 97
Jardine, Mignon 97
Jay, Mrs. William 81
Jensen, Marie 53
jewelers, as bike retailers 87
jewelry, for cycling 92
Johnson, Ike 169

Kenosha, Wisconsin 149
Kern, W.H. 146
Kipley, Joseph 149
Kirkwood, Margaret 70
Knickerbocker Cycling Club of Chicago 175
knickerbockers 24, 82, 130, 161, 174–176; France 169; male 164; and society women 169
Kraemer, Gosta 178
Krauskopf, Charles G.W. 40

Ladies Bicycle Riding School 62
Ladies Cycling League (Minneapolis) 68
Ladies' Home Journal 154
lampooned 46
League of American Wheelmen 40, 46
Le Bon Marche 185
leggings 192
legislation 12, 32; New Jersey 72; Wisconsin 149
legs 126; bare 192, 193; display of 174–175
lessons: costs 62, 74, 82; number needed 66, 74
letter carriers 40
licensing female cyclists 149
Lightning Hot Drops 85
Livermore, Mary 130
Lockwood, Belva 20–21, 25, 41–42, 51–52
Logan, Mrs. John A. 25
loitering 143
Los Angeles 58
low income 80
Luccock, George 141
lust in males, stirred 124–125

Madison Square Garden 55
magazine, special supplement 99–101

maids 81
manual, for women 133
manufacturers 43, 69, 81, 87–89; numbers 74; statistics 81, 87–89
masculinity 110
Mason, Mrs. Elliott 46
masquerading, as male 47, 194–196
McAllister, Ward 34–35, 123, 127–128
McHenry, Nellie 85
McWilliams, Mrs. J.E. 164
Melba, Nellie 89–91
Memphis Tennessee Bicycle Club 23–24
men's apparel, laws against, women 168
men's bikes, and women 37
merits, relative 51
Michaux Club 184
middle class 80–81
Mills, Harriet H. 51, 105
Minneapolis 62, 68
Minnesota 79
mobility, female 12
mockery 25, 27, 46
moderation 111
modesty 23, 78, 125, 129–130, 138, 141, 157, 166, 173; screen, for bikes 87
Moore, Carrie 13
Moore, William C. 194–196
morality 123–150; influence 181; injured 113; negative 107; ruination 148
Morrison, Mamie 40–41
motivations, to cycle 66
mounting, cycles 46, 50, 53, 54, 77, 127

nervous system 119
new woman 48, 87, 101, 135, 181
New York City 24–25, 32, 87
Newport RI 82
newspapers, special supplement 98–101
novelty 73; fading 71

ordinances 149
ordinary bicycle *see* high wheeler
Orlando FL 172
Osborn, Ellen 171–172
outfits, invented 176
overexertion 112
Overman Wheel Company 44
Owen, Bert 94

Palo Alto CA 79
panniers 9
pantaloons 13
pants 9, 17, 23, 194
Paris 8, 13–14, 91, 97, 164–165, 166
Parisian Velo Troupe 11
Park Bicycle Rink (Philadelphia) 53–54
Parker, Georgie 174
parks, New York City 32
patent medicines 85–86
patriarchy 16, 19, 31, 123

Peckham, Grace 128–130
pedestrian costume 152
penny farthing *see* high wheeler
petticoats 154, 169
Phelps, A.M. 112
Philadelphia 53
Philadelphia Bicycle Club 58
physical appearance 14, 110, 130, 136; negative 18, 21, 26, 41–42, 52, 125
physical culture 108–109
physical destruction 137
physicians 40, 71; female 110; homeopathic 106–107; opinions 107, 113–114; polled 109, 112–113
Pittsburgh 58–60
Place, H.S. 143
Platt, Isaac Hull 181–183
pneumatic tires 36, 45
pockets 130, 188
policemen 40
Pope, Albert A. 44
Pope Manufacturing Company 44
popularity 62; class-based 36; negative 68–69
Potomac Tricycle Club 22–23
prejudice 96
Proctor, Isabella 74, 108
Professional Woman's League 109
progress 80
propriety 12, 25–26, 34–35, 50, 123–150
propulsion 5
prudery 127–128, 191
Pry, Pauline 80
public opinion 67–68, 79, 111
publicity 109
purchases, as gifts 87

Quebec City 159
Queens NY 131

racers, women 55
races 55, 71
railroads 82
Reimer, A.F.W. 131
religious attack 124–126, 133–135
religious leaders: against 132; favoring 131–132
rental rates 32–33, 57, 72
restaurants 82
Reynolds, W.W. 148
Rhode Island 58
Rich, A.M. 141
Richmond VA 78–79
riders: class divisions 104; demographics, from actual count 87–89; descriptions (1888) 48–49; descriptions (1893) 107–108; descriptions, hyperbolic 70; male vs. female 112; physical count 87; professional 10–11; statistics 87
riding: alone 123–124, 132, 168; appearance,

male vs. female 74; costumes 30, 67, 89, 130; day vs. night 74; daylight 30; posture 108, 112, 121
Ritson, Mrs. William 153–154
roads 28, 41, 66
Rochester NY 64–65
royalty, English 15, 16, 32
rules for cyclists, women 132
Russell, Lillian 53, 85, 101
Russia 147, 148

Sabbath 136; desecration 141
saddles 29, 46, 119; tilting 166
safety bikes 7, 41; development 42–43; first 36; weight 45; women 36–37, 42–43
safety machines 35–36
Sage, Mrs. Russell (Margaret) 178–179
St. Louis 62, 141, 146
St. Paul 79
Salt Lake Cycle Club 58
San Francisco 72
San Francisco Bicycle Club 73
San Jose CA 110–111
satire 128
Sayre, Lewis A. 119–120
Schmults, Kittie 72
schools 62, 72–73, 80, 82; school boards 131
scientific opinion 111
Scudder, J.L. 131–132
self-confidence 182
self-consciousness 30
self-reliance 120
servants 81
sewing machines 108, 109
sexism 149–150; foreign 148
sexuality 124
shamefulness 65–66
Sherwood, Mrs. John 128–130
Shorten John W. 146–147
Shuler, Edith 11–12
skirts 23, 27, 36–37, 47, 49, 78, 143, 156; anti 182–184; divided 22, 72, 121, 153–154, 160–161, 163, 169, 173–174; and femininity 173; length 28, 160, 173, 179; removable 79; symbolism 174; versus bloomers 147
sleeves, baggy 191
Smith, Charlotte 137
Smith, W.E. 94
Smith, Mrs. W.E. 73
Snow's Bicycle House 62
sociables 16, 22
society leaders 80–81, 130–131
society women 73, 78–79, 82, 168; and autos 102–104; instruction 169
socks 193
Somerset, Mrs. Henry 128–130, 164
stage and bicycle 174
stage play 85, 174
Stanford University 79
Stanton, Elizabeth Cady 133, 136

Starley, John Kemp 36
steering wheel 44
step through frame *see* drop frame
Stevens, W.X. 42–43
storage facilities 83
stout women, costumes 173–174
straddling 13, 16, 58, 108, 127; morality 16
street clothing, impractical 151
streetcars, business loss 83
Strugnell, H. 162, 170–171
suffrage 133, 162
Sundays 132, 136; riding 140
Surprise, W.L. 24
syncope 109

talking 120–121
tandem machines 16, 41, 49
teachers 141–143; and bloomers 181; New York City 141; public schools 131
textile industry 153
theaters 95, 174
Thomas, T. Gaillard 107
tights 171, 174
timidity 74
Toronto School Board 181
transportation changes 7–8, 10
treadmill action 108
tricycles 5, 15–35, 50, 57; clubs 18, 22–23, 26; costs 25, 29, 31, 32; demise of 16, 33–35; dimensions 16; distances 32; exercise value 27; and fashion 16–17, 22, 23; fitness 21; girl, description 17; inline third wheel 29; and men 15–16; men vs. women 19; negative aspects 52; numbers 21; parties 32; popularity 19, 27; riders 19, 24, 30; vs. bicycles 15, 18; vs. horses 29–30; and White House 29
Tricyclist Club (Philadelphia) 32
trousers 159–160, 165–166
tuberculosis statistics 117
Turkish trousers 176

underclothing 23, 24, 191
unisex bicycle, predictions 76–78, 94
universities 79
upper class 81

Vanderbilt, Mrs. William K. 81, 102
velocipede 5–14, 43; and advertising 10; clothing 7; commercialization 10–12; commuting 9; craze 5; death of 14; dimensions 9, 10; dress for 13; 1868–1869 7; legislation 12; lights 8; schools 8, 12; speed 9; vs. horse 9; wheels 8
verbal abuse, passersby 23
Victoria BC 172
voice 120–121; improvement 105
von Berg, Bertha 53
von Blumen, Elsa 40
voting 13

Walker, Mary 194–196
Wallace, Lew 143–144
Wallace, Maggie 40
Walsh, Frank 146
wardrobe 154–157; advice 171; criticisms 155, 156–157; ideal 155
Washington Cycle Club 40
Washington DC 25, 32–33, 41, 95
Washington Tricycle Club 26
Waugh, Alice 69
wealthy class 31–32; as leaders 67, 78–79
Weippiert, G.W. 68
White Pigeon Michigan 180
Wiggins, Mrs. Frank 176

Willard, Frances 128–130, 164
Winslow, Forbes 113
Woman's Bicycle Club of Washington 51
woman's place 144
woman's rights 162
women: and athletics 29; fallen 143; prominent, opinions 128–130; stereotypes 128; wealthy 104
Women's Rescue League 133, 136–139
wooden construction 43
W.W. Cole traveling circus 38

Zulia 38

www.ingramcontent.com/pod-product-compliance
Ingram Content Group UK Ltd.
Pitfield, Milton Keynes, MK11 3LW, UK
UKHW021849210426
5322IPUK00022B/568